Phenomenology and Naturalism

At present, 'naturalism' is arguably the dominant trend in both Anglo-American and European philosophy. Owing to the influence of the works of W.V.O. Quine, Wilfred Sellars and Hillary Putnam, among others, naturalism both as a methodological and as a ontological position has become one of the mainstays of contemporary analytic approaches to knowledge, mind and ethics. From the early 1990s onward, European philosophy in the English-speaking world has been witnessing a turn from the philosophies of the subjects of phenomenology, hermeneutics and existentialism and a revival of a certain kind of vitalism, whether Bergsonian or Nietzschean, and also of a certain kind of materialism that is close in spirit to Spinoza's *Ethics*, and to the naturalism and monism of the early Ionian thinkers.

This book comprises chapters written by experts in both the European and the Anglo-American traditions such as John Sallis, David Papineau, David R. Cerbone, Dan Zahavi, Paul Patton, Bernhard Weiss, Jack Reynolds and Benedict Smith, who explore the limit of naturalism and the debate between naturalism and phenomenology. This book also considers the relation between Deleuze's philosophy and naturalism as well as the critique of phenomenology by speculative realism. This book was originally published as a special issue of the *International Journal of Philosophical Studies*.

Rafael Winkler is an Associate Professor in the Department of Philosophy at the University of Johannesburg, South Africa. He is the editor of *Identity and Difference: Contemporary Debates on the Self* (2016), the co-editor of three special issues with the *International Journal of Philosophical Studies*, the *Journal of the British Society for Phenomenology* and the *South African Journal of Philosophy*, and the co-founder and co-chair of the Centre for Phenomenology in South Africa.

Phenomenology and Naturalism

Edited by
Rafael Winkler

LONDON AND NEW YORK

First published 2017
by Routledge
2 Park Square, Milton Park, Abingdon, Oxon, OX14 4RN, UK

and by Routledge
711 Third Avenue, New York, NY 10017, USA

Routledge is an imprint of the Taylor & Francis Group, an informa business

© 2017 Taylor & Francis

All rights reserved. No part of this book may be reprinted or reproduced or utilised in any form or by any electronic, mechanical, or other means, now known or hereafter invented, including photocopying and recording, or in any information storage or retrieval system, without permission in writing from the publishers.

Trademark notice: Product or corporate names may be trademarks or registered trademarks, and are used only for identification and explanation without intent to infringe.

British Library Cataloguing in Publication Data
A catalogue record for this book is available from the British Library

ISBN 13: 978-1-138-71848-7

Typeset in MinionPro
by diacriTech, Chennai

Publisher's Note
The publisher accepts responsibility for any inconsistencies that may have arisen during the conversion of this book from journal articles to book chapters, namely the possible inclusion of journal terminology.

Disclaimer
Every effort has been made to contact copyright holders for their permission to reprint material in this book. The publishers would be grateful to hear from any copyright holder who is not here acknowledged and will undertake to rectify any errors or omissions in future editions of this book.

Contents

Citation Information		vii
Notes on Contributors		ix
Introduction: Phenomenology and Naturalism *Rafael Winkler, Catherine Botha and Abraham Olivier*		1
1	The end of what? Phenomenology vs. speculative realism *Dan Zahavi*	5
2	Naturalism, Experience, and Hume's 'Science of Human Nature' *Benedict Smith*	26
3	Against representationalism (about conscious sensory experience) *David Papineau*	40
4	Deleuze and Naturalism *Paul Patton*	64
5	Exile and return: from phenomenology to naturalism (and back again) *David R. Cerbone*	81
6	Return to Nature *John Sallis*	97

CONTENTS

7 Phenomenology and naturalism: a hybrid and heretical proposal 109
  Jack Reynolds

8 Two Facets of Belief 129
  Bernhard Weiss

  Index 149

Citation Information

The chapters in this book were originally published in the *International Journal of Philosophical Studies*, volume 24, issue 3 (July 2016). When citing this material, please use the original page numbering for each article, as follows:

Introduction
Phenomenology and Naturalism
Rafael Winkler, Catherine Botha and Abraham Olivier
International Journal of Philosophical Studies, volume 24, issue 3 (July 2016) pp. 285–288

Chapter 1
The end of what? Phenomenology vs. speculative realism
Dan Zahavi
International Journal of Philosophical Studies, volume 24, issue 3 (July 2016) pp. 289–309

Chapter 2
Naturalism, Experience, and Hume's 'Science of Human Nature'
Benedict Smith
International Journal of Philosophical Studies, volume 24, issue 3 (July 2016) pp. 310–323

Chapter 3
Against representationalism (about conscious sensory experience)
David Papineau
International Journal of Philosophical Studies, volume 24, issue 3 (July 2016) pp. 324–347

CITATION INFORMATION

Chapter 4
Deleuze and Naturalism
Paul Patton
International Journal of Philosophical Studies, volume 24, issue 3 (July 2016)
pp. 348–364

Chapter 5
Exile and return: from phenomenology to naturalism (and back again)
David R. Cerbone
International Journal of Philosophical Studies, volume 24, issue 3 (July 2016)
pp. 365–380

Chapter 6
Return to Nature
John Sallis
International Journal of Philosophical Studies, volume 24, issue 3 (July 2016)
pp. 381–392

Chapter 7
Phenomenology and naturalism: a hybrid and heretical proposal
Jack Reynolds
International Journal of Philosophical Studies, volume 24, issue 3 (July 2016)
pp. 393–412

Chapter 8
Two Facets of Belief
Bernhard Weiss
International Journal of Philosophical Studies, volume 24, issue 3 (July 2016)
pp. 413–432

For any permission-related enquiries please visit:
http://www.tandfonline.com/page/help/permissions

Notes on Contributors

Catherine Botha is an Associate Professor in the Department of Philosophy at the University of Johannesburg, South Africa. Her research is focused mainly on aesthetics, most especially the philosophy of dance. Her interest lies also in the phenomenological tradition and its precursors in the continental tradition, especially in the works of Nietzsche and Heidegger.

David R. Cerbone is a Professor in the Department of Philosophy at the University of West Virginia, USA. His research centres on both the phenomenological tradition, emphasising the work of Heidegger and Husserl, and on Wittgenstein and early analytic philosophy. He is the author of *Understanding Phenomenology* (2006) and *Heidegger: A Guide for the Perplexed* (2008).

Abraham Olivier is a Professor and the Head of the Department of Philosophy at the University of Fort Hare, South Africa. He is the co-founder and co-chair of the Centre for Phenomenology in South Africa, is the author of *Being in Pain* (2007), and was previously the editor of the *South African Journal of Philosophy*.

David Papineau is a Professor of Philosophy of Science at King's College London, UK. He works on issues in metaphysics, philosophy of science, and the philosophy of mind and psychology. His most recent books include *Thinking about Consciousness* (2002), *The Roots of Reason: Philosophical Essays on Rationality, Evolution, and Probability* (2003) and *Philosophical Devices: Proofs, Probabilities, Possibilities, and Sets* (2012).

Paul Patton is a Professor of Philosophy at the University of New South Wales, Australia. His research interest includes political philosophy in the analytic and continental traditions. He has published on French poststructuralist approaches to political philosophy, including the work of Deleuze, Derrida and Foucault. He is the author of *Deleuzian Concepts: Philosophy, Colonization, Politics* (2010).

NOTES ON CONTRIBUTORS

Jack Reynolds is a Professor in the Faculty of Arts and Education at Deakin University, Australia. His research interests include phenomenology, contemporary European philosophy, metaphilosophy and intersubjectivity. He is the author of *Chronopathologies: Time and Politics in Deleuze, Derrida, Analytic Philosophy, and Phenomenology* (2012).

John Sallis is a Professor of Philosophy at Boston College, USA. He is the founding editor of *Research in Phenomenology*; author of *The Figure of Nature: On Greek Origins* (2016), *The Return of Nature: Coming as if from Nowhere* (2016) and *Senses of Landscape* (2015); and the editor of *The Philosophical Vision of Paul Klee* (2014), amongst many others.

Benedict Smith is a Lecturer in the Department of Philosophy at Durham University, UK. His current research focuses on a number of issues in moral philosophy, including the nature of moral experience, motivation, trust, and the role of concepts in our moral thought and practice. He is the author of *Particularism and the Space of Moral Reasons* (2011).

Bernhard Weiss is a Professor in the Department of Philosophy at the University of Cape Town, South Africa. His areas of interest include philosophies of language, logic and mathematics, realism and anti-realism. He is the author of *Michael Dummett* (2002), *How to Understand Language: A Philosophical Inquiry* (2009) and *Reading Brandom: On Making It Explicit* (2010).

Rafael Winkler is an Associate Professor in the Department of Philosophy at the University of Johannesburg, South Africa. He is the editor of *Identity and Difference: Contemporary Debates on the Self* (2016); the co-editor of three special issues with the *International Journal of Philosophical Studies*, the *Journal of the British Society for Phenomenology* and the *South African Journal of Philosophy*; and the co-founder and co-chair of the Centre for Phenomenology in South Africa.

Dan Zahavi is a Professor in the Department of Media, Cognition and Communication at the University of Copenhagen, Denmark. His recent authored books include *The Phenomenological Mind* (with Shaun Gallagher, 2nd ed., 2012) and *Self and Other: Exploring Subjectivity, Empathy, and Shame* (2014). He is also the editor of *The Oxford Handbook of Contemporary Phenomenology* (2012).

INTRODUCTION

Phenomenology and Naturalism

Rafael Winkler[a], Catherine Botha[a] and Abraham Olivier[b]

[a]University of Johannesburg; [b]University of Fort Hare

'Naturalism' is arguably the dominant trend currently in both Anglo-American and European philosophy. Owing to the influence of the works of W.V.O. Quine, Wilfred Sellars, and Hillary Putnam among others, naturalism both as a methodological and ontological position has become one of the mainstays of contemporary analytic approaches to knowledge, mind and ethics. From the early 1990s onward, European philosophy in the English-speaking world has been witnessing a turn from the philosophies of the subject of phenomenology, hermeneutics and existentialism and a revival of a certain kind of vitalism, whether Bergsonian or Nietzschean, and also of a certain kind of materialism that is close in spirit to Spinoza's *Ethics* and to the naturalism and monism of the early Ionian thinkers. There are, to be sure, quite a few reasons for this turn in European thought. Not all of them are easily perceivable or identifiable, at least not at the present historical junction where we find ourselves. The reasons for this turn that most emphatically stand out include the reception of the post-structuralist critique of the subject in French philosophy since the late 1960s, the translation and reception of the works of Gilles Deleuze, Alain Badiou, and Slavoj Zizek, among others, the current popularity of speculative realism, and recent explorations in neuroscience and the philosophy of mind by continental authors such as Catherine Malabou and others.

There are no doubt important differences, which it would be naïve to overlook, between the naturalism that dominates the Anglo-American tradition and the kind of 'naturalistic monism' (for want of a more suitable expression) that is becoming increasingly more pervasive in current trends in the European tradition. One of these differences includes the fact that for the former the terms of naturalism, or what constitutes the meaning or concept of 'nature', are dictated in the final analysis by the method and outlook of the mathematical-physical and biological sciences, whereas for the latter art is sometimes held to deliver equally authoritative insights into the meaning or concept of 'nature'. In spite of these differences, however, which we cannot hope to explore in this introduction, it is evident that they share some common goals, in particular and above all the rejection of the first-person standpoint of the philosophies of the subject to the question of mind, meaning, knowledge, normativity and art – a rejection that challenges one of the founding claims of phenomenology, notably that no satisfactory account can be given of these issues from a naturalistic standpoint.

This special issue, which is in part the result of an international conference hosted by the Centre for Phenomenology in South Africa at the University of Johannesburg in April 2014, is largely concerned with the debate between phenomenology and naturalism in contemporary Anglo-American and European philosophy. It also considers the relation between Deleuze's philosophy and naturalism as well as the critique of phenomenology by speculative realism. This special issue contains the work of leading figures in both traditions, including John Sallis, David Papineau, David Cerbone, Dan Zahavi, Paul Patton, Bernhard Weiss Jack Reynolds, and Benedict Smith.

In 'The End of What? Phenomenology vs. Speculative Realism' Dan Zahavi provides a critical overview of some of the main positions and arguments levelled against phenomenology by some proponents of speculative realism, including Graham Harman, Ray Brassier and Quentin Meillassoux. Zahavi shows that many of their claims are questionable because they rest on a superficial, highly selective or straightforwardly false reading of classical phenomenological texts, and argues that other claims made by proponents of speculative realism are dubious for genuinely philosophical reasons. Zahavi turns to a defence of correlationism, which speculative realism claims is a dead-end and must be overcome at all cost, by linking phenomenology to other thinkers such as Putnam, Davidson and others, who also see a profound connection between epistemology and metaphysics while espousing some form of 'realism' – a form that resembles, in many ways, Husserl's own position. Zahavi concludes his article by summarising his claims against speculative realism in a list showing to what extent the latter's criticisms of phenomenology are flawed in various ways. While Zahavi admits that the future of phenomenology is not secure, he demonstrates that it has genuine power and substance that is untouched by anything the speculative realists have said.

In 'Naturalism, Experience, and Hume's "Science of Human Nature"', Benedict Smith critically considers the standard interpretation of Hume's naturalism as paving the way for a scientistic and 'disenchanted' conception of the world. Smith shows that this is a restrictive reading of Hume and that it obscures a more profitable interpretation of Humean naturalism. Examining the two senses of 'experience' in the *Treatise*, the psychological and intersubjective one, Smith argues that the latter is a principal and irreducible element of Hume's science of man and that this has implications for a different interpretation of Hume's naturalism that phenomenologists (such as Samuel Todes) and conceptualists (such as John McDowell) alike tend to obscure in their focus on and critique of Hume's atomistic empiricism.

In 'Against Representationalism (about Conscious Sensory Experience)', David Papineau develops an argument against the view that conscious sensory experience is essentially representational. The fault lies, so he contends, not in the details of different versions of representationalism, but in the whole idea that sensory experience is intrinsically representational. Discussing a series of examples, he argues that the broadness of representational properties in any case renders them unsuitable to constitute conscious properties. Furthermore, the equation of conscious sensory and representational properties faces the problem of implying that conscious sensory properties are constituted by relations to propositions or other abstract objects not instantiated in space and time. As an alternative to the representational account, Papineau defends an equation of conscious sensory properties with intrinsic non-relational properties of subjects. Showing how this view can deal with all the difficulties facing representationalism, he concludes by defending this non-relational account of conscious experience against arguments from the transparency and the intrinsic intentionality of experience.

Contrary to prevailing views, Paul Patton argues against the conclusion that Gilles Deleuze was a thoroughgoing scientific naturalist in 'Deleuze and Naturalism'. Admitting that Deleuze's method and his experimentation with novel philosophical vocabularies make it challenging to identify something we can call 'Deleuze's philosophy', Patton nonetheless creatively interrogates the ontological and methodological naturalist credentials of a number of Deleuze's major texts. Patton deftly shows how Deleuze's work on the nature of events cannot be reconciled with ontological naturalism. While Deleuze's philosophy does not admit to a contemporary scientific naturalism in Patton's view, he does show how it resonates with some aspects of a more liberal and pluralist naturalism.

In 'Exile and Return: From Phenomenology to Naturalism (and Back Again)', David Cerbone considers the opposition between phenomenology and naturalism as an opposition between two philosophical approaches with regards to conceptual schemes. The phenomenological approach, most forcefully expressed in Husserl, consists in holding that a description of our conceptual schemes can be achieved from without, that is, from the privileged standpoint of the subject that is external to the schemes. The naturalistic approach, which Quine introduced in analytic philosophy, claims that such a description cannot be achieved except from within. In the course of his article, Cerbone demonstrates the unsoundness of Husserl's position no less than Quine's temptation to account for our conceptual schemes as a result of something less than what our schemes purport to be about which, Cerbone insists, 'creates a kind of exile from within' that faces some of the same difficulties as in Husserl. In the concluding section of his article, Cerbone considers Merleau-Ponty's phenomenology, showing how it avoids some of the pitfalls he identifies in both Husserl and Quine.

In 'Return to Nature', John Sallis examines the question of the return to nature as it was raised in antiquity and developed in all of its consequences in modern philosophy culminating in Schelling and Hegel. He shows how, beginning with Nietzsche, the character of such return is interrupted. This interruption is, in turn, shown to put in question the very concept of nature, so that a thorough rethinking of the sense of nature is demanded. Sallis identifies two fundamental reorientations that philosophical thought is called on to address: the turn to the elemental in nature and the turn from nature to the cosmos at large.

Jack Reynolds' paper 'Phenomenology and Naturalism: A Hybrid and Heretical Proposal' advocates the compatibility of phenomenology and naturalism, defending the necessity of phenomenology for philosophy, but acknowledging that the version of phenomenology defended cannot preserve a domain that is entirely distinct and autonomous from empirical science, either methodologically or substantively. Reynolds proposes a hybrid and heretical version of phenomenology that claims to be incompatible with scientific naturalism but compatible with liberal naturalism and weak forms of methodological naturalism, understood as advocating 'results continuity' with the relevant empirical sciences. His conclusion is that phenomenology and naturalism need each other, albeit in a manner that troubles the standard acceptations of each, as well as the standard understandings of the lines of demarcation between philosophy and science.

In 'Two Facets of Belief', Bernhard Weiss distinguishes between two plausible facets of our everyday conception of belief: on the one hand, 'Threshold Views' that claim that when the evidence in favour of a proposition exceeds a certain threshold then one should endorse it by forming the appropriate belief; and, on the other, 'Representational Views', which claim that a believer's beliefs form – or ought to form – a description of reality, that is, such beliefs ought to be true. Since they form a description of reality, they ought to be logically coherent, have explanatory power and/or make narrative sense. Weiss then argues that Representationalism and Thresholdism are incompatible since the former requires Logical Coherence and Logical Coherence is incompatible with Thresholdism. He subsequently discusses the Preface Paradox, showing how this debate is instructive in the choice between the two conceptions of belief.

The end of what? Phenomenology vs. speculative realism

Dan Zahavi

Center for Subjectivity Research, University of Copenhagen, Denmark

ABSTRACT
Phenomenology has recently come under attack from proponents of speculative realism. In this paper, I present and assess the criticism, and argue that it is either superficial and simplistic or lacks novelty.

The question of how to understand and respond to naturalism has been of concern to phenomenology ever since its commencement. It figured centrally in Husserl's discussion of psychologism in *Logische Untersuchungen*, in his programmatic manifesto *Philosophie als strenge Wissenschaft*, in his last work *Die Krisis der europäischen Wissenschaften und die transzendentale Phänomenologie*, and in his 1919 lectures *Natur und Geist*, to mention just a few relevant texts. It was also at the forefront of Merleau-Ponty's first major work *La structure du comportement*. More recently, Francisco Varela's work on neurophenomenology has been decisive in rekindling interest in the issue and has led to an intense discussion of whether it is possible to naturalize phenomenology (Varela 1996). One important milestone in this debate was the landmark volume *Naturalizing Phenomenology* from 1999, where Varela and his three co-editors argued that it was crucial for the advancement of cognitive science that it adapted some of the methodological tools that were developed by Husserl and Merleau-Ponty (Petitot et al. 1999).

Seventeen years later, the discussion continues. In a number of previous publications, I have argued that the answer to the question of whether a naturalized phenomenology is a desideratum or a category mistake very much depends on what one takes the question to be, and that it is urgent to be clear on what notion of phenomenology and what notion of nature and naturalization one has in mind (Zahavi 2004a, 2010a, 2013). One obvious challenge to any happy marriage obviously derives from the *transcendental* character of phenomenology. Contrary to some proposals, it is not naturalism's classical endorsement of some form of physicalism that constitutes the main obstacle to a reconciliation. It is not as if matters would improve if naturalism opted for some version of emergentism or property dualism. The real problem has to do with naturalism's commitment to metaphysical realism, and with its treatment of consciousness as a mere object in the world.

Much of the recent discussion of these issues has taken place in the border area between phenomenology, cognitive science and analytic philosophy of mind. Recently, however, a new discussion partner has appeared on the scene. One that very much wants to get non-human nature back on stage, whose relation to naturalism is complicated, and whose attitude towards phenomenology can only be described as deeply hostile. This new partner, called *speculative realism*, is heralded (by its proponents) as one of the most exciting and promising new currents in Continental philosophy.

1. The end of phenomenology

In a recent book entitled *The End of Phenomenology*, Sparrow offers an overview of speculative realism and highlights its relation to phenomenology. Sparrow's own explanation of his title is twofold. On the one hand, he argues that the rise of speculative realism brings phenomenology to a close. Why is that? Because speculative realism delivers what phenomenology always promised, but never provided: a wholehearted endorsement of realism (Sparrow 2014, xi). On the other hand, however, Sparrow also argues that phenomenology never really got started. It began and ended with Husserl. Since Husserl, according to Sparrow, was never able to settle on what phenomenology should become 'it is not clear that it ever was anything at all' (Sparrow 2014, xi). In fact, the case could be 'made that phenomenology never really existed' (2014, 204), since no proponent of phenomenology has ever been able to 'adequately clarify its method, scope, and metaphysical commitments' (Sparrow 2014, xiii). That many self-declared phenomenologists have failed to realize this merely attests to the fact that they are a kind of living dead. Sparrow (2014, 187) even goes so far as to suggest that phenomenology is a form of *zombie philosophy*, 'extremely active, but at the same time lacking philosophical vitality and methodologically hollow'.

The harshness of Sparrow's rhetoric is reminiscent of the work by Tom Rockmore, whom Sparrow often quotes as a source of authority. In his book *Kant and Phenomenology*, for instance, Rockmore maintains that Husserl never managed to make it clear precisely what he meant by phenomenology; that he was unable to clarify his basic account of the relationship between phenomenology and epistemology; that he repeatedly failed to address his own questions, and often just obscured the issues at stake. Thus, for Rockmore, Husserl's methodology, as well as most of his central concepts, including notions such as intuition, essence, representation, constitution, *noesis*, *noema* and phenomenological reduction, remain fundamentally obscure (Rockmore 2011, 116, 127, 131, etc.).

Sparrow's own interpretation is as tendentious as Rockmore's.[1] To select just one example among many, consider Sparrow's (2014, 48) claim that Merleau-Ponty in *Phenomenology of Perception* 'affirms that yes, phenomenology is impossible'. How does Sparrow reach such a conclusion? In his preface to *Phenomenology of Perception*, Merleau-Ponty characterizes phenomenology as a perpetual critical (self-)reflection. It should not take anything for granted, least of all itself. It is, to put it differently, a constant meditation (Merleau-Ponty 2012, lxxxv). Merleau-Ponty's point is that phenomenology is always on the way, but Sparrow equates this anti-dogmatic attitude with the view that phenomenology can never get started. In addition, Sparrow also takes issue with Merleau-Ponty's (2012, lxxvii) famous assertion that 'the most important lesson of the reduction is the impossibility of a complete reduction', and interprets it as amounting to the claim that the reduction is a methodological step that cannot be undertaken (Sparrow 2014, 48). If the reduction is crucial to phenomenology – as some would insist – it would again show that phenomenology is impossible. As a closer engagement with the text will show, however, this is not what Merleau-Ponty is saying. The reduction is a form of reflective move (see Zahavi 2015), and Merleau-Ponty's point is rather that we as finite creatures are incapable of effectuating an absolute reflection that once and for all would allow us to cut our ties to our world-immersed life and permit us to survey it from a view from nowhere. Even the most radical reflection depends upon and is linked to an unreflected life that, as Merleau-Ponty (2012, lxxviii) puts it, remains its initial, constant, and final situation. To say that the reduction cannot be completed is not to say that it cannot be carried out. After all, it is only by distancing ourselves, if ever so slightly, from our world-immersed life that we can describe it. It is only by slacking them slightly, that we can make the intentional threads that connect us to the world visible (Merleau-Ponty 2012, lxxvii). But this procedure is something that has to be performed repeatedly, rather than completed once and for all. To that extent, Merleau-Ponty's remarks about the unfinished character of phenomenology and about the incomplete reduction are two ways of making the same point. None of this entails that Merleau-Ponty should affirm that phenomenology or the reduction is impossible, which, of course, is also why he can insist that Heidegger's analysis of being-in-the-world presupposes the reduction (Merleau-Ponty 2012, lxxviii).

Sparrow's misinterpretation of Merleau-Ponty aside, his main criticism is obviously directed at what he takes to be the ambiguities of the phenomenological method. Husserl's inability to come up with a definite account of his own method, the fact that he never bequeathed us with something like Descartes's *Regulae ad directionem ingenii* is, according to Sparrow, a fatal vice and weakness, since it entails that it is entirely unclear how phenomenology is supposed to be carried out (Sparrow 2014, 5–6). That subsequent phenomenologists have rebelled against Husserl's methodological requirements only makes matters even worse. There is for Sparrow no consensus, and no criteria, that will allow us to differentiate what is phenomenological, from what is not (Sparrow 2014, 3–4, 10).[2]

At this point, Sparrow starts to vacillate between three different positions. The first is the one just mentioned, namely that phenomenology has no method and stable identity. The second is that phenomenology is indeed unified by its commitment to a transcendental method: As he writes,

> for a philosophical description, study, or conclusion to count as phenomenological – that is, to mark it as something other than everyday description, empirical study, or speculative metaphysics – that description must take place from within some form of methodological reduction that shifts the focus of description to the transcendental, or at least quasi-transcendental, level. (Sparrow, 2014, 14)

According to Sparrow, however, the price for this methodologically unifying transcendental commitment is too high: it entails that phenomenology has to abandon and prohibit metaphysics. But if that is the case, phenomenology cannot offer or provide a defence of full blown metaphysical realism, or as Sparrow (2014, 13) puts it: 'when this book proclaims the end of phenomenology, it means that phenomenology *as a method for realists* has worn itself out.'

After having argued at length that the execution of the epoché and transcendental reduction prevents phenomenology from making any judgments regarding the existence of things, for which reason phenomenology has to remain metaphysically neutral or agnostic, Sparrow (2014, 26) makes his final move and claims that phenomenology cannot remain neutral, but that it ultimately must align itself with a form of antirealism or idealism. It is not clear how Sparrow can reconcile the claim that phenomenology has no method, that it has a transcendental method that prohibits metaphysical commitments, and that its method commits it to idealism, but given his general interpretational tactics, it cannot wonder that he faults the phenomenologists (rather than his own interpretation) for the inconsistency (see Sparrow 2014, 31, 80).

Let me not spend more time on Sparrow's interpretation and accusations. His main conclusion and objection is that phenomenology cannot yield metaphysical realism. Despite its promise of returning us to the 'things themselves' it keeps us chained to the phenomenal. To that extent, phenomenology remains committed to a form of Kantianism, rather than providing a real realist alternative (Sparrow 2014, 1). If we want to get out of 'Kant's shadow' we shouldn't turn to phenomenology, but to speculative realism, since only 'speculative realism returns us to the real without qualification and without twisting the meaning of realism' (Sparrow 2014, xii).

2. Speculative realism

What is speculative realism? It takes its name from a conference held at Goldsmiths College, University of London, in April 2007. The conference featured presentations by Ray Brassier, Iain Hamilton Grant, Graham Harman, and Quentin Meillassoux (Brassier et al. 2007). As quickly became apparent, these four protagonists diverged rather significantly when it came to their own positive proposals. Their philosophical progenitors included so diverse figures as Whitehead, Latour, Heidegger, Churchland, Metzinger, Sellars, Nietzsche, Levinas, Badiou and Schelling, but they were united by what they opposed. They all had one common enemy: *Correlationism*.

Correlationism is the view that subjectivity and objectivity cannot be understood or analysed apart from one another because both are always already intertwined or internally related. It is the view that we only ever have access to the correlation between thinking (theory) and being (reality) and never to either in isolation from or independently of the other. On this view, thought cannot get outside itself in order to compare the world as it is 'in itself' with the world as it is 'for us'. Indeed, we can neither think nor grasp the 'in itself' in isolation from its relation to the subject, nor can we ever grasp a subject that would not always-already be related to an object.[3]

It was allegedly Kant who introduced this type of philosophy.[4] Prior to Kant, one of the principal tasks of philosophy was to comprehend the universe, whereas since Kant, its primary focus and locus has been the correlationist circle. Rather than engaging in straightforward metaphysics, the effort has in turn been devoted to investigations of intentional correlations, language games, conceptual schemes, and discourses.

The speculative realists are unequivocal in their criticism of this development, which is described as the 'Kantian catastrophe' (Meillassoux 2008, 124) that enduringly has 'poisoned philosophy' (Badiou 2009, 535). Their hostility towards phenomenology is partially explained by the fact that it very much is a tradition 'that seeps from the rot of Kant' (Bogost 2012, 4). That phenomenology is indeed a form of correlationism is easy to illustrate:

> The first breakthrough of this universal a priori of correlation between experienced object and manners of givenness (which occurred during work on my *Logical Investigations* around 1898) affected me so deeply that my whole subsequent life-work has been dominated by the task of systematically elaborating on this a priori of correlation. (Husserl 1970, 166)

> The genuine transcendental epoché makes possible the 'transcendental reduction' – the discovery and investigation of the transcendental correlation between world and world-consciousness. (Husserl 1970, 151)

> [O]ne must not let oneself be deceived by speaking of the physical thing as transcending consciousness or as 'existing in itself' [...] *An object existing in itself is never one with which consciousness or the Ego pertaining to consciousness has nothing to do.* (Husserl 1982, 106)

> World exists – that is, it is – only if Dasein exists, only if there is Dasein. Only if world is there, if Dasein exists as being-in-the-world, is there understanding of being, and only if this understanding exists are intraworldly beings unveiled as extant and handy. World-understanding as Dasein-understanding is self-understanding. Self and world belong together in the single entity, the Dasein. Self and world are not two beings, like subject and object, or like I and thou, but self and world are the basic determination of the Dasein itself in the unity of the structure of being-in-the-world. (Heidegger 1982, 297)

> The world is inseparable from the subject, but from a subject who is nothing but a project of the world; and the subject is inseparable from the world, but from a world that it itself projects. The subject is being-in-the-world and the world remains 'subjective,' since its texture and its articulations are sketched out by the subject's movement of transcendence. (Merleau-Ponty 2012, 454)

Speculative realist, by contrast, insist that the 'world in itself – the world as it exists apart from us – cannot in any way be contained or constrained by the question of our *access* to it' (Shaviro 2011, 2). Their aim is to break out of the correlationist circle, and once more reach 'the *great outdoors*, the *absolute* outside of pre-critical thinkers: that outside which was not relative to us […] existing in itself regardless of whether we are thinking of it or not' (Meillassoux 2008, 7).

Kant warned us 'never to venture with speculative reason beyond the boundaries of experience' (Kant 1998, B xxiv). The speculative realists by contrast urge us to do exactly that: 'Pace Kant, we *must* think outside of our own thought; and we must positively conceive the existence of things outside our own conceptions of them' (Shaviro 2011, 2). Indeed, on Sparrow's (2014, 22) view, only speculative realism offers 'the kind of speculation required for grounding realism in philosophical argument'. Although Sparrow does not explain why only speculation should be able to ground realism philosophically, let us follow his suggestion and see where these speculations lead us.

According to Graham Harman, the only way to reverse Kant's *human-world duopoly* and the anthropocentric bias of phenomenology is by opting for equality. The human-world relation is just a special case of the relation between any two entities whatsoever, or as Harman and Bogost phrase it:

> All relations in the cosmos, whether it be the perceptual clearing between humans and world, the corrosive effect of acid on lime stone, or a slap-fight between orangutans in Borneo, are on precisely the same philosophical footing. (Harman 2005, 75)

> [T]here is no reason to believe that the entanglement in which a noodle finds itself is any less complex than the human who shapes, boils, vends, consumes, or digests it. (Bogost 2012, 30)

At first sight, the claim that causal relations between non-human objects are no different in kind from subject-object relations (Harman 2011, 198) seems rather familiar. It is strongly reminiscent of various reductionist attempts to naturalize intentionality, i.e. attempts to account for intentionality in terms of non-intentional mechanisms. But appearances are (in this case) misleading.

When insisting on equality, the aim is not to reduce the mind (and its cognitive and affective relation to the world) to mindless mechanics. No, if anything the aim seems the reverse, namely to finally recognize that all objects, including fireplaces, lawnmowers or slices of rotting pork possess an inner infinity of their own (Morton 2012, 132). Indeed, as Harman (2005, 104) insists, the real weakness of phenomenology has precisely been its failure to capture the '"I" of sailboats and moons'. Phenomenology has been too restrictive, and has failed to recognize that it is entirely appropriate to ask 'What's it like to be a computer, or a microprocessor, or a ribbon cable? [...] What do they *experience*? What's their proper phenomenology? In short, what is it like to be a thing?' (Bogost 2012, 9–10).

Pan- or (as Harman prefers to label it) polypsychism emerges, on his view, 'directly from the rejection of the Kantian Revolution' (Harman 2011, 170). One might wonder how direct and necessary that link is. On closer consideration, however, one might also wonder whether such a move really undermines correlationism, or whether it rather supports and expands it. Such worries also seem to have troubled Harman since he in other publications has argued that panpsychism and human exceptionalism share a common feature: the idea that the psyche is one of the key building blocks in the universe (Harman 2005, 220). This is the fundamental assumption that has to be rejected. There might indeed be a difference between humans and minerals, but there is also a difference between the hum of a refrigerator and a bucket of yellow paint, and ultimately we just have to face up to the fact that consciousness is simply one type of object among many others. There is no reason to prioritize it. If anything has to be prioritized, it is *sincerity*. As Harman (2005, 220) writes, '[R]ocks and dust must be every bit as sincere as humans, parrots or killer whales'. Some readers will undoubtedly be puzzled by now. But there is more puzzlement in store for us. As Harman (2008, 334) also declares, 'philosophy's sole mission is *weird realism*. Philosophy must be realist because its mandate is to unlock the structure of the world itself; it must be weird because reality is weird'. Indeed, one reason to be dissatisfied with Husserl is that he is 'neither weird, nor a realist, and even looks like the opposite: a "non-weird antirealist"' (Harman 2008, 348).[5]

Despite his criticism of correlationist subjectivism, Harman is no friend of naturalist objectivism. In fact, on his account, scientific naturalism is itself a form of correlationism. It is merely yet another attempt to squeeze and conform reality to our (current scientific) mindset: 'The thing as portrayed by the natural sciences is the thing made dependent on our knowledge, and not the thing in its untamed, subterranean reality' (Harman 2011, 80). But if science doesn't reveal or disclose the mind-independent uncorrelated objects, how do we then gain access or knowledge about them? We do not. We can only know the appearance of the thing and never its true being. On Harman's account, the real objects, the things-in-themselves, forever remain inaccessible. As he remarks polemically against Heidegger: 'To use a hammer and to stare at it explicitly are both distortions of the very reality of that hammer as it goes about just being itself, unleashed in the world like a wild animal' (Harman 2005, 74). Importantly, this inaccessibility of the in-itself is not due to some specific human cognitive flaw or incapacity, since Harman also holds the view that objects are hidden from and inaccessible to each other. The wind blowing on the banana, the hail hitting the tent, the rock colliding with the window, the flame consuming the cotton: in each case, the objects recede and withdraw from each other (Harman 2005, 19). Everything is isolated from everything else; nothing is ever in direct contact with anything else. This principle holds not only on the inter-objective level, but even on the intra-objective level: an object also withdraws from and has no direct contact with its constituent parts (Harman 2005, 94, 172).

Harman criticizes phenomenology for its alleged anti-realism and argues that it chains us to the phenomenal. Whatever merit there is to this criticism, it certainly seems like a rather fitting description of his own position. Harman's fervent endorsement of realism goes hand in hand with a radical global scepticism that forever makes reality inaccessible to us. A fact that has not prevented him from making various claims about the structure and nature of this inaccessible realm.

Not all speculative realists share Harman's scepticism, however. Some of them have a far more positive view of science. In *After Finitude*, for instance, Meillassoux argues that phenomenology because of its commitment to correlationism is unable to accept the literal truth of scientific statements concerning events happening prior to the emergence of consciousness. When faced with a statement like 'The accretion of the Earth happened 4.56 billion years ago', phenomenology is forced to adopt a two-layered approach. It has to insist on the difference between the immediate, realist, meaning of the statement, and a more profound, transcendental, interpretation of it. It can accept the truth of the statement, but only by adding the codicil that it is true 'for us'. Meillassoux finds this move unacceptable and claims that it is dangerously close to the position of creationists (Meillassoux 2008, 18, cf. Brassier 2007, 62). He insists that fidelity to science demands that we take scientific statements at face value and that we reject correlationism. No compromise is possible. Either scientific statements have a literal realist sense and only a realist sense or they have no sense at all (Meillassoux 2008, 17).[6] To put it differently, science gives us access to a reality that cannot be contained in or captured by any correlationist framework. More specifically, Meillassoux endorses a kind of Cartesian rationalism and rehabilitates the distinction between primary and secondary qualities. The former are mathematically graspable features of the things-in-themselves. Mathematics is consequently able to describe a world where humanity is absent; it can describe the great outdoors; it can give us absolute knowledge from a view from nowhere (Meillassoux 2008, 26). In the course of his argumentation, Meillassoux also defends the view, however, that everything is without reason and therefore capable of becoming otherwise without reason. Meillassoux (2008, 53) takes this ultimate absence of reason to be an absolute ontological property, and describes it as 'an extreme form of chaos, a *hyper-Chaos*, for which nothing is or would seem to be, impossible, not even the unthinkable' (2008, 64). As he admits himself, it is quite a task to reconcile this view, which maintains that the laws of nature can change at any time for no reason whatsoever (2008, 83), with an attempt to secure the scientific discourse and the idea that mathematical science can describe the in-itself and permit knowledge of the ancestral (2008, 65).

An even more extreme form of anti-correlationist scientism can be found in the work of Brassier. On his account, the ultimate aim and true consummation of the Enlightenment project is a radical demolishment of the manifest image (Brassier 2007, 26). Brassier consequently lauds Churchland's eliminativist criticism of Folk Psychology, and sees speculative realism as a metaphysical radicalization of eliminativism (Brassier 2007, 31); a radicalization that ultimately leads to nihilism:

> Nihilism is the unavoidable corollary of the realist conviction that there is a mind-independent reality, which, despite the presumptions of human narcissism, is indifferent to our existence and oblivious to the 'values' and 'meanings' which we would drape over it in order to make it more hospitable. (Brassier 2007, xi)

The world as it is in itself is inherently devoid of intelligibility and meaning. To realize this, to realize the senselessness and purposelessness of everything is a mark of intellectual maturity (Brassier 2007, xi, 238). This realization has also implications for our assessment of the value of philosophical thinking. As Brassier concludes *Nihil Unbound*: '[P]hilosophy is neither a medium of affirmation nor a source of justification, but rather the organon of extinction' (Brassier 2007, 239). One inevitable wonders how such a verdict affects the assessment of Brassier's own philosophy, just as one might wonder whether one can consistently celebrate the virtue of intellectual maturity at the same time as one denies the reality of sense, meaning, intelligibility and purpose.

3. Forms of realism

How fatal is this criticism of phenomenology? How much of a threat to phenomenology does it constitute? Let us for a moment return to Harman, and consider another statement of his:

> We have seen that one of the worst effects of phenomenology was to cement the notion that the dispute between realism and anti-realism is a 'pseudo-problem.' Since intentionality is always directed toward something outside itself, perceiving or hating some object, phenomenology supposedly gives us all the realism we will ever need, and without falling into the 'naïve' realism that posits entities beyond all possible perception. The problem is that the objects of intentionality are by no means real, as proven by the fact that we hate, love, or fear many things that turn out not to exist in the least. By confining itself to sensual objects and leaving no

room for real ones, phenomenology is idealist to the core, and cannot get away with dismissing as a 'pseudo-problem' a difficulty that happens to threaten its own views about the world. (Harman 2011, 197)

This criticism is unconvincing. It is an obvious *non sequitur* to argue that since some objects of intentionality are non-existing, all objects of intentionality are non-existing (or unreal). Furthermore, already in *Logische Untersuchungen* Husserl rejected any facile distinction between intentional objects (which Harman terms sensual objects) and real objects, and argued that

> *the intentional object of a presentation is the same as its actual object, and on occasion as its external object, and that it is absurd to distinguish between them.* The transcendent object would not be the object of *this* presentation, if it was not *its* intentional object. This is plainly a merely analytic proposition. The object of the presentation, of the 'intention', *is* and *means* what is presented, the intentional object. (Husserl 2001, 127)

This is not to say that all intentional objects are real, but only that if the intended object really exists, then it is this real object, and no other, which is our intentional object. In other words, for Husserl the distinction to keep unto is not the one between the intentional object and the real object, but the one between the merely intentional object, and the real and intentional object:

> 'The object is merely intentional' does not, of course, mean that it exists, but only in an intention, of which it is a real (*reelles*) part, or that some shadow of it exists. It means rather that the intention, the reference to an object so qualified, exists, but not that the object does. If the intentional object exists, the intention, the reference, does not exist alone, but the thing referred to exists also. (Husserl 2001, 127)

What about Harman's claim that the recurrent attempt by phenomenology to dismiss the dispute between realism and anti-realism as a pseudo-problem is disingenuous, since phenomenology is idealist to its core? This claim is not merely quite controversial; it is also historically incorrect. Whereas it is true that some phenomenologists have suggested that one should stay clear of the realism/anti-realism (idealism) controversy, it is certainly not a position shared by all. Husserl often expressed his commitment to a form of idealism – though the precise nature and character of this idealism remains contested. Whether it amounts to a metaphysical idealism or whether it is compatible with a form of realism is debated in the scholarly literature (Zahavi 2008, 2010b). More importantly, however, many early phenomenologists (including members of the Munich and Göttingen circles of phenomenology, i.e. figures like Reinach, Pfänder, Scheler, Stein, Geiger, Hildebrand and Ingarden) were committed realists who were quite disappointed by what they saw as Husserl's turn towards transcendental idealism. They considered this turn a betrayal of the realist thrust of phenomenology and very much saw themselves as defending realism (Smith 1997). Finally, to mention one further example, Heidegger is often portrayed by the speculative realists as an even more fierce idealist and correlationist than Husserl (see Sparrow 2014, 36). This characterization, however, is by no means univocally accepted by Heidegger scholars. Many see him as a realist (Dreyfus and Spinosa 1999; Carman 2003). There are even those who interpret him as a scientific realist (Glazebrook 2001). Recently, even Husserl has been interpreted along similar lines. In his 2014 book *Nature's Suit: Husserl's Phenomenological Philosophy of the Physical Sciences*, Hardy defends the view that Husserl's transcendental idealism and his claims concerning the dependence of physical objects on consciousness must be understood within a justification-theoretic context and is wholly compatible with scientific realism (Hardy 2014, 201).

Matters are in short far more complex than suggested by the speculative critics, and ultimately one has to wonder whether they are reliable and knowledgeable interpreters of the tradition they are criticizing.[7]

But back to the main issue, the criticism of correlationism and the articulation and defense of robust realism. The speculative realists are certainly right in their assessment of how widespread correlationism is. It has indeed been 'the reigning *doxa* of post-metaphysical philosophy' (Brassier 2007, 50), and although Husserl (1970, 165) in *Krisis* claims to have been the first to investigate the correlation philosophically, correlationism cannot be dismissed as a Husserlian idiosyncrasy. To illustrate its presence also in recent analytic philosophy, consider the case of Putnam.[8]

Putnam is known as a(n occasional) critic of *metaphysical realism* and has at one point conceived of his own alternative – which he in turn labelled 'internal realism', 'natural realism', 'pragmatic realism' or 'commonsense realism' – as an attempt to find a third way beyond classical realism and subjective idealism, and between 'reactionary metaphysics and irresponsible relativism' (Putnam 1999, 5).

According to metaphysical realism, there is a clear distinction to be drawn between the properties things have 'in themselves' and the properties that are 'projected by us' (Putnam 1990, 13). One can illustrate this way of thinking by way of the following metaphor: Whereas reality as it is in itself, independently of us, can be compared to a dough, our conceptual contribution can be compared to the shape of a cookie cutter. The world itself is fixed and stable, but we can conceive of it in different ways. But as Putnam insists, this view suffers from an intolerable naiveté:

> What the Cookie Cutter Metaphor tries to preserve is the naive idea that at least one Category – the ancient category of Object or Substance – has an absolute interpretation. The alternative to this idea is not the view that, in some inconceivable way, it's all *just* language. We can and should insist that some facts are there to be discovered and not legislated by us. But this is something to be said when one has adopted a way of speaking, a language, a 'conceptual scheme'. To talk of 'facts' without specifying the language to be used is to talk of nothing; the word 'fact' no more has its use fixed by Reality Itself than does the word 'exist' or the word 'object'. (Putnam 1987, 36)

Thus, according to Putnam (1992, 120), it is an illusion to think that the notions of 'object' or 'reality' or 'world' have any sense outside of and independently of our conceptual schemes. Putnam is not denying that there are 'external facts'; he even thinks that we can say what they are. But as he writes, 'what we cannot say – because it makes no sense – is what the facts are *independent of all conceptual choices*' (Putnam 1987, 33). This is not to say that our conceptual schemes create the world, but they do not just mirror it either (Putnam 1978, 1). Ultimately, what we call 'reality' is so deeply suffused with mind- and language-dependent structures that it is altogether impossible to make a neat distinction between those parts of our beliefs that reflect the world 'in itself' and those parts of our beliefs that simply expresses 'our conceptual contribution'. The very idea that our cognition should be nothing but a re-presentation of something mind-independent consequently has to be abandoned (Putnam 1990, 28).

Given this outlook, it cannot surprise that Putnam is sceptical when metaphysical realists insist that there is a gap between epistemological and ontological issues, and when they deny that epistemological distinctions have any ontological implications. As Putnam (1988, 120) retorts, the 'epistemological' and the 'ontological' are intimately related, and any serious philosophical work must respect their interconnection.

In his discussion of these issues, Putnam sometimes accuses scientific realists of not being sufficiently realist. Occasionally the claim is being made that science is the sole legitimate source of empirical knowledge. Thereby a certain theoretical outlook is made the measure of what counts as real, and the existence of everyday objects and events such as tables, marriages, economic crises, and civil wars are denied, with the argument that none of them figures in the world as described by physics (Putnam 1987, 12). Although scientific realism was once heralded as a strong antidote against idealism and scepticism, Putnam consequently argues that it has joined forces with what it was supposed to combat.

When Putnam insists that the metaphysical realists do not take realism sufficiently seriously, and when he argues that it is the philosophers traditionally accused of idealism, namely the Kantians, the Pragmatists, and the Phenomenologists, who actually respect and honour our natural realism (Putnam 1987, 12), he is following in the footsteps of Husserl. As Husserl declared in a famous letter to Émile Baudin: 'No ordinary "realist" has ever been so realistic and so concrete as I, the phenomenological "idealist"' (Husserl 1994, 16).

Although the main speculative criticism of phenomenology concerns its alleged failure to be sufficiently realist, although Sparrow (2014, xii) insists that speculative realism 'returns us to the real without qualification and without twisting the meaning of realism', it should by now be obvious that the realism on offer is of a rather peculiar kind. Harman defends a radical scepticism that denies us any glimpse of reality (while making various claims about the character of this ungraspable reality-in-itself), and whereas Meillassoux seeks to reconcile an old-style rationalism according to which only that which is amenable to mathematization counts as real with the idea that chaos is the primary absolute, Brassier opts for a nihilist eliminativism. How robustly realist are these divergent positions? If realism is about affirming the reality of everyday objects, the speculative realists fail miserably.

Husserl was in part led by similar considerations as Putnam. It was in order to ward off scepticism, it was in order to save the objectivity of the world that we know, that Husserl embraced transcendental idealism and insisted that reality involves a necessary intertwining of subject and object. Thus not unlike Kant, Husserl did not merely think that transcendental idealism and empirical realism are compatible; he thought that the latter required the former. By developing a sophisticated non-representationalist theory of intentionality, Husserl sought to rule out the possibility of a gap between the world that we investigate and the real world, thereby allowing global scepticism no purchase. In defending such a view, it is again important to realize that Husserl isn't a lone and late excrescence of German Idealism. There are striking parallels to views also found in analytic philosophy. As Davidson declares in 'The Structure and Content of Truth', realism – understood as the position that truth is 'radically non-epistemic' and that all our best researched and established beliefs and theories may be false – is a view he considers incomprehensible (Davidson 1990, 308–309). As he would later write in *Subjective, Intersubjective, Objective*: 'A community of minds is the basis of knowledge; it provides the measure of all things. It makes no sense to question the adequacy of this measure, or to seek a more ultimate standard' (Davidson 2001, 218).[9]

It might be tempting to accuse the correlationists of committing hubris, by defining reality in terms of what we can have access to. But as Braver (2012, 261–62) has pointed out, one might also reverse this particular criticism. Not only do the speculative realists make claims about that which transcends us, but they (at least some of them) are also the ones who aspire to absolute knowledge. It is no coincidence that Meillassoux's book is called *After Finitude*. By contrast, correlationism might be a way of acknowledging the finite and perspectival character of our knowledge.

4. The end of speculative realism

Given the hostility towards and proclaimed showdown with phenomenology, one might have expected more in terms of scholarly engagement with the tradition. As already mentioned, there are serious problems with the critical interpretation being offered and it falls short of the best work done by scholars of Husserl, Heidegger, Merleau-Ponty etc. One of the utterly puzzling features of the criticism is the following. The main point of contention is the alleged idealist or anti-realist orientation of phenomenology. Because of this metaphysical commitment, phenomenology has come to an end. But the fallacy of this argument should be obvious. Even if some of the phenomenologists did indeed contribute to the realism-idealism debate, even if some of their analyses, in particular those pertaining to the very status of the phenomenon or to the scope of transcendental phenomenology, bear directly on this issue, it is certainly not as if phenomenologists were exclusively concerned with this issue. What about their investigations of intentionality, experience, emotions, self-consciousness, perception, imagination, social cognition, action, embodiment, truth, temporality, ethics, community, historicity, etc.? What about the fruitful interaction that is currently taken place between phenomenology and the (cognitive) sciences? What about the influence the phenomenological analyses have had on such disciplines as psychiatry, architecture, education, sports science, psychology, nursing, comparative literature, anthropology, sociology etc? To what extent are these analyses or contributions dependent upon phenomenology's transcendental commitment? To what extent are they undermined by speculative realism's attack on correlationism? To what extent is speculative realism in a position to offer its own more convincing analyses?

But – the critics might retort – even if speculative realism might lack the ability to do the latter, you are just sidetracking the issue. You are not responding to the ancestrality objection. Is correlationism really incompatible with the findings of science? Does an endorsement of the former make certain interpretations of scientific findings nonsensical? And if yes, is that not a *reductio ad absurdum* of correlationism? This would undoubtedly be the view of some scientists. As Hawking and Mlodinow put it in their book *The Grand Design: New Answers to the Ultimate Questions of Life*: 'Philosophy is dead' (Hawking and Mlodinow 2010, 5). I doubt many philosophers would endorse this verdict, but ultimately we need to ask whether science ought to be the final arbiter of deep philosophical questions.[10] Is it appropriate to dismiss Kant's *Kritik der reinen Vernunft* (or Husserl's *Ideen I*) by appealing to the findings of astrophysics and evolutionary history (Brassier 2001, 28), or does such a 'refutation' merely testify to a conflation of levels and categories? Although I veer towards the latter view, my aim is not to settle this issue here. My point is rather that regardless of which choice one makes, it will leave the speculative realists in an uncomfortable bind. If they simply defer to the authority of science, their criticism of phenomenology (and any other kind of correlationism) is not only bereft of philosophical import, it also lacks novelty. If they do not take that route, they lose one of their supposedly weightiest arguments, and will then have to buttress their criticism with proper philosophical arguments, for instance arguments taken from philosophy of science. But as Wiltsche has recently pointed out in a critical discussion of Meillassoux' work, the latter's treatment of and engagement with philosophy of science is astonishingly sparse (Wiltsche under review). In *After Finitude*, Meillassoux seems to take it for granted that scientific realism is the only available option. That, however, is hardly correct (for an informative overview see Chakravartty 2011). Furthermore, most standard textbooks in philosophy of science contain more arguments for – and against – scientific realism than *After Finitude* (see Sankey, 2008).

To put it differently, speculative realism's most substantial challenge to phenomenology is an old hat, and can be found in more potent form in analytic philosophy. Russell (1959, 213) held the view that philosophers should strive towards becoming undistorting mirrors of the world, and claimed that results from astronomy and geology could refute Kant and Hegel by showing that the mind is of a recent date and that the processes of stellar evolution proceeded according to laws in which mind plays no part (1959, 16). If tempted by eliminativism, one can simply read the Churchlands, Metzinger, or Alex Rosenberg. It is harder to find an analytic counterpart to Harman's weird realism, but that is less surprising, and might also – depending on one's philosophical inclinations – be a good thing.

Let me try to take stock. The allegedly devastating criticism that speculative realism directs at phenomenology is flawed in various ways.

- It is too superficial: it misinterprets the classical texts and fails to engage sufficiently with relevant scholarship in the area
- It is too simplistic: it misses out on important differences internal to phenomenology, such as the difference between early realist phenomenology and the transcendental idealism of Husserl, and claims to be able to assess the value and significance of phenomenological analyses *tout court* by criticizing what phenomenology has to say, or not to say, on the topic of metaphysics.
- It lacks novelty: the central objections have already previously been raised by (some) phenomenologists, analytic philosophers, and empirical scientists.

My focus has primarily been on the negative or critical contribution of speculative realism. Let me conclude with a few remarks concerning its positive contribution, with the obvious proviso that a definitive verdict would have to await (somebody else's) more exhaustive and thorough treatment and analysis:

- Its realist credentials are somewhat questionable, ranging from Harman's scepticism (with its paradoxical revival of something akin to Kant's noumenal realm) to Brassier's radical nihilism. It is an open question whether any of these positions are coherent.
- It is epistemologically underdetermined. Even when rejecting Putnam's (and the phenomenologists') claim that the ontological and the epistemological are deeply interconnected, many scientific realists would consider it of paramount importance to explain how human cognition can give rise to genuine knowledge of a mind-independent reality: how is knowledge possible? The phenomenologists likewise were led to their views regarding the status of reality through a focused exploration and analysis

of intentionality. The speculative realists, by contrast, do not really offer much in terms of a theory of knowledge that could justify their metaphysical claims.

- Given the significant divergence between the positive views of Harman, Meillassoux and Brassier, one might finally wonder whether it at all makes sense to employ the collective label *speculative realism*. Sparrow obviously thinks so, although he does admit that the defenders of speculative realism do not actually share a critical method (Sparrow 2014, 19). 'What then legitimates its speculative claims?' (Sparrow 2014, 19). The answer given by Sparrow is as brief as it is unsatisfactory. He writes that the speculative realists share 'a set of commitments', including a 'commitment to speculation' (Sparrow 2014, 19). But this merely restates the problem. What is the justification for the various (outlandish) claims being made? How should we distinguish speculation from free phantasy? A question that is particularly pressing when reading Harman. As Sparrow (2014, 20) continues, to different degrees the speculative realists are committed to 'a blending of fiction and fact', they have 'a taste for the weird, the strange, the uncanny', and their aim 'is to clear the ground for new advances in the thinking of reality. This is, after all, the end of philosophy' (Sparrow 2014, 20). Perhaps speculative realism does indeed constitute the end of philosophy, or perhaps it has merely reached its own dead-end. If so, Sparrow's unfounded verdict on phenomenology would turn out to be an impressively accurate assessment of speculative realism: It never really got started and it is not clear that it ever was anything at all. This also seems to be a conclusion eventually reached by Brassier:

> The 'speculative realist movement' exists only in the imaginations of a group of bloggers promoting an agenda for which I have no sympathy whatsoever: actor-network theory spiced with pan-psychist metaphysics and morsels of process philosophy. I don't believe the Internet is an appropriate medium for serious philosophical debate; nor do I believe it is acceptable to try to concoct a philosophical movement online by using blogs to exploit the misguided enthusiasm of impressionable graduate students. I agree with Deleuze's remark that ultimately the most basic task of philosophy is to impede stupidity, so I see little philosophical merit in a 'movement' whose most signal achievement thus far is to have generated an online orgy of stupidity. (Brassier and Rychter 2011)[11]

As for phenomenology, I think it currently finds itself at a crossroad. It continues to remain a source of inspiration for other disciplines, and at least certain of its ideas have also been taken up by analytic philosophy and cognitive science. At the same time, phenomenology remains under attack from a variety of different positions, including hard-nosed naturalism and neurocentrism, and after the death of Henry, Levinas, and Derrida it is not clear who, if any, their natural successors are. It is not easy to identify new thinkers who in equal measures are innovating phenomenology. As shown by *The Oxford Handbook of Contemporary Phenomenology* (Zahavi 2012b), what we rather find is a lot of work being done in two directions: inward (and backward) and outward (and forward). On the one hand, we find a continuing engagement and conversation with the founding fathers (and mothers). The philosophical resources and insights to be found in Husserl's, Heidegger's and Merleau-Ponty's work are evidently not yet exhausted. On the other hand, an increasing amount of dialogue is taking place between phenomenology and other philosophical tradition and empirical disciplines.

It is hard to predict how many self-avowed phenomenologists there will be 100 years from now. But I am quite confident that the basic insights found in phenomenology will continue to appeal to and attract and inspire gifted thinkers. In fact, if there is any truth to phenomenology, it should be able to renew itself, and continue to flourish in new forms and perhaps also under new names.

Notes

1. One of Rockmore's (2011, 8) claims is that one should reject the often repeated 'myth' that Husserl is the inventor of phenomenology and instead credit Kant as the first true phenomenologist. In fact, Rockmore (2011, 210) even questions whether Husserl, Heidegger and Merleau-Ponty deserve being classified as phenomenologists. For a critical review of Rockmore's book, see Zahavi 2012a.
2. On previous occasions, I have defended the coherency of Husserl's transcendental phenomenology (see Zahavi 1996, 2003, 2010b), just as I have also argued that there are a number of overarching concerns and common themes that unifies the major figures of classical phenomenology (Zahavi 2007, 2008). I will not rehearse these arguments here. When discussing the question of whether a philosophical tradition is sufficiently unified to count as a tradition, it might, however, be unwise to adopt such rigid criteria that one ultimately risks proving just about any philosophical tradition out of existence. Were one to accept Sparrow's approach, it is hard to see how critical theory, hermeneutics, pragmatism or analytic philosophy could survive. Indeed, if consensus concerning a fixed set of methodological tools is a necessary condition for the existence of a research program, hardly any would exist. A somewhat similar remark holds true in the case of individual figures. It is hard to point to any influential thinker in the history of philosophy whose work has not given rise to scholarly disagreements and conflicting interpretations. A purist might insist that such disagreement simply reveals that the thoughts of the philosopher under examination are fundamentally confused and unclear, and that they therefore ought to be rejected. A contrasting and more sensible view would be that any philosophical work worth discussing decades and centuries later has a scope and depth to it that allows for conflicting interpretations and that the continuing critical engagement with the tradition is part of what philosophy is all about. Should one be so unwise as to choose the first option, however, it should be obvious that one cannot then single out a few figures for condemnation, one should at the very least be consistent, and then reject the whole lot: Plato, Aristotle, Augustine, Aquinas, Descartes, Leibniz, Locke, Hume, Kant, Nietzsche, etc.
3. Although Meillassoux (2008, 5) is often credited with the coinage of the term, 'correlationism' was in fact used and defined much earlier. Here is Beck in 1928:

'"Korrelativismus" soll hier als Terminus dienen zur Bezeichnung eines von Husserl und Dilthey erarbeiteten Standpunktes, der die alten Disjunktionen Idealismus oder Realismus, Subjektivismus oder Objektivismus, Immanenzphilosophie und Phänomenalismus oder Realphilosophie überwunden hat zugunsten der These: Weder existiert eine Welt an sich, unabhängig von einem Bewußtsein von ihr, noch existiert bloß ein Bewußtsein, resp. Bewußtseinssubjekt und nur als des Bewußtseins, resp. Subjekts bloßer Modus (Erlebnis, Funktion oder Inhalt) die Welt. Und: weder erkennen wir die Welt, wie sie an sich, d. i. unabhängig von unserem Bewußtsein ist, noch erkennen wir bloß eine Scheinwelt, jenseits derer die eigentliche, wahre Welt an sich existierte. Die korrelativistische Gegenthese lautet positiv: Bewußtsein und Welt, Subjekt und Objekt, Ich und Welt stehen selbst in einem derartigen korrelativen, d. i. sich gegenseitig bedingenden Seinszusammenhang, daß obige Disjunktionen überhaupt keinen Sinn haben' (Beck 1928, 611). I am indebted to Genki Uemura for this reference.

4 The fact that Kant kept on to the idea of the thing-in-itself was of course an affront to the German Idealists, who saw it as an expression of Kant's inability to carry through his own revolutionary project. Whereas Kant would claim that things outside of the correlation are nothing to us, Hegel would downgrade the 'nothing to us' to a 'nothing at all' (Braver 2007, 81). Whether Kant's view commits him to a two-world theory is debated, however. For a recent rejection of this idea, see Allais 2004.

5 Some of Harman's ideas are reminiscent of ideas found elsewhere, namely in phenomenology. Consider, for instance, Merleau-Ponty's claim that idealism and constructivism deprive the world of its transcendence. Had the former positions been true, had the world really been a mere product of our constitution, the world would have appeared in full transparency, it would only have possessed the meaning we ascribe to it, and would have had no hidden aspects. In truth however, the world is an infinite source of richness, it is mystery and a gift (Merleau-Ponty 2012, lxxv, lxxxv). Consider also Levinas' claim that object-intentionality cannot provide us with an encounter with true otherness. When I study or utilize objects, I am constantly transforming the foreign and different into the familiar and same, thereby making them lose their strangeness. This is also why, according to Levinas, Husserlian phenomenology cannot accommodate and do justice to the transcendence of the other. The other is exactly that which cannot be conceptualized or categorized. Any attempt to grasp or know the other necessarily domesticates and distorts what is ultimately an ineffable and untotalizable exteriority (Levinas 1972). It is debatable whether Merleau-Ponty's criticism of idealism is a criticism of Husserlian idealism, or whether it is rather targeting Kant and French neo-Kantians like *Brunschvicg*. It is also a matter of dispute whether Levinas' criticism of Husserl is justified (see Overgaard 2003). In either case, however, it is important to realize that the criticism in question is an internal criticism, it is a criticism pre-empted by and developed within phenomenology.

6 Despite being sympathetic to Meillassoux's criticism of correlationism, Brassier has argued that the former's focus on ancestrality and on arch-fossils (materials indicating the existence of events anterior to terrestrial life) is unfortunate. To 'insist that it is only the ancestral dimension that transcends correlational constitution, is to imply that the emergence of consciousness marks some sort of fundamental ontological rupture, shattering the autonomy and consistency of reality, such that once consciousness has emerged on the scene, nothing can pursue an independent existence any more. The danger is that in privileging

the arche-fossil as sole paradigm of a mind-independent reality, Meillassoux is ceding too much ground to the correlationism he wishes to destroy' (Brassier 2007, 60).

7   For an in-depth engagement with and criticism of Harman's Heidegger-interpretation, see Wolfendale 2014. For a more well-informed, though in my view still too uncharitable, critical reading of Husserl, see Sebold 2014.
8   For a more extensive discussion of the relation between Putnam and Husserl, see Zahavi 2004b.
9   For more on the relation between Davidson and Husserl, see Zahavi and Satne 2016.
10 In 1922, Moritz Schlick gave a talk where he argued that the general theory of relativity had disconfirmed transcendental philosophy and vindicated empiricist philosophy. This view has found much resonance, but as Ryckman observes in *The Reign of Relativity: Philosophy in Physics 1915–1925*, it happens to be quite incorrect. The outstanding mathematician Hermann Weyl, who was one of Einstein's colleagues in Zürich, and who contributed decisively to the interpretation and further development of both the general theory of relativity and the field of quantum mechanics, did not only draw quite extensively on Husserl's criticism of naturalism, but was also deeply influenced by Husserl's transcendental idealism (Ryckman 2005, 6, 110). Another distinguished physicist heavily influenced by Husserl was the quantum theorist Fritz London (see French 2002). Ultimately, one might wonder whether the decisive advances in theoretical physics at the beginning of the twentieth century really leave our standard conception of subjectivity, objectivity and knowledge untouched.
11 Brassier's assessment points to an important aspect of speculative realism that I have not been able to address: the specific sociological context of its emergence and diffusion. What institutional establishment was it a reaction against, and why did it gain popularity at the time and in the way it did?

Disclosure statement

No potential conflict of interest was reported by the author.

References

Allais, L. (2004) 'Kant's One World: Interpreting "Transcendental Idealism"', *British Journal for the History of Philosophy* 12(4): 655–684.
Badiou, A. (2009) *Logics of Worlds: Being and Event 2*, London: Continuum.
Beck, M. (1928) 'Die neue Problemlage der Erkenntnistheorie', *Deutsche Vierteljahrsschrift für Literaturwissenschaft und Geistesgeschichte* 6: 611–639.
Bogost, I. (2012) *Alien Phenomenology, or What it's Like to be a Thing*, Minneapolis, MN: University of Minnesota Press.
Brassier, R. (2001). *Alien Theory: The Decline of Materialism in the Name of Matter*. PhD thesis, University of Warwick.
Brassier, R. (2007) *Nihil Unbound: Enlightenment and Extinction*, Palgrave Macmillan.
Brassier, R., I. H. Grant, G. Harman, and Q. Meillassoux (2007) *Speculative Realism*. *Collapse* III: 306–449.
Brassier, R., and Rychter, M. (2011). "I Am a Nihilist Because I Still Believe in Truth". *Kronos*. Retrieved October 5, 2015 from http://www.kronos.org.pl/index.php?23151,896

Braver, L. (2007) *A Thing of This World: A History of Continental Anti-realism*, Evanston: Northwestern University Press.
Braver, L. (2012) 'A Brief History of Continental Realism', *Continental Philosophy Review* 45(2): 261–289.
Carman, T. (2003) *Heidegger's Analytic: Interpretation, Discourse, and Authenticity in Being and Time*, Cambridge: Cambridge University Press.
Chakravartty, A. (2011) 'Scientific Realism'. In E. N. Zalta (ed.) *The Stanford Encyclopedia of Philosophy*, http://plato.stanford.edu/entries/scientific-realism/
Davidson, D. (1990) 'The Structure and Content of Truth', *Journal of Philosophy* 87(6): 279–328.
Davidson, D. (2001) *Subjective, Intersubjective, Objective*, Oxford: Oxford University Press.
Dreyfus, H. L., and C. Spinosa (1999) 'Coping with Things-in-Themselves: A Practice-Based Phenomenological Argument for Realism', *Inquiry* 42(1): 49–78.
French, S. (2002) 'A Phenomenological Solution to the Measurement Problem? Husserl and the Foundations of Quantum Mechanics', *Studies in History and Philosophy of Science Part B* 33(3): 467–491.
Glazebrook, T. (2001) 'Heidegger and Scientific Realism', *Continental Philosophy Review* 34(4): 361–401.
Hardy, L. (2014) *Nature's Suit: Husserl's Phenomenological Philosophy of the Physical Sciences*, Athens, OH: Ohio University Press.
Harman, G. (2005) *Guerrilla Metaphysics: Phenomenology and the Carpentry of Things*, Chicago, IL: Open Court.
Harman, G. (2008) 'On the Horror of Phenomenology: Lovecraft and Husserl', *Collapse IV.* 333–364.
Harman, G. (2011) *The Quadruple Object*, Alresford: Zero Books.
Hawking, S., and Mlodinow, L. (2010) *The Grand Design*, New York, NY: Bantam Books.
Heidegger, M. (1982) *The Basic Problems of Phenomenology*, Bloomington: Indiana University Press.
Husserl, E. (1970) *The Crisis of European Sciences and Transcendental Phenomenology*, Evanston: Northwestern University Press.
Husserl, E. (1982) *Ideas pertaining to a pure Phenomenology and to a Phenomenological Philosophy. First Book: General Introduction to a Pure Phenomenology*, The Hague: Martinus Nijhoff.
Husserl, E. (1994) *Briefwechsel – Wissenschaftlerkorrespondenz* Husserliana Dokumente III/7 K.Schuhmann (ed.), Dordrecht: Kluwer.
Husserl, E. (2001) *Logical Investigations II*, London: Routledge.
Kant, I. (1998) *Critique of Pure Reason*, Cambridge: Cambridge University Press.
Levinas, E. (1972) *Totality and Infinity: An Essay on Exteriority*, Pittsburgh, PA: Duquesne University Press.
Meillassoux, Q. (2008) *After Finitude. An Essay on the Necessity of Contingency*, London: Continuum.
Merleau-Ponty, M. (2012) *Phenomenology of Perception*, London: Routledge.
Morton, T. (2012) 'Art in the age of asymmetry: Hegel, objects, aesthetics', *Evental Aesthetics* 1(1): 121–142.
Overgaard, S. (2003) 'On Levinas' Critique of Husserl', In D. Zahavi, S. Heinämaa, H. Ruin (eds) *Metaphysics, Facticity, Interpretation*, 115–138). Dordrecht: Kluwer.
Petitot, J. et al. (eds.) (1999) *Naturalizing phenomenology: Issues in contemporary phenomenology and cognitive science*, Stanford: Stanford University Press.
Putnam, H. (1978) *Meaning and the Moral Sciences*, London: Routledge & Kegan Paul.
Putnam, H. (1987) *The Many Faces of Realism*, LaSalle, Illinois: Open Court.

Putnam, H. (1988) *Representation and Reality*, Cambridge, MA: MIT Press.
Putnam, H. (1990) *Realism with a Human Face*, Cambridge, MA: Harvard University Press.
Putnam, H. (1992) *Renewing Philosophy*, Cambridge, MA: Harvard University Press.
Putnam, H. (1999) *The Threefold Cord. Mind, Body, and World*, New York, NY: Columbia University Press.
Rockmore, T. (2011) *Kant and Phenomenology*, Chicago, IL: University of Chicago Press.
Russell, B. (1959) *My Philosophical Development*. New York: Simon and Schuster.
Ryckman, T. (2005) *The Reign of Relativity: Philosophy in Physics, 1915–1925*, Oxford: Oxford University Press.
Sankey, H. (2008) *Scientific Realism and the Rationality of Science*, Aldershot: Ashgate.
Sebold, R. (2014) *Continental Anti-Realism: A Critique*, London: Rowman & Littlefield International.
Shaviro, S. (2011) 'Panpsychism and/or Eliminativism'. Retrieved October 5, 2015 from http://www.shaviro.com/Blog/?p=1012
Smith, B. (1997) 'Realistic Phenomenology', In L. Embree (ed.) *Encyclopedia of Phenomenology*, 586–590). Dordrecht: Kluwer.
Sparrow, T. (2014) *The End of Phenomenology: Metaphysics and the New Realism*, Edinburgh: Edinburgh University Press.
Varela, F. J. (1996). 'Neurophenomenology a Methodological Remedy for the Hard Problem', *Journal of Consciousness Studies* 3(4): 330–349.
Wiltsche, H. (under review) 'Science, Realism and Correlationism. A Phenomenological Critique of Meillassoux' Argument from Ancestrality'.
Wolfendale, P. (2014) *Object-Oriented Philosophy: The Noumenon's New Clothes*, Falmouth: Urbanomic.
Zahavi, D. (1996) *Husserl und die transzendentale Intersubjektivität. Eine Antwort auf die sprachpragmatische Kritik*. Phaenomenologica 135, Dordrecht: Kluwer.
Zahavi, D. (2003) *Husserl's Phenomenology*, Stanford: Stanford University Press.
Zahavi, D. (2004a) 'Phenomenology and the project of naturalization', *Phenomenology and the Cognitive Sciences* 3(4): 331–347.
Zahavi, D. (2004b) 'Natural Realism, Anti-Reductionism, and Intentionality. The 'Phenomenology' of Hilary Putnam', in D. Carr and C. F. Cheung (eds) *Time, Space, and Culture*, 235–251. Dordrecht: Springer.
Zahavi, D. (2007) *Phänomenologie für Einsteiger*, München: Wilhelm Fink Verlag.
Zahavi, D. (2008) 'Phenomenology', in D. Moran (ed) *Routledge Companion to Twentieth-Century Philosophy*, 661–692. London: Routledge.
Zahavi, D. (2010a) 'Naturalized Phenomenology', in S. Gallagher and D. Schmicking (eds) *Handbook of Phenomenology and Cognitive Science*, 2–19. Dordrecht: Springer.
Zahavi, D. (2010b) 'Husserl and the 'absolute'', in C. Ierna, H. Jacobs, and F. Mattens (eds) *Philosophy, Phenomenology, Sciences: Essays in Commemoration of Husserl*, Dordrecht: Springer. (71–92). Phaenomenologica Vol. 200.
Zahavi, D. (2012a) 'Noesis and noema', *The Times Literary Supplement*, June 29, 28.
Zahavi, D. (ed.) (2012b) *The Oxford Handbook of Contemporary Phenomenology*, Oxford: Oxford University Press.
Zahavi, D. (2013) 'Naturalized Phenomenology: A Desideratum or a Category Mistake?', *Royal Institute of Philosophy Supplement* 72: 23–42.
Zahavi, D. (2015) 'Phenomenology of reflection', in A. Staiti (ed) *Commentary on Husserl's Ideas I*, 177–193. Berlin: De Gruyter.
Zahavi, D., and G. Satne (2016) 'Varieties of shared intentionality: Tomasello and classical phenomenology', in J. Bell, A. Cutrofello, and P. Livingston (eds) *Beyond the Analytic-Continental Divide: Pluralist Philosophy in the Twenty-First Century*, 305–325. London: Routledge.

Naturalism, Experience, and Hume's 'Science of Human Nature'

Benedict Smith

Durham University, UK

ABSTRACT
A standard interpretation of Hume's naturalism is that it paved the way for a scientific and 'disenchanted' conception of the world. My aim in this paper is to show that this is a restrictive reading of Hume, and it obscures a different and profitable interpretation of what Humean naturalism amounts to. The standard interpretation implies that Hume's 'science of human nature' was a reductive investigation into our psychology. But, as Hume explains, the subject matter of this science is not restricted to introspectively accessible mental content and incorporates our social nature and interpersonal experience. Illuminating the science of human nature has implications for how we understand what Hume means by 'experience' and thus how we understand the context of his epistemological investigations. I examine these in turn and argue overall that Hume's naturalism and his science of man do not simply anticipate a disenchanted conception of the world.

Naturalism and Disenchantment

Book I of Hume's *Treatise* culminates in considering the disturbing predicament that the 'current of nature' determines us, inescapably, to possess beliefs for which we can find no rational justification (1978, 269). By way of response Hume is said to have provided a powerful 'naturalized epistemology', seeking to account for our knowledge and epistemic practices more generally in a scientifically acceptable way. If successful, such a naturalistic approach promises to surmount any sceptical conclusions implied by the disturbing predicament, since the uneasy relation between reason and nature may be resolved by recasting the relation between them. For example, in adopting what he considers a Humean perspective, Quine proposed that naturalized epistemology need not assume that questions of justification are a distinctive part of a self-standing subject matter; rather, naturalized epistemology would describe the psychological processes of belief formation. Accordingly naturalism subsumes epistemology and makes it, famously, 'simply ... a chapter of psychology and hence of natural science' (Quine 1969, 82).[1]

Strawson's (1985, 12) alternative view characterizes Hume's naturalism as a kind of refuge from his epistemological reflections. We would need a refuge since the discoveries of reason are, inevitably, sceptical ones which threaten to destabilize our everyday understandings of the world and of our experience. From inside the refuge, as it were, we can look upon the discoveries of reason as intellectual curiosities but never as genuine opportunities for our theoretical or practical assent. Thus a third 'biperspectivalist' approach, suggests Michael Williams, claims that at best we oscillate between the perspectives of naturalism and scepticism, turning (or perhaps being driven) from one to the other depending on context. A plausible interpretation of Hume's project might ensure that both the rational and natural elements are adequately recognized but, so far, it seems that interpreters have tended to focus on just one of them (Williams 2004, 271).[2]

Whatever the most successful interpretive strategy it is important to be clear that the subject matter of Hume's 'science of man' (e.g., 1978, 16) incorporates the relation between nature and reason, this relation is thus part of what we would expect Hume's naturalism to encompass. Whilst the importance of this 'science of human nature' cannot be overstated its character and implications have been overlooked by some influential interpretations of Hume. The result is that what is meant by 'Humean naturalism' is needlessly restrictive and the possibility of appreciating the breadth of Hume's naturalism is subsequently blocked.

The restriction in question occurs because of a tendency, displayed by both critics and supporters alike, to read Hume's naturalism to involve a narrowly psychological view of human practice. Hume's appeal to psychology presupposes metaphysical assumptions distinctive of what nowadays is described as a scientific world view. Accordingly Hume's science of man is assumed to be an investigation into our epistemic practices that takes for granted the privileged status of the scientifically described world. This has the effect of characterizing Hume's project as one that tries to 'place' our practices and our human nature more widely *within* the world as scientifically described.[3]

Hume is read as being committed to an austere metaphysics and was, in McDowell's (1998, 174–175) words, the 'prophet par excellence' of a so-called disenchanted conception of the world, the view according to which the world is an 'ineffable lump'.[4] Similarly David Lewis (1986, ix) writes that Hume's world is exhausted by 'a vast mosaic of local matters of particular fact, just one little thing after another'. These images, although quite different in some respects, both reflect a view about the metaphysics deemed to be characteristic of the Humean natural-scientific framework. On the face of it such a metaphysical view is not easy to reconcile with the aspiration to conduct the science of man as Hume characterizes it. The constraints of an austere naturalist ontology might jeopardize the idea that 'man' or 'human nature' in the relevant senses can themselves be appropriate objects of study. The conception of the world as disenchanted might be supposed as the context from which a science of man is subsequently conducted. But as I understand it *that* conception of the world is already a partial conclusion of a particular kind of philosophical inquiry, not its condition. For Hume, human beings are not only the possible but the principal objects of philosophical inquiry and the science of man is not some attempt to understand ourselves against the backdrop of the world construed as an ineffable lump.

As Hume explains human nature is the cardinal focus of the science of man, the study of which is not additional to but is presupposed by other sciences:

> 'Tis evident, that all the sciences have a relation, greater or less, to human nature; and that however wide any of them may seem to run from it, they still return back by one passage or another. Even Mathematics, Natural Philosophy, and Natural Religion, are in some measure dependent on the science of Man ... [T]he science of man is the only solid foundation for the other sciences (1978, xv-xvi).[5]

Here, in the Introduction to the *Treatise*, Hume explicitly articulates the idea that the science of man is of foundational importance. Hume (1978, xix) also takes care to explain that when the science of man proceeds via the 'cautious observation of human' life it incorporates ordinary features of our lives that are to be described as far as possible 'as they appear in the common course of the world'. These remarks refer to aspects of our lives that cannot be identified as, let alone solely explained in terms of, psychological properties or tendencies. Yet an influential way of interpreting Hume is to reduce or restrict his naturalism to a thesis about how are minds process and render intelligible the data provided by the senses – our 'experience' – and the interrelations between psychological mechanisms such as the role of memory and the felt 'force' or 'vivacity' of impressions and ideas (Hume 1978, 96).

There should be no objection to Hume being described as a naturalist. But, in addition to the logical point that the science of man is presupposed by what is nowadays meant by scientific naturalism, what is open to cautious observation is more than what can be characterized in psychological terms. This at least raises a question about what constitutes the subject matter of or the input to the science of man. Any answer, I suggest, ought to distinguish between two different senses of experience. I do this in the next section before turning to the implications for characterizing Hume's epistemology.

Hume on Experience

Hume means different things when he uses the term 'experience'. One use is individualistic and introspectionist, experience of sense and memory which can be reached or recalled by turning reflection inwards, to the interior of our psychic domain. But Hume also invokes another sense of experience, less solipsistic and more social, experience of 'common life and observation'. We ought not to cleave too cleanly between these different kinds of experience since they overlap. For example, whilst all our experience for Hume involves perceptions of sense and memory, the majority of our experience occurs on a social level (Traiger 1994, 253).[6]

In the majority of cases where Hume invokes experience in Book I of the *Treatise* it is used in a fairly narrow sense as part of the analysis of, for example, the nature and origin of causal inference (e.g., 1978, 163). In this context and others such as the discussion about the existence of objects when unperceived (e.g., 1978, 188) experience is broken down into particular discrete instances. Merleau-Ponty (2002, 256) would later describe how this led Hume to 'dissect' experience. Yet Books II and III of the *Treatise*, for example, as well as the first *Enquiry* are replete with examples of experience used in the wider sense. Hume frequently refers to 'daily experience' and 'common experience' and does so in order to demonstrate the truth (or otherwise) of some proposed analysis of our ideas. For example, the causes of love and hatred are revealed by 'undeniable proofs drawn from daily experience' and the 'phaenomena that occur to us in common life and conversation' help to explain how we regard persons in authority (1978, 347, 361).

Hume explains that a person's experience can be expanded through interaction with others. In the first *Enquiry* Hume (1975, 107) talks of processes that 'enlarge ... the sphere of one man's experience and thought'. Enlarged experience is achieved, for example, through engaging 'testimony, books and conversation' (1975, 107) all explicit examples of interpersonal experience, not experience construed as inner states or as instances as we find in Book I of the *Treatise*. What I want to emphasize here is that this sense of experience, of common life and conversation in the ordinary course of the world, is a principal and irreducible element in Hume's science of man.[7] This has implications for a different interpretation of Hume's naturalism, one that arguably provides a form of intelligibility different from that provided by modern science and aims instead to elucidate the ordinary features of human experience living in a world with other people.

When describing how the science of man is presupposed by the other sciences, Hume (1978, xvi) goes on to say that the 'only solid foundation' of the science of man, in turn, 'must be laid on experience and observation'. What Hume must have in mind here is the experience and observation of 'common life' and not, or not just, experience in the sense of inner states or instances of sensory experience. Hume insisted that philosophical reflection ought to be constrained by experience and it never should attempt to reach beyond it (e.g. 1978, xvii). But this does not mean that the constraint in question is provided by introspection; the relevant sense of experience is not, or not just, a stock of private, inner episodes. The cautious observation of human life does not equate to the cautious observation of inner psychological states.

What Hume's pluralism about experience implies is that there are different ways in which we make the subject matter of the science of human nature intelligible. I have been suggesting that there is at least one sense of experience in Hume that refers irreducibly to our intersubjective interaction. The cautious observation of human life reveals that the activity of reflecting on common experience is interestingly different from the activity of reflecting on our inward or private experience. It is different because it distinguishes between what is and what is not possible to entertain (or, better, to *do*) as a reflective agent. We are bound to hold beliefs, such as those about necessary connection for instance, irrespective of the conclusions of rational reflection. This – to repeat – is not just a psychological point about what is or is not possible to entertain or imagine. It is a point about our nature as embodied, intersubjective creatures, a point about our human nature.

Another way to distinguish between the different contents is to contrast the abstract reflection of the solitary thinker, descending into the familiar sceptical *cul de sac*, with the engaged person who is immersed in common life. In the first case, rational reflection on the grounds of belief 'entirely subverts itself' and leaves the thinker in a state of spectatorial alienation (1978, 267). Such a person is detached not only from the ordinary world of external objects and other people, but also from their own ideas and experience. No wonder Hume portrays such a state in terms that are reminiscent of descriptions of psychiatric illness. In the conclusion of Book I, Hume (1978, 264) writes:

> I am first affrighted and confounded with that forelorn solitude, in which I am plac'd in my philosophy, and fancy myself some strange uncouth monster, who not being able to mingle and unite in society, has been expell'd all human commerce, and left utterly abandon'd and disconsolate ... no one will hearken to me. Every one keeps at a distance, and dreads that storm, which beats upon me from every side.

The sceptical conclusions are the outcome of applying reason in the search for the grounds of our ideas, yet this application and its results are examples of *abstract* reasoning; a mode of reflection that presupposes common life. Hume explains that when reason subverts itself the result is 'total scepticism' since we are left with no reasons to believe one thing rather than any other thing 'either in philosophy or common life'. But Hume does not think that the 'refin'd or elaborate reasoning' that leads us to scepticism is thereby shown to be mistaken. Were we to refuse to employ abstract reasoning then we would 'cut off entirely all science and philosophy' (Hume 1978, 268). The mistake, if there is one, is to construe the scepticism as if it revealed the basic condition of our experience and thought, a condition from which we are merely distracted when engaged in common life. Insisting that we ought to believe that scepticism is foundational in this sense would involve a 'manifest contradiction'; the subverting effect of rational reflection provides us with no reasons to believe anything at all.

The point is that abstract reasoning and the content of our experience and thought at the level of common life are both part of what we consider in the science of man. They are different expressions of our human nature, different ways in which we make things intelligible. Likewise, the disenchanted conception of the world that Hume is supposed to champion is not foundational, as if it were a more genuine or authentic conception of the way things are. Formulating a disenchanted conception of the world should not be seen as the principal aspiration of Hume's naturalism. My objection is specifically to the assumption that Hume's primary commitment *qua* naturalist is a metaphysical one, a commitment that is emblematic of what is nowadays referred to as a scientistic standpoint. Hume's naturalism is more complex and more humane than this. Appreciating this is has implications, as I have been trying show, for how we characterize experience and for how we construe Hume's epistemology.

What I have been urging is that reading Hume as the 'prophet of disenchantment' has a significant effect on what we then come to see as the subject matter of the science of man. If Hume's method really was to, firstly, set forth a disenchanted conception of the world and then, secondly, to explain the grounds of our experience and thought in light of that, then no sense can made of how Hume himself conceived of the science of man. If we describe Hume's method in this way then the vital role that Hume gave to common life is obscured.[8] A result is that the main focus becomes the narrow epistemological investigations that occupy the majority of Book I of the *Treatise*.

I have objected to the idea that Hume is primarily a scientistic naturalist, and elaborated that objection by drawing attention to what constitutes the subject matter of the science of man. The influence of what I am objecting to is widespread, and has affected what is understood to be the chief aim of Hume's work. The dominance of the so-called 'Oxford view' casts Hume as primarily an epistemologist with a notable enthusiasm for the explanatory potential of psychology.[9] The Oxford view underpins the reception of Hume in 'analytic' philosophy but it is also influential in how the phenomenological tradition has characterized the nature and role of experience in Hume's work.

Phenomenology and Hume's Epistemology

Inspired by Merleau-Ponty the phenomenologist Samuel Todes (2001) developed an account of embodied perception, describing experience as articulating a 'life-field' – a domain of enticements and opportunities in which the nature of perceptual objects reflect our bodily capacities. Todes claims that it is through our responsive actions and our embodied agency more widely that the field of experience is engaged, sustained and negotiated. Todes characterized perception as an active and more or less skilled practical accommodation and receptiveness to what the world affords by way of opportunities to have our needs (as Todes puts it) satisfied.[10] According to Todes (2001, 72) our perceptual-bodily responsiveness is a form of practical engagement with the world, an engagement that incorporates a preparation to encounter the ongoing affordances and meanings that present themselves in our experience. Like Merleau-Ponty, Todes regards such affordances and meanings as mediated by our bodies understood as the vehicles of our perceptual relatedness to the world.

In Todes's (2001, 72) terminology we operate with non-conceptual 'bodily inferences' that conjoin our anticipation of experience to its actual occurrence; the anticipated nature of the hidden side of coffee cup, say, is fulfilled when the previously hidden side is actually experienced.[11] The structure of this anticipation is, for Todes, a bodily achievement not a function of habitual mental processes trained through brute repetition to react in particular ways to relevant stimuli. This is, then, allegedly a counterpart to Hume's emphasis on mental inference, a kind of felt determination of the mind toward possessing and maintaining particular beliefs in the face of a suitable diet of instances.[12] Todes also suggests that there is another counterpart here, one that concerns 'habit'.

The refinement of our perceptual skills, the refinement of our 'poise' as Todes (2001, 81) puts it, is a refinement of our anticipations and habits:

> The field of our experience [can] endure only so long as we, by responsive action, can make it *habitable*: habitable, as our habitation, or dwelling place, *where* we live: and habit-able, as a place to which we can become *accustomed* as the determinately skilled percipients (marked by our past experience) we gradually create ourselves to be.

According to Todes this diachronic conception of experience is unavailable to Hume. Presumably, Todes has in mind the thin conception of experience that Hume discusses in Book I of the *Treatise*. For Todes (2001, 6), Hume's view culminates in eliminating the active body from experience, equating experience with the 'visual point of view' of a 'pure spectator'. Hume draws the 'necessary though incredible' conclusion that experiences are, in fact, discrete instances and nothing about one of these instances implies anything about other experiences. Thus, Todes (2001, 6) claims, according to Hume 'there is no justification for believing that our experience is even likely to be ordered'. Todes argues that Hume cannot conceive of experience construed as a 'life field', the anticipatory structure and interconnected character of perceptions is undermined by a commitment to an atomistic model of empirical content. Such a model in Merleau-Ponty's words (and which anticipate Sellars's critique of 'the given') construes experience as an 'instantaneous, dotlike impact' and thus cannot appreciate its holistic character (Merleau-Ponty, 2002, 3).

But this raises a worry, apart from the fact that it would be a needlessly restrictive reading of Hume on experience. McDowell's account of experience, for example, has emphasized the irreducible conceptuality of experience in order to avoid characterizing experience as a dotlike impact; such an impact could not account for how experience provides reasons and plays a role in grounding a world-view (McDowell 1996). This commits McDowell to a form of conceptualism about experience which has been the subject of much discussion in recent years.[13] Particularly relevant for the present context is how conceptualism appears to run counter to a broadly phenomenological account of experience and how both conceptualism and phenomenology are critical of Hume's atomistic empiricism.

McDowell's conceptualism about the content of experience is partly motivated by the attempt to portray experience as meaningful and to show how it can provide an adequately rational constraint on our thinking. For Todes, and other phenomenologists, such an attempt overlooks a more basic and less intellectual way that we find phenomena, and the world at large, meaningful. Phenomenologists have long insisted that meaningful experience need not presuppose the possession and exercise of concepts; the meaning and world-disclosing character of experience can be perfectly well enjoyed at a nonconceptual level, where that involves what Dreyfus (e.g. 2005, 2007a, 2007b, 2013) has described as our being 'absorbed in coping' with the world, not distanced from it through the critical employment of concepts. Dreyfus argues that conceptualists such as Davidson and McDowell do not describe perceptual objects 'as they are in themselves' but rather focus their attention on highly specialized cases of 'judgements of detached thought'. Conceptualists then construe such detachment as if it were the primary or perhaps the only way that our experience of the world can be made intelligible (Dreyfus 2001, xvi). Dreyfus interprets Todes as showing how, through an account of the nature of our embodiment, the nonconceptual character of experience is in fact presupposed by intelligibility in the conceptualist's sense.

According to conceptualists Hume offers an account of experience that tries to explain its meaning and reason giving capacity yet in a way that presupposes no concepts or understanding (Sellars 1997, 33).[14] Such a view, they suggest, is incoherent. A phenomenologist might emphasize the non-conceptual nature of our embodiment in order to undercut their opponent's insistence that concepts and the theoretical, detached understanding they enable, are primary. But phenomenologists such as Merleau-Ponty and Todes regard Hume's account of experience to be impoverished, and thus Hume's view and the account of experience provided by a phenomenological account exploit different senses of 'non-conceptual'.[15] Yet criticizing Hume for 'dissecting' experience and providing an impoverished account has only limited success; the criticism only has purchase on the account of experience as described in the early parts of the *Treatise*. Our experiences at the level of 'behaviour in company, in affairs, and in [our] pleasures' cannot even make sense, let alone successfully explained, if experience is characterized as a dotlike impact. Recall that the *explananda* in the science of man incorporates our experience at the level of social interaction and of our ordinary commerce with the world, in Stroud's (1977, 222) words 'what people actually think, feel and do in human life'. When Hume *does* dissect experience into 'instances', he does so in the service of producing a 'philosophical', abstract analysis. But, as Hume explains, such an account is part – not the grounds – of a wider characterization of human nature.

Focusing exclusively on the impoverished conception of experience is bound up with interpreting Hume's concerns as primarily epistemological, specifically sceptical. For instance, Todes (2001, 81) claims that what moves us toward and around in the world are our 'desires' or 'needs' which are constrained by nature:

> Our desires are somewhat restricted by the facts, which eliminate unrealistic desires. But what can be countenanced as a perceptual fact is also limited by our indispensable human needs. Hume would agree that the percipient and his impressions would cease to be, if his needs were inadequately met. But for Hume this would be no more than an (unjustifiable) empirical generalization.

But the qualification 'no more than' is misleading and arises because of reading Hume as primarily a sceptic. Todes quotes a very famous moment at the end of Book I of the *Treatise* where Hume reaches out to Nature to help disperse the clouds of scepticism:

> Most fortunately, it happens that since reason is incapable of dispelling these clouds, Nature herself suffices for that purpose ... I dine, I play backgammon, I converse, and am merry with my friends; and when I return to these speculations, they appear so cold, so strain'd, so ridiculous (Hume 1978, 269).[16]

Todes (2001, 87) describes this passage as an example of Hume's recognition that his own philosophical system is inadequate. But, in my view, this appeal to Nature is not just the *result* of an epistemological investigation it is rather part of the condition of any such investigation. Part of Hume's aim was to illuminate the taken-for-granted sense of what it is to be a human being, a sense presupposed by questions of how our beliefs are or are not justified, warranted, and so forth, a sense elucidated by the cautious observation of common life.

I am not recommending that we should simply ignore how Hume frames his epistemology in apparently anti-social terms, especially during Book 1 of the *Treatise*.[17] The process of delving into one's private supply of perceptions and experiences in the attempt to identify the relevant rational relations between mental contents is an important feature of Hume's overall project. But I have argued that care is needed over the interpretation of 'experience'. I am suggesting that an alternative and perfectly consistent meaning of experience and thus what it implies for the rational status of our impressions, ideas and beliefs, should not be ignored either – an alternative which is irreducibly interpersonal. Hume's epistemology need not be construed in exclusively individualistic terms.

Emphasizing Hume's interpersonal epistemology, his social science, is a familiar aspect of some interpretations such as Baier's for example. She writes that 'Hume's naturalism in epistemology takes human nature as the nature closest to hand, and takes our nature to be social and passionate, before it is cognitive' (Baier 1991, 28–29).[18] My point here is that both aspects of Hume's epistemology, the social and the solipsistic (if the distinction is best drawn in these terms) can be characterized naturalistically. The science of man, when focused on our wider non-solipsistic experience, delivers insights about ourselves and our epistemic situation as irreducibly practical creatures.[19]

Concluding Remarks

If Baier is right, Hume

> was initiating not the science (in our sense) of psychology, either introspective or experimental, but a broader discipline of reflection on human nature, into which Charles Darwin and Michel Foucault, as much as William James and Sigmund Freud, can be seen to belong. (Baier 1991, 25)

I suggest that the reading of Hume developed here accounts for how his naturalistic epistemology forms part of this broad discipline, part of a systematic reflection on human nature: a human science. A common reading of Hume is that his naturalism is expressed in the first place as a commitment to a conception of the world as disenchanted. This, in my view, is incorrect as a description of Hume's naturalism and it has a distorting effect on how we might understand Hume's aims in the *Treatise* and elsewhere. What I have been arguing is that Hume's naturalism does not proceed by starting with a set of metaphysical commitments and then move to consider how to explain our practices in light of them. Rather, Hume's science of man is principally a study of human nature as articulated in the common course of our existence.

Hume's project, according to Lewis (1986), seems to assume an austere metaphysics, an assumption that others such as McDowell (1998) take to indicate a primary commitment to a disenchanted conception of the world. I have argued that Hume's naturalism involves more than this, a wider naturalism that has been overlooked by both scientific naturalists and also their critics. Whether or not Hume's alleged ontological austerity deserves approval or criticism, that aspect of Hume's naturalism would need to be singled out and extracted from its place alongside other aspects of the broader naturalist attitude that I have sought to illuminate. There must be conceptual space for naturalisms other than what has generally been taken as scientific naturalism, and being inclusive with respect to naturalism is itself a proper lesson of what a more liberal naturalism teaches.[20] Hume's naturalism does not incorporate an attitude toward our experience that attempts to 'locate' it in some prior characterization of the world, a characterization supplied by science. Whilst it is true to say that an important element in Hume's approach was the appeal to psychological explanations of the content and significance of experience, the restrictive reading of experience and of the naturalist background overextends the role assigned to psychology.

If we consider Book I of the *Treatise* we are, compared to other passages, presented with the solipsistic, detached, intellectual engagement with sceptical questions. But elsewhere in (Book II and III, and in the *Enquiries*) we have the return of what Baier (1991, p. 138) describes as 'flesh and blood persons' and the redeployment of a non-scientific sort of naturalism. Hume is not obviously the founding father of scientism and, moreover, he has more to offer the phenomenological tradition than has previously been recognized.[21] McDowell (1998, 181) has characterized the attitude of scientistic naturalism to involve compensating for the effects of a scientific investigator, perhaps discounting 'even his humanity' as he puts it. Whatever the desirability or plausibility of such an attitude, it should be clear that Hume does not hold it. Hume explicitly places our humanity at the very centre of a naturalist standpoint: 'Human Nature is the only science of man' (Hume 1978, 273). If we overlook this then Hume's naturalism will be misunderstood. The idea that Hume's naturalism only, or even primarily, amounts to a science-inspired metaphysics is a mistake. Whilst it may be granted that the creed of scientistic naturalism is mistaken, it is just as mistaken to regard Hume as its prophet.

Notes

1. In characterizing philosophical naturalism it is usual to distinguish between interrelating ontological, epistemological and methodological aspects. What unifies these aspects, if anything, is a matter of continuing dispute. But an overarching thesis is that natural science is to have priority in giving us an account of what exists and that philosophical inquiry is to be guided by, if not become part of, natural scientific investigation. A proper treatment would need to distinguish the subcategories within each of these aspects, also interrelating with each other and other subcategories. For ontological versions see, for example, Maddy 2007; Papineau 1993. For examples of naturalism's epistemological aspects see Quine 1969; Kornblith 2002.
2. See also Stroud 2006, 342. 'Naturalist' readings of Hume include Norman Kemp Smith 1905a, 1905b, 1941; Stroud 1977; Fogelin 1985; Mounce 1999. Perhaps the most famous 'sceptical' interpretation is presented in Kant 1998. More recent versions include Strawson 1985. Williams also suggests a 'critical' reading such as that found in Ayer (1980) and Bennett (1971).
3. For a characterization of the 'placement problem' in the context of contemporary accounts of naturalism see Price 2011.
4. Such remarks suggest that Hume himself had a 'scientistic' conception of the world, but McDowell emphasizes that Hume was innocent of the historical explanation of the modern disenchanted view of the world. Stroud (1977, 223) also remarks that 'scientism' was alien to Hume's thought and to the eighteenth century more generally.
5. See also the 'Abstract'.
6. Traiger distinguishes between four senses of experience in Hume: (1) evidence of sense and memory; (2) common life and conversation; (3) testimony of history; (4) the fidelity of 'printers and copists'. See Traiger 1994, 253.
7. In Book I of the *Treatise* Hume also uses enlargement to explain how the repetition of experiences (in the narrow sense) can in some cases not just 'multiply' our ideas but 'enlarge' them; that is, that we come to form new ideas on the basis of multiplicity, but which not to have their direct source in any instance of experience. See Hume 1978, 163).
8. See Fogelin (2009, 6–7) for a characterization of the different 'voices' to be found in Hume and a warning that the standpoint of common life can be easily overlooked.
9. The 'Oxford view' refers to the interpretation described by Duncan Forbes as 'the Locke-Berkeley-epistemology-only Hume'. See Forbes's (1970, 9) introduction to Hume's *History of England*. I learned this from R.W. Connon's (1979) essay 'The Naturalism of Hume Revisited': see his footnote 4 for further details and explanation.

10. Although 'satisfaction' is not a form of *terminus*. See Rouse 2005, 43.
11. See also Husserl 1999.
12. Recent accounts of Hume's theory of belief emphasize the role of 'stability'. See, for example, Loeb 2002.
13. See, for example, the essays collected in Schear 2013.
14. See Allison (2008) for a discussion of the relation between Hume's account of experience and belief and how Sellars characterizes the 'logical space of reasons'.
15. On Hume's impoverished conception of experience, see Bell and McGinn 1990, and Stroud 2006.
16. Note how in both this passage, and the one slightly earlier in the conclusion of Book I where Hume describes himself as a 'strange uncouth monster', the role of other people is fundamental. Firstly, in the fragmentation of interpersonal relations ('utterly abandon'd and disconsolate … no one will hearken to me. Every one keeps at a distance…') and then, secondly, as part of what restores a more agreeable state.
17. As Baier (1991, 3) puts it, throughout Part 4 of Book 1 of the *Treatise* Hume had 'sailed a one-person ship, albeit in an ocean where other manned ships were clearly visible'.
18. Baier (1991, 298, n.18) cites Gilles Deleuze's work as suggesting this kind of view in his work from 1953, translated as *Empiricism as Subjectivity: An Essay on Hume's Theory of Human Nature*: 'Hume is a moralist and a sociologist, before being a psychologist' (Deleuze 1991).
19. At the start of the first *Enquiry*, Hume (1975, 5) identifies the science of human nature with 'moral philosophy' as opposed to 'natural philosophy'.
20. See De Caro and McArthur 2010, 9.
21. Although, writing in 1929, Husserl wrote of Hume's unrecognized 'greatness' since, according to Husserl (1969, 256), Hume was 'the first to grasp the *concrete problem* of transcendental philosophy'. See also Salmon 1929.

Acknowledgements

An earlier version of this paper was presented at the University of Johannesburg in 2014 as part of the 'Phenomenology and Naturalism' conference, organised by Rafael Winkler, Catherine Botha, Abraham Olivier, Andrea Hurst and Marianna Oelofsen. Many thanks to them and to the other participants for a number of very helpful discussions and to an anonymous referee for their comments on a previous version. Thanks also to colleagues at Durham University especially Matthew Ratcliffe, Nathan Shannon, Andy Hamilton and Simon P. James.

Disclosure Statement

No potential conflict of interest was reported by the author.

References

Allison, H. E. (2008) *Custom and Reason in Hume: A Kantian Reading of the First Book of the Treatise*, Oxford: Oxford University Press.

Ayer, A. J. (1980) *Hume*, New York, NY: Hill and Wang.

Baier, A. (1991) *A Progress of Sentiments: Reflections of Hume's Treatise*, Cambridge, Mass: Harvard University Press.

Bell, M., and M. McGinn (1990) 'Naturalism and Scepticism', *Philosophy* 65(254): 413–414.

Bennett, J. (1971) *Locke, Berkeley, Hume: Central Themes*, Oxford: Oxford University Press.

Connon, R.W. (1979) 'The Naturalism of Hume Revisited' in D. F. Norton, N. Capaldi, and W. L. Robison (eds.) *McGill Hume Studies*, San Diego, CA: Austin Hill Press, 121–145.

De Caro, M., and D. McArthur (eds.) (2010) *Naturalism and Normativity*, New York, NY: Columbia University Press.

Deleuze, G. (1991) *Empiricism and Subjectivity: An Essay on Hume's Theory of Human Nature* (Trans. C. Boundas), New York, NY: Columbia University Press.

Dreyfus, H. (2001). 'Introduction I', in S. Todes (ed.) *Body and World*, xv–xxvii.

Dreyfus, H. (2005) 'Overcoming the Myth of the Mental: How Philosophers Can Profit From the Phenomenology of Everyday Expertise', *Proceedings and Addresses of the American Philosophical Association* 79: 47–65.

Dreyfus, H. (2007a) 'The Return of the Myth of the Mental', *Inquiry* 50(4): 352–365.

Dreyfus, H. (2007b) 'Response to McDowell', *Inquiry* 50(4): 371–377.

Dreyfus, H. (2013) 'The Myth of the Pervasiveness of the Mental', in J. K. Schear (ed.), *Mind, Reason, and Being-in-the-World The McDowell-Dreyfus Debate*, London: Routledge.

Fogelin, R. (1985) *Hume's Scepticism in the Treatise of Human Nature*, London: Routledge.

Fogelin, R. (2009) *Hume's Skeptical Crisis*, Oxford: Oxford University Press.

Hume, D. (1970) *History of England*, in D. Forbes (ed.) Middlesex: Penguin Books.

Hume, D. (1975) *Enquiries Concerning Human Understanding and Concerning the Principles of Morals*, Oxford: Oxford University Press.

Hume, D. (1978) *A Treatise of Human Nature*, Oxford: Oxford University Press.

Husserl, E. (1969) *Formal and Transcendental Logic* (trans. D. Cairns), The Hague: Martinus Nijhoff.

Husserl, E. (1999) *Cartesian Meditations: an Introduction to Phenomenology*, London: Kluwer Academic Publishers.

Kant, I. (1998) *Critique of Pure Reason* (trans. P. Guyer and A. Wood), Cambridge: Cambridge University Press.

Kemp Smith, N. (1905a) 'The Naturalism of Hume (I)', *Mind* 14: 149–173.

Kemp Smith, N. (1905b) 'The Naturalism of Hume (II)', *Mind* 14: 335–347.

Kemp Smith, N. (1941) *The Philosophy of David Hume*, London: MacMillan.

Kornblith, H. (2002) *Knowledge and its Place in Nature*, Oxford: Oxford University Press.

Lewis, D. (1986) *Philosophical Papers vol. 2*, Oxford: Oxford University Press.

Loeb, L. (2002) *Stability and Justification in Hume's Treatise*, Oxford: Oxford University Press.

Maddy, P. (2007) *Second Philosophy: A Naturalistic Method*, Oxford: Oxford University Press.

McDowell, J. (1996) *Mind and World*, Cambridge, MA: Harvard University Press.

McDowell, J. (1998). 'Two Sorts of Naturalism' in J. McDowell (ed.) *Mind, Value and Reality*, Cambridge, MA: Harvard University Press, 167–197.

Merleau-Ponty, M. (2002) *Phenomenology of Perception*, London: Routledge.

Mounce, H. O. (1999) *Hume's Naturalism*, London: Routledge.

Papineau, D. (1993) *Philosophical Naturalism*, Oxford: Blackwell.

Price, H. (2011) *Naturalism Without Mirrors*, Oxford: Oxford University Press.

Quine, W. V. O. (1969) 'Epistemology Naturalized', in *Ontological Relativity and Other Essays*, New York, NY: Columbia University Press.

Rouse, J. (2005) 'Mind, Body, and World: Todes and McDowell on Bodies and Language', *Inquiry* 48(1): 38–61.

Salmon, C. V. (1929). *The Central Problem of David Hume's Philosophy. An Essay Towards a Phenomenological Interpretation of the First Book of the Treatise of Human Nature*, Halle: Max Niemeyer Verlag.

Schear, J. K. (ed.) (2013) *Mind, Reason, and Being-in-the-World: The McDowell-Dreyfus Debate*, London: Routledge.

Sellars, W. (1997) *Empiricism and the Philosophy of Mind*, Cambridge, MA: Harvard University Press.

Strawson, P. F. (1985) *Scepticism and Naturalism: Some Varieties*, London: Methuen.

Stroud, B. (1977) *Hume*, London: Routledge.

Stroud, B. (2006) 'The constraints of Hume's naturalism', *Synthese* 152: 339–351.

Todes, S. (2001) *Body and World*, London: The MIT Press.

Traiger, S. (1994). 'Beyond Our Senses: Recasting Book I, Part 3 of Hume's *Treatise*, *Hume Studies* 20(2): 241–259.

Williams, M. (2004) 'The Unity of Hume's Philosophical Project', *Hume Studies* 30(2): 265–296.

Against representationalism (about conscious sensory experience)

David Papineau

King's College London, United Kingdom

ABSTRACT
It is very natural to suppose that conscious sensory experience is essentially representational. However this thought gives rise to any number of philosophical problems and confusions. I shall argue that it is quite mistaken. Conscious phenomena cannot be constructed out of representational materials.

1. Introduction

It is very natural to suppose that conscious sensory experience is essentially representational. However this thought gives rise to any number of philosophical problems and confusions. I shall argue that it is quite mistaken. Conscious phenomena cannot be constructed out of representational materials.

There are two rather different motivations for the thesis that the conscious features of sensory experience are essentially representational – 'representationalism' henceforth.[1] One comes from cognitive science, the other from phenomenological introspection.

A number of different lines of evidence have persuaded cognitive scientists that the neural processes underlying conscious sensory experience do not simply relay the structure of sensory stimulations impacting on our bodily peripheries, but rather construct hypothetical representations of distal features of our environment. This tradition goes back to Helmholtz in the nineteenth century and has received increasing support in recent decades. Much of the focus has been on vision, but the approach has been applied to other sensory modalities too.

This tradition in cognitive science leads naturally to a representationalist view. We need only identify the conscious features of sensory experience with the representational contents of the outputs of sensory processing. According to this line of thought, we feel consciously as we do when we see a table, say, because we are in a cerebral state which represents the presence of a table.

The phenomenological motivation for representationalism is different. Here we start, not with information about brain processing, but simply with the introspectible phenomenal structure of sensory experience. When we focus introspectively on our visual experience of a table, say, is it not obvious that our conscious state presents us with a mind-independent object of a certain shape, size, colour and distance? It seems built into the introspectible nature of our experience that it lays claim to the presence of this table. And isn't this just to say, so this thought goes, that our conscious sensory experience essentially represents such a table?

The two different motivations for representationalism are often found together in the same representationalist writers. But it is worth distinguishing them, because they raise different issues. In what follows, I shall respect the first motivation, to the extent of accepting the claims about sensory representation made by cognitive science – though I shall accommodate those claims without embracing representationalism as a metaphysical thesis. By contrast, I shall argue that the ideas about representation involved in the second phenomenological motivation rest on a series of mistakes.

2. Problems of broadness

An initial indication that something is amiss with representationalism comes from representational externalism. There is good reason to suppose that representation is broad. But it would seem odd to hold that conscious experience is broad too.

Much recent discussion assumes that broadness is an internal issue for representationalism, and that the right response is somehow to refine the way in which representationalism is formulated. But in my view the issue is a symptom of a deeper malaise. The fault lies, not in the details of different versions of representationalism, but in the whole idea that sensory experience is intrinsically representational.

Representational externalism is the view that the truth conditions of representational mental states can depend, not just on their subjects' intrinsic properties, but also on facets of their environments, histories and social milieus. Truth conditions like this are called 'broad' representational contents. Broadness occurs when two intrinsically identical subjects have corresponding mental states with different representational contents.

The problem that broadness raises for representationalism about conscious sensory experience should be clear. Representationalism wants to say that the conscious properties of sensory experiences consist in those experiences representing the world to be a certain way. But if two intrinsically identical individuals can have experiences with different truth conditions, because of different environments, histories or social milieus, then it would seem to follow that those individuals must be consciously different, in virtue of representing the world differently in sensory experience. But it would seem odd, to say the least, that two individuals should be consciously different, despite their intrinsic identity, because of differences in environment, history or social milieu.

3. Examples of broadness

The idea of broad contents was introduced to philosophers in the 1960s and 1970s with a series of examples designed to show how the truth conditions of *statements* or *beliefs* can vary across intrinsically identical subjects. So, for example, Hilary Putnam's tale of twin water aimed to show how a statement's truth condition can depend on which liquid is present in a subject's environment. Similarly, Tyler Burge's story about Alf and arthritis argued that a belief's truth condition can depend on which ailment a subject's community refers to by a certain term. And before them Saul Kripke had in effect suggested that the truth condition of a statement involving a proper name can depend on the origin of the causal chain leading up to the subject's use of the name (Putnam 1975; Burge 1979; Kripke 1980).

Statements and beliefs are not sensory experiences. So perhaps there is room for defenders of representationalism to allow broadness for statements and beliefs, but to deny that it ever characterizes sensory experiences. It is not hard, however, to come up with plausible examples of sensory experiences with broad representational contents, analogous to beliefs with broad contents. Here are three cases featuring pairs of subjects who are intrinsically identical, yet whose corresponding sensory states intuitively represent different things.

Particular Objects. Suppose I am viewing a yellow lemon; Jane is viewing another yellow lemon that looks just the same; and John is being manipulated by scientists to have a sensory impression as of a yellow lemon even though no lemon is present at all. Let us suppose that what is going on inside our skins is just the same in all three cases: our visual systems are engaging in just the same processes, despite our differing external circumstances. Yet on the face of things the representational contents of our states are different. I am representing that *this lemon* is yellow; Jane is representing that a *different particular lemon* is yellow; and John's sensory experience has no such singular content at all, since there is no particular object in play in his case.

Inverted Earth. On Inverted Earth the sky is yellow and daffodils are blue, and so on. You are kidnapped, drugged and taken there, but while you are drugged you have inverting lenses inserted in your eyes so you don't notice the difference when you wake up. What is going on inside your skin when you look at the sky on Inverted Earth will be just the same as what happened inside your skin when you looked skywards on Earth. But on Earth your experience represented blueness, yet (once you have been on Inverted Earth for a while) your experience there arguably represents yellowness. (Block 1990).

Cosmic Swampbrain. Suppose that a perfect duplicate of your brain coagulates by cosmic happenstance in interstellar space together with sustaining vat, and for some while engages in just the same neural processes as your brain. Your own conscious states represent features of your Earthly environment. But the Swampbrain's conscious states arguably represent nothing at all.

These examples bring out the awkward dilemma facing representationalists. Either they need to resist the natural broad interpretations which make the intrinsic identicals come out representationally different, or they have to embrace the implication that intrinsic identicals sometimes differ consciously. Neither horn seems attractive.

4. Broadness analysed

Some philosophers are suspicious of broad contents. They are not persuaded by intuitive reactions to possible cases. In their view, there are strong theoretical reasons why truth conditions *must* be narrow (that is, determined by intrinsic properties of subjects). As a result, they hold that the kind of thought experiments outlined above are misleading, and the intuitive conclusions drawn from them confused.

It will be worth briefly examining the theoretical issues involved here, as it will help bring the phenomenon of representation into sharper focus.

One theoretical reason for thinking representation must be narrow relates to the phenomenological motive for representationalism aired in the Introduction above. Suppose that you think that the introspectible structure of conscious sensory experience is the fundamental source of representation. Then this itself provides reason to think that intrinsic identicals must always share representational contents. For it is natural to suppose that intrinsic identicals will always be consciously identical. And then, if representational content derives from conscious structure, it follows that intrinsic identicals will always end up representing the world the same way.

A rather different theoretical argument for narrowness relates to the explanation of action. A number of philosophers think that the essential features of mental representations are grounded in the way that they generate behaviour, from the inside, as it were (Fodor 1980; Segal 2002). What shows that I believe that *an apple is on the table*, say, rather than, say, *an apple is in the cupboard* is that I approach the table when I am hungry. But, if this is accepted, then broadness once more looks suspicious. Any two intrinsic identicals will surely behave the same way. So, if mental representation is constituted by its role in generating behaviour, it will make no sense to suppose that intrinsic identicals can have mental states with different representational contents.

However, it is not obvious that either of these motivations for narrowness is compelling. Note that both run counter to the natural thought that an essential feature of mental representation is the way it relates subjects to the world around them and assists them in finding their way through it. Perspectives on representation that focus purely on the internal structure of consciousness, or on the way mental states causally prompt behaviour from within, seem in danger of leaving out this world-involving aspect of representation. After all, if our primary interest were in the internal structure of consciousness, or the internal springs of behaviour, it is not clear why we should think of mental states as ever laying claim to matters beyond the skull in the first place. Maybe broadness appears problematic if we think of mental representation as somehow limited to what goes on inside the skull. But once we think of representation in a world-involving way, then broadness can seem less puzzling.

There is a range of theories which seek to understand representation in terms of how subjects are embedded in their environments. Some such theories aim to analyse a cognitive state representing that p in terms of its normally being *caused by p*; others focus of the way such cognitive states will *guide actions in a way appropriate to the presence of p*; and there are also theories that invoke a mixture of these two ideas. This is not the place to assess the relative merits of these options.[2] For present purposes we need only observe that any such theory will render it quite unsurprising that representation should be broad. If the representational content of a cognitive state hinges on which features of the environment the subject is responding to, or orientating its behaviour to, then we should positively expect that intrinsically identical subjects embedded in different environments will be in states with different representational contents.

5. Options for representationalists

Representationalists have two ways to go in the face of examples that purport to show that the same conscious state can represent different broad truth conditions in different intrinsically identical individuals. On the one hand, they can seek to resist the broadness, and argue that the states in question are better understood as sharing some common narrow truth condition. Alternatively, they can grasp the nettle and argue that the states in question are consciously different, in line with their differing broad truth conditions, despite the intrinsic identity of the individuals involved.

The former narrow strategy is adopted by effectively all representationalists in connection with 'singular contents'; that is, with the putative contribution of *particular objects* to truth conditions, of the kind that is at issue with *Particular Objects*. Some representationalists attempt a similar narrow strategy with respect to the represented *properties* that are also at issue in *Inverted Earth* and *Cosmic Swampbrain*; but with such 'general contents' we also find representationalists who are prepared to allow that consciousness itself is sometimes broad.

This is not the place to explore all the moves that have been made in this area. From my own perspective, the whole need to make consciousness and representation line up is a problem of representationalism's own making, and simply dissolves away once we drop the idea that conscious experience is intrinsically representational. In due course I shall give some indication of how that might work. But first it will be useful to run over a few aspects of the representationalist literature.

6. Singular experiential contents

There is a general reason why representationalists characteristically go narrow with respect to possible singular contents of experience. Representationalists typically adhere to the 'common factor principle': they hold that subjects who are perceiving veridically will share their conscious sensory properties with those who have matching illusions or hallucinations. But there will no singular contents shared across these three cases. The different experiencers in such matching cases will be related to different particular objects, or to no particular object at all. So if representationalists want to equate the conscious property they take to be shared across these cases with some representational property, they need to find some non-singular content that the cases share.

Despite their best efforts, representationalists have not been particularly successful at locating such a shared singular content. A natural first thought is to appeal to a general existential content: that is, to take all the matching cases to be representing simply that *there is a lemon before me that is yellow*. But then there are objections involving cases where this existential claim is true by accident: imagine that there is indeed a yellow lemon in front of you, but this isn't the cause of your experience; there is in fact a screen between you and the lemon, and your experience is in fact produced by ingenious scientists stimulating your optic nerve. Intuitively, this is not a veridical sensory experience – we take the experience to be aiming to refer to some more directly related object than the lemon behind the screen, and so not to be vindicated merely by that obscured lemon being yellow.

This kind of example might suggest that we should build some causal requirement into the desired content, along the lines of *there is a lemon before me that is yellow and is causing this experience*. But this now threatens to make the content overly self-referential. It seems wrong to have experiences making meta-claims about their own aetiology. Surely it is possible to represent the world experientially without representing your own experiences.[3]

In response to these difficulties, many representationalists settle for 'gappy contents'. The idea is that relevant sensory experiences don't in the end refer to particular objects, but merely present general properties as such. Somehow they answer to a local instantiation of yellowness, and perhaps local instantiation of lemonness, without any commitment to some specific object being supposed to possess these properties. On this analysis, the contents of sensory experience never themselves amount to conditions that can be true or false, just to something that would make up such a truth condition if combined with a particular object (Tye 2014).

To my mind, all these manoeuvrings around singular contents reflect badly on the overall representationalist programme. The initial representationalist idea was to equate the conscious properties of sensory experiences with their representational ones. But as soon as we focus on the singular dimension of representation, it quickly appears that conscious properties do not cut as fine as representational ones. I take this to cast doubt on the original representationalist idea. After all, it is not as if there is any independent reason to deny singular contents to sensory experiences, apart from the need to satisfy the theoretical demands of representationalism.

7. In favour of singular contents

To bring out the naturalness of singular experiential contents, and the consequent ad hoc-ness of the lengths to which representationalism is drawn on this issue, consider a slightly different pair of examples. I see my wife Rose come through the door. I have a doppelganger in Australia whose wife Ruby looks just the same, and he sees her come through the door. It seems entirely natural to say that my experience represents *Rose* and his represents *Ruby*. The fact that I and my doppelganger share the same conscious properties (I specified that our wives look just the same) seems no reason at all to deny that our states have these different representational contents – unless, that is, we are in the theoretical grip of representationalism.

Perhaps we should not take it for granted that all sensory experiences have the same kind of singular contents as experiences of familiar reidentifiable objects. It is one thing to say that experiences can represent well-known objects like wives, another to say that they can represent randomly encountered everyday objects, like that particular lemon. Still, even if that were right, experience of familiar objects like spouses would already be an awkward thorn in the side of representationalism. And, in any case, I see no reason not to allow the same kind of singular contents to sensory experiences in general.

There is every ecological and biological reason to suppose that a primary function of sensory perception is to enable us to track and reidentify particular objects, the better to allow us to gear our actions to their particular idiosyncrasies. This aspect of perception is highlighted when the objects in question are familiar and subject is already acquainted with a rich range of idiosyncrasies. But I would say that the same point applies even in the case, say, where someone sees a random lemon to be yellow, and has yet acquire any specific information about it. The truth condition of their experiential states is still that *the particular lemon in question is yellow*. The experience of someone who is looking at a different lemon has a correspondingly different truth condition. And, in the hallucinatory case, where no particular is in play at all, no complete truth condition has been constituted (though it is here also true that this state *would* have a truth condition involving yellowness if it *did* refer to an object).

8. General experiential contents

So much for singular contents. What about general contents, like the colours at issue in *Inverted Earth*, or all the properties with respect to which *Cosmic Swampbrain* is arguably representationally inferior to its earthly counterpart?

Now, one option here would be once more to seek narrow contents that are shared across the intrinsic duplicates, by analogy with the representationalist moves just explored in connection with singular contents. But of course, once we come to general properties, the strategy of 'gappy contents' is no longer available, since the problem is precisely that the counterparts are now arguably referring to different *properties*, not particulars. So the defenders of narrow general contents are driven back to ascribing existential general contents (there is some property that …), perhaps augmented with a causal requirement (… and is causally responsible for certain effects in me). The problems that faced these moves with singular contents now arise again. Moreover, in the case of the cosmic swampbrain in particular, there is the extra problem that every property that is not intrinsic to the subject will need this treatment, arguably including the notion of *cause*, which will make the cosmic swampbrain and its earthly counterparts end up with very thin shared experiential contents indeed.[4]

In the face of these difficulties, some representationalists are prepared to resort to the other option, and maintain that the intrinsic duplicates involved would not in fact be consciously identical. According to this line, your colour experiences will be phenomenologically altered once you have been on inverted earth for a while (even though everything inside your skin is still just as it was on earth). And, in similar spirit, why suppose that the cosmic swampbrain is conscious at all, given that it has never enjoyed interaction with any real environments? (Dretske 1995, 1996; Tye 1995; Lycan 1996, 2001; Byrne and Tye 2006).

I do not want to dismiss these moves out of hand. Still, many philosophers will find it hard to swallow the idea that two beings can end up consciously different solely because of their environmental differences, even though everything is the same inside their skin.[5] Perhaps once more the moral to draw from the hard choices facing representationalists is that there is something wrong with their starting point.

9. Non-relationism

In support of this diagnosis, let me now introduce an alternative way of understanding sensory experience that avoids all the problems of broadness while preserving much of the spirit of representationalism. This alternative will respect the scientific idea that conscious sensory experiences are the outputs of processes designed to construct hypothetical representations of distal features of our environment, but will do so without embracing the metaphysical tenets of representationalism.

Consider an analogy. Written sentences are the outputs of processes designed to produce representations that will convey information to readers. It does not follow that all the properties of sentences are essentially representational. Their typographical properties are not, for instance. It is entirely contingent that this arrangement of marks on paper means what it does. In different circumstances, just that arrangement of marks could easily have meant something different, or nothing at all.

I think the same about the relation between the conscious and representational properties of sensory experiences: the former stand to the latter just as the typographical properties of sentences stand to their representational contents. It is not essential to a given conscious experience that it stand for the truth condition it does. In different circumstances, just that conscious state could have had a different a truth condition, or no truth condition at all.

In effect, this is to view the consciously constituted experience as the *vehicle* of representation, rather than the content. With sentences, we distinguish between vehicle properties – the shape and arrangement of the letters and so on – and the representational properties – that the sentences has a certain truth condition. So with sensory experiences. The conscious features of the experience are one thing, the experience having a truth condition is another.

Note how all the problems of broadness immediately disappear once we adopt this non-relationist perspective.[6] Just as given typographically constituted sentences can have different meanings in different languages, so can a given consciously constituted sensory state stand for different truth conditions when embedded in different environments and histories. The same narrow vehicle can have different truth conditions, or none, depending on broad circumstances.[7]

Thus with all our problem pairs. With *Particular Objects*, the same conscious vehicle refers to different particular objects in different normal cases, but to no object in the hallucinatory case. With *Inverted Earth*, the same conscious vehicle refers to blue on earth, but to yellow on inverted earth. With *Cosmic Swampbrain*, the same conscious vehicles have their normal referents in me, but no referents at all in swampbrain.

Of course, this allows that vehicle and representational properties may be tightly correlated within certain contexts. Once you fix a language, you fix a one-to-one correspondence between typographical and semantic properties (at least until ambiguity and synonymy intrude). Similarly, we are likely to find one-to-one correspondences between the conscious and representational properties of certain sensory experiences within biological species, say, or within individuals, or within individuals at given times.

10. Transparency

Given how easily non-relationism bypasses all the problems of broadness, it is surprising that it is almost entirely absent from the contemporary philosophical literature on perception. Introductions to the area will typically start with a brief mention of sense datum theory, and then quickly move on to the debate between representationalism and direct realist disjunctivism, without any suggestion that non-relationism might be a serious option.

One explicit reason sometimes offered for dismissing non-relationism is the 'transparency of experience'. Imagine that you are looking at some visible scene – some fruit on a table say. Now try to turn your attention from the features of the fruit to the conscious features of your visible experience. All that will happen is that you will stare harder at the fruit and their properties, and not instead at some supposed realm of inner experience. A number of philosophers take this to argue that the properties present in your experience are ordinary properties of physical objects, like the shape and colour of the fruit, and not some special range of private non-relational conscious properties possessed by subjects rather than physical objects (Harman 1990; Tye 2002).

How exactly is this argument supposed to work? We can focus things by adopting a useful convention due to Christopher Peacocke. Let us refer to the conscious properties that subjects instantiate when they have sensory experience as properties*. So for example, subjects will instantiate redness*, squareness* and so on, when they see objects that are red, square and so forth. The transparency argument is then supposed to show that the properties we encounter directly in experience are properties like redness and squareness, not redness* and squareness*, as non-relationism would have it (Peacocke 1983).

Now, as we shall see in a minute, talk about properties being 'in' experience needs to be treated with care, but let us go along with this way of talking for the moment, and moreover let us allow that non-relationism implies that the only properties we encounter directly 'in' experience are properties*.

Why now is the transparency argument supposed to undermine non-relationism? At bottom the transparency argument hinges on the observation that when you try to shift your attention from the properties of physical objects to the properties of your experience, your visual phenomenology remains unchanged. But, put like this, it seems that the argument should be consistent with pretty much any account of the metaphysical nature of conscious experience. On the sense datum theory, this nature consists in my relation to some sense datum and its properties; on the representationalist theory, it consist in my relation to a representational content; on direct realist disjunctivism, it consists (at least in the veridical case) in my relation to the perceived fact itself; and on the non-relationist view, it consists in my instantiating some intrinsic non-relational non-representational property.

On any of these accounts of conscious sensory experiences, why shouldn't my experiences remain unaffected when I 'turn my attention' from their physical objects to the experiences themselves? I take it that such attentional shifts are *cognitive* acts, and as such there seems no obvious reason why they should have any impact at all on the mechanisms responsible for my *sensory* state when I am looking, say, at some fruit with my eyes open. In general we don't expect occurrent cognitive activities to alter our perceptual states, and it is not clear why we should do so here.

Perhaps the transparency argument would be a good argument against theories that take conscious sensory experience to involve 'qualia' *in addition* to having constitutive representational properties. (For example, I take Block 2004 and Peacocke 2008 to endorse such theories.) On a portmanteau view like this, an experience of a square physical object, say, could have a squareness* property, say, due to representing the square from a certain perspective, in addition to the conscious representational property of representing the object itself to be objectively square. A view like this would indeed seem to be in the transparency argument's line of fire. Now there are two sets of properties 'in' the experience, and we ought arguably to be able to shift attention from one set to the other.

But the non-relationist view I am proposing does not have this portmanteau structure. The idea isn't that somehow both the qualitative 'mental paint' *and* the represented objective properties are 'in' the experience. Rather my view is that our conscious experience is *all paint*, and any representational or represented features are quite external to our consciousness. So from my point of view there is no reason to expect that that we ought somehow to be able switch attention away from the *other* properties 'in' our experience and towards the qualia. The qualia are all that were there in the first place – so the whole idea of turning away from the other features of experience and towards them doesn't get off the ground.

11. Sensory 'awareness'

Still, even if the transparency argument doesn't knock out non-relationism, doesn't it highlight its unattractiveness? Do we really want to hold that conscious experiences are constituted entirely by intrinsic non-relational qualia, and that there is no sense at all in which the properties of objects themselves are ever 'in' our experience? It is certainly a natural thought, when we reflect on our conscious sensory experience, to suppose that the objects and properties that we are perceiving are somehow 'in' our experience.

Well, I agree that this is a natural thought, and in the final sections of this paper will explain why. But I think it must be resisted. In the next few sections I shall explain how representationalism gets itself into a nasty tangle when it tries to accommodate this thought. But first, in this section, it will be useful briefly to make clear how the non-relationalist view is at least consistent in denying that the properties of objects enter into our experience, even though this may seem initially unnatural.

You might think that non-relationism would be committed to denying that we are ever 'aware of' ordinary properties of objects. And that would seem absurd. Surely I can be aware of the colour of a lemon when I look at it in good lighting?

However, I do not take non-relationism to have any such implication. I take it that we are 'aware of' things when we are in mental states that represent them. In this sense, it is always physical objects and their properties that my sensory states make me 'aware of'. My sensory state represents the colour of the lemon, and thereby makes me aware of it.

My sensory state itself has a conscious property, yellowness*, which is distinct from the yellowness of the lemon. It is this property* that is conscious, not the yellowness itself. I become aware of the yellowness of the lemon *by* instantiating yellowness*. But I am not, in the normal course of events, aware *of* the yellowness*. The yellowness* is conscious, but as long as my mental states are focused on the lemon rather than my experience, I will not be aware *of* my conscious property.

Of course, I may sometimes introspect, or otherwise think about the conscious sensory properties that I currently possess. And this will make me 'aware of' my sensory properties themselves, as well as of any physical properties that I am currently perceiving. But note that in this case it still won't be my sensory experience that makes me 'aware of' my conscious sensory properties, but some further cognitive state that is about those properties. The sensory state will still be about physical objects and *their* properties.

12. The properties of experience

Perhaps the non-relationist position can be cogently articulated. But many will still feel that it flies in the face of good sense.

Suppose you are looking at a bright yellow lemon. Now think of the yellowish property that you know to be present when you are introspectively aware of the nature your experience. Surely we would like to think of this property as just the same yellowness that lemons often possess, and not as some mental symbol yellowness* that bears no more relation to that property than the word 'yellow' does.

Plenty of philosophers think that deliverances of introspection are unequivocal on this issue. For example, Gilbert Harman insists that, if we try to introspect a visual experience of a tree, we will find that

the only features there to turn your attention to will be features of the presented tree. (Harman 1990, 39)

And Michael Tye (2002, 448), in similar vein, describing a visual experience of the Pacific Ocean, tells us that

what I found so pleasing in the above instance, what I was focusing on, as it were, were a certain shade and intensity of the colour blue.

Still, while it may be initially plausible that introspection relates us directly to ordinary properties of physical objects, this intuitive idea conceals a number of hidden difficulties. It is not at all clear that representationalists have any defensible explanation of how ordinary properties of objects can be 'present in' our experiences.

Note for a start that, however this is supposed to work, it is presumably not via the ordinary properties of objects being *instantiated* when we have experiences. As noted earlier, representationalists are common factor theorists, taking the same conscious properties to be present when I am mistakenly seeing a green lemon to be yellow as when I am veridically perceiving a yellow one. In both cases I have the property of *representing* the lemon to be yellow, and the conscious nature of my experience is constituted by this common fact. So now focus on the case where I have this conscious experience, yet the lemon is green. Yellowness is still supposed somehow to be 'present in' my experience. But clearly it is not there in virtue of being instantiated. Nothing in this case instantiates yellowness. The lemon is not yellow, I am not yellow, and none of my mental states is yellow.

The idea, presumably, is that the properties get into our experience, not by being instantiated, but by being *represented*. In experience we represent the uninstantiated property of yellowness, and this somehow constitutes the conscious state we are in when so experiencing. Some representationalists are quite explicit on this matter.

Thus Fred Dretske (2003, 73):

> In hallucinating pink rats we are aware of something – the properties, *pink* and *rat-shaped* that something is represented as having – but we are not aware of any object that has these properties – a pink, rat-shaped, object. We are aware of pure universals, uninstantiated properties.

And MichaelTye (2014, 304) again:

> Along with (most) other representationalists, I am happy to say that, in the hallucinatory case, the perceiver is conscious of an un-instantiated property. This seems to me to be part of naïve commonsense.

13. Comparison with direct realist disjunctivism

I must say that I find the representationalist view hard to understand at this point. Uninstantiated properties are not located within space and time. It seems strange that a mental relation to such an abstract entity could constitute the phenomenal character of my experience. My conscious states are here-and-now, local, the kind of things that have causes and effects. How could a mental relation to an uninstantiated universal constitute this kind of state?

It is worth briefly comparing representationalism with direct realist disjunctivism on this point. Disjunctivists also hold that ordinary physical properties can be constitutive parts of our conscious experiences. But in their view this always depends on the property in question being instantiated. When we have a veridical perception, our conscious state involves the fact perceived: when we see a yellow lemon, the actual yellowness of the lemon plays a role in fixing our conscious properties. Of course, disjunctivists cannot say this about illusions or hallucinations of yellow lemons, precisely because yellowness is not instantiated in those cases. But that is all right for them, as they are not common factor theorists, and take the conscious properties in those cases to be different.

Now, you might well be uneasy about the disjunctivist suggestion that my conscious state in the veridical case depends on matters outside my skin. But the representationalist account of how ordinary properties get 'into' our experiences strikes me as much more puzzling that that. It is one thing for yellowness to contribute to the conscious character of my experience in virtue of being instantiated before my eyes. It would another for it somehow to enter into my consciousness even though nothing in my field of view or anywhere else nearby is actually yellow.

Somehow the representationalists are thinking that the yellowness is 'present in' my experience, not because it is instantiated there, but in some other way. My mind reaches out and grasps the property yellowness itself, the property that is sometimes instantiated, in lemons and other things, but is not, let us take it, currently being instantiated in or around me – and this grasping is somehow supposed to be responsible for the distinctive feel that characterizes our visual experiences as of yellow things. As I said, I find this suggestion difficult to understand.

14. Representational properties

Perhaps I am in danger of proving too much. I am expressing scepticism about relations between thinking subjects and uninstantiated properties. But there are independent reasons for recognizing some such relations. After all, sensory experiences and other mental states do in fact represent possible states of affairs, and such representational facts do create relationships between thinking subjects and uninstantiated properties. Unless I am prepared to eliminate representational facts, this then argues that mental relations to uninstaniated properties must be legitimate after all.

This is a reasonable point. I certainly do not want to eliminate representation. Representational facts play an important role in the unfolding of the natural world. And I agree that representational facts involve relations to uninstantiated properties. However, I don't think that this is of any real help to representationalists about sensory experience. When we unravel exactly what kind of relations to uninstantiated properties representational facts commit us to, we will see that they are quite unsuitable to serve as the basis for conscious properties.

Let us assume that when someone represents that p in some mode (cognition, visual perception, audition . . .), this will involve their being in some state S that represents that p.

Further, let us assume that
S represents that p
can be equated with
S is true if and only if p, in virtue of the way that S operates as a representation[8]
and that this in turn can be equated with
S will fulfil its aim if and only if p, in virtue of the way that S operates as a representation.

I myself am inclined to understand 'fulfil its aim' in this context in terms of such naturalistic categories as causation and biological design, but I intend this formulation to be neutral between different accounts of the nature of representation: after all, any such account will presumably agree that the essential feature of representational states is that they answer to some condition for their truth, and moreover that the aim of representations is, in some sense or other, to be true.

Now, if this much is agreed, then it follows from subjects representing that they will be related to properties. When a subject represents that a given lemon is yellow, for example, that subject is in a state that will fulfil its aim if and only if the lemon in question has the property of yellowness. And this in itself is a relation between the subject and yellowness.

But note how indirect and conditional a relation this is. In particular, note that a subject can bear this relation to yellowness even if yellowness is not instantiated anywhere in the subject's vicinity, as when the lemon being represented is not in fact yellow. The way that the subject's state is hooked up to yellowness, so to speak, does not demand that yellowness be presently instantiated.[9] It only imposes the *conditional* requirement that the state will do its job if and only if the lemon instantiates yellowness – that is, *either* it does its job and the lemon is yellow *or* it doesn't do its job and the lemon is not yellow. And in some cases – where the representation is false – this disjunction will be made true by the latter disjunct, and no actual instance of yellowness will currently be in play at all.[10]

Given this, it seems very strange to hold that the representational relation to yellowness can account for the 'presence' of yellowness, that very property that some surfaces possess, in our conscious experiences. Defenders of standard representationalism are committed to this ('only features *there* to turn your attention to' Harman 1990, 39; 'It seems to me that what I found so pleasing *in* the above instance...' Tye 1992, 160, my italics in both cases), but the nature of the representational relation, once clearly spelt out, does nothing to substantiate the thought that the properties of objects are to be found 'in' our conscious experience.

Consider an analogy. I harbour certain antibodies X whose job is to protect me against some antigen Y. They will fulfil their aim if and only if they repel an infection by Y. As it happens, I am not currently infected by Y, and so antibody X isn't fulfilling its aim. It take it that nobody would want to say on this account that nevertheless the antigen Y is currently 'present' in me, in virtue of my harbouring X, whose aim involves Y. Yet this is effectively what representationalists say about represented properties. The represented property Y is 'present' in my consciousness, in virtue of my harbouring S, whose aim involves Y, even when that aim isn't being fulfilled.

We have been considering the suggestion that representationalism about sensory experience is preferable to non-relationism because it respects the intuitive thought that in conscious experience we are acquainted with ordinary properties of physical objects, like colours and shapes, and not just with properties*. But this suggestion has not stood up to examination. There is no good way to make sense of the idea that ordinary properties of objects are somehow present in conscious sensory experiences.

So on this score, representationalism turns out to fare no better than non-relationism. It offers no real alternative to the view that the only properties of conscious experience with which we can make introspective contact are properties*, instrinsic properties of subjects that have no essential connection with the objectual properties that they contingently represent.[11] Moreover, given that non-relationism also avoids all the difficulties that broadness poses for representationalism, we would seem to have ample reason to prefer it.

15. Phenomenal intentionality

Let me now return to the phenomenological motive for representationalism mentioned at the beginning of this paper. This appealed to the idea that introspection can show us directly that conscious sensory experience is representational. Many philosophers who are moved by this thought side with non-relationism in holding that instrinsic properties of subjects suffice to fix their conscious properties. Where they differ is in holding that these intrinsic properties are by their nature representational: conscious sensory states are not like the typographical words that we use to write English sentences, which could well have meant other things, or nothing at all; rather, introspection shows that our conscious sensory states necessarily have a definite representational content, necessarily represent the world to be thus-and-so.

Let us call this position *'phenomenal intentionalism'*, following Uriah Kriegel (2013). Phenomenal intentionalists typically point to certain introspectible feature of sensory consciousness to support their contention that it is intrinsically representational. I am happy to agree that sensory consciousness displays the features in question. But I do not accept that these features suffice to establish representationalism.

In the first instance, the relevant features consist of certain constancies that are displayed by interlinked sensory experiences as we move through time and space. As I move my head, or walk around, or stand up and sit down, my successive sensory experiences will have a number of salient common elements, corresponding to the ordinary physical objects in my environment, such as chairs, table, trees, people and so on. What is more, the relationships between my successive experiences will mean that these common elements maintain a constant position in my visual space (or a continuous trajectory in those cases where the corresponding objects are moving). In addition, my sensory experience will contain constant elements corresponding to various properties of the relevant objects, including their shapes, colours, facial characteristics and so on (see Farkas 2013; Masrour 2013).

It is no doubt these structural feature in sensory experience that makes it so natural to suppose that properties of ordinary physical objects can be found 'within' experience. But, as we saw earlier, there are fundamental difficulties facing any representationalist who wants to understand things in this way. The alternative is to take the constancies found within sensory experience to be intrinsic features of experience itself. There may be a genuine chair-ish entity in my experience all right, in the sense of a sensory item that maintain its visual position, shape and colour, even as I move around, shift perspective and undergo changes in illumination. And, given such structural feature of experience, we might usefully talk of 'phenomenal objects' and their properties, and even acknowledge that they display a kind of 'mind-independence', in that they maintain certain constancies even as we walk around and bob up and down. But nothing in this requires us to think of these objects and properties as anything more than modulations of the intrinsic structure of experience.

Sometimes philosophers speak of experience being 'intentional' rather than 'representational'. It is not always clear what this commits them to. If all they mean is that our sensory conscious experience contains 'phenomenal objects', in the sense just outlined, then I am quite happy to agree that sensory experience is 'intentional'. There is no doubt that sensory experience has the internal structural features in question. But if it is supposed to be part of sensory 'intentionality' that sensory experiences have essential correctness conditions, and thereby lay claim to the world being a certain way, then I deny that sensory experiences are intentional.

Representation, as I am understanding it, requires a mental state to lay claim to something other than itself. Something beyond the state is required for the state to be true. Representation requires the representer to reach out beyond itself, so to speak, in an attempt to hook up with some putative fact. It is not immediately obvious how the mere presence of phenomenal objects in our conscious sensory states could bring this about. Those objects are intrinsic features of conscious experiences, features that the experiences have in themselves, independently of anything else. It is difficult to see how such features on their own could ensure any representational powers.

16. Checking for accuracy

Even so, some philosophers are explicit in maintaining that the intrinsic features of sensory consciousness suffice to determine everything needed for representation. Terence Horgan and John Tienson (2002), in their influential paper 'The Intentionality of Phenomenology and the Phenomenology of Intentionality', argue that the experiences of any two 'phenomenal duplicates' will have the same truth conditions, independently of their environments, histories or anything else. ('Phenomenal duplicates' are beings who are consciously the same; Horgan and Tienson agree that my cosmic swapmbrain counterpart, for instance, will be a phenomenal duplicate of me.)

Thus Horgan and Tienson (2002, 225):

> Consider any creature who is a complete phenomenal duplicate of yourself – its mental life is phenomenally exactly like yours. Assume nothing *else* about this creature ... suppose that you have the experience of seeing a picture hanging crooked. Each of your phenomenal duplicates has a phenomenally identical experience. Some of these experiences will be accurate and some will be inaccurate ... Thus, the sensory-phenomenal experience, by itself, determines conditions of accuracy: i.e., a class of ways the environment must be in order for the experience to be accurate. In order for such an experience to be accurate, there must be a picture before oneself, and it must be crooked.

I see no reason to accept this. From my perspective, conscious sensory experiences only represent contingently. Whether a given conscious experience represents a picture, or something else, or nothing at all, depends on factors beyond itself, such as historical correlations to feature of an environment, and is not fixed by its phenomenal nature.

Horgan and Tienson (2002, 226) offer an immediate argument for their view.

> That these phenomenally identical experiences all have the same truth conditions is reflected in the fact that each of the experiences is subject in the same way to investigation as to whether it is accurate. For example, you and your phenomenal duplicate each might have the experience of seeming to oneself to be testing one's

perceptual experience for accuracy by making measurements or using a level. You and your phenomenal duplicate each might have the subsequent experience of seeming to oneself to discover that the picture merely appears to be crooked because of irregularities of the wall, or tricks of light.

However, this argument does not serve. I agree that my phenomenal duplicates will go through the same motions, so to speak, in checking their experiences for veridicality (though of course my cosmic swampbrain counterpart won't literally go through any motions, as opposed to initiating motor signals that terminate at its cerebral boundaries). But this is no reason to suppose that my duplicates' states represent, as opposed to accepting that my duplicates *think* that their states represent.

In my view, my sensory states do not represent essentially, but they certainly represent contingently, and it does not require too much sophistication on my part to figure this out. All I need to do is to reflect on such facts as that: any given type of conscious sensory state will normally be caused by a given type of fact in my immediate environment, and will incline me to behave in ways appropriate to that fact; while at the same time that type of state will occasionally be produced in the absence of the relevant fact, but even then will still cause me to behave in the same way. A few simple considerations like these seem quite enough to lead me to regard my experiences as *representing* the possible facts that they stand proxy for – and no doubt on occasion to wonder whether they are representing accurately, and to take steps to check this.

And, if I can come to think that my states represent, and as a result be moved on occasion to check them for accuracy, then so can my phenomenal duplicates, including my cosmic swampbrain counterpart. After all, that counterpart is intrinsically identical to me, and so will have states corresponding to my belief that my sensory experiences represent, and to my intention to check whether the picture is indeed crooked, and so on. Of course, by my lights it isn't *true* that the sensory states of my swampbrain counterpart represent, and so there isn't any *point* in its trying to check them for accuracy. But that does not alter the fact that it will go through the same mental motions as I do, even though its sensory states do not represent anything.

To digress for a moment, there is of course a question of whether the cosmic swampbrain's *cognitive* states really represent anything, analogous to the issue of whether its sensory states represent anything. Let us assume that cognitive states like occurrent thoughts, beliefs, and so on, have a phenomenology – that is, that there are conscious properties that we instantiate when are in such states. This is of course contentious, but it is something that will be agreed by most phenomenal intentionalists. Now, are these conscious cognitive properties essentially representational? This is just the same question that we have been asking about conscious sensory properties, and I want to give just the same answer. In the actual world, these conscious cognitive states do indeed represent, but only contingently, in virtue of their environmental and historical embedding.

So from my point of view the cosmic swampbrain's cognitive states won't actually represent. They will feel just like my cognitive states, but lack representational content. In particular, the 'thought' prompted by 'reflection' on its 'crooked picture' sensory state won't actually have the truth condition that *this sensory state represents a crooked picture*. It will only feel the same as the cognitive state which has this content in me.

Still, this by itself is enough to answer Horgan and Tienson's argument. What must be conceded to their argument is that my phenomenal duplicates are in a position to form cognitive states which correspond to my (true) beliefs about the representational contents of my sensory states. But it does not follow that the sensory states of my duplicates have representational contents, nor even that their cognitive states have representational contents.[12]

17. Mind and world

We need to be careful that we are not seduced by the following line of thought:

Sensory experience, whether veridical, illusory or hallucinatory, presents us with properties that ordinary physical objects can possess, such as colours and shapes and so on. But the presence of these properties in experience does not guarantee that they really are possessed by any physical object, or even that such an object exists. So sensory experience by its very nature poses a further question, of whether there really is an independent physical object with the properties we are experientially presented with. That is, experience by its nature is representational.

This line of thought would indeed be compelling, if only the initial idea that ordinary objectual properties are present in experience were granted. However, as we saw earlier, this idea does not stand up to examination. The property of yellowness is not 'in' our experience when we have an experience as of a yellow lemon. Rather the property that we know introspectively to be instantiated in such cases, whether veridical, illusory or hallucinatory, is yellowness*, a conscious property of mental subjects, not a surface property of physical objects. These properties* might represent object properties, but in themselves they are like typographical words, items that have no constitutive tie to what they contingently represent.

This point isn't altered by the sense in which sensory experiences do contain 'phenomenal objects' with constant features. These 'objects' and their features are still on the side of properties*, aspects of experiences that contingently represent, not the kinds of things that are so represented. These aspects may display structural features that invite us to characterize them as displaying a kind of 'mind-independence', but this doesn't mean that they are the kinds of things that can exist outside experience.

It is of course very tempting to think of the properties that are present in experience as the same properties that physical objects might or might not have.[13] And it would indeed follow from this that experiences are intrinsically representational. (For they would intrinsically pose the question: are those properties also present in reality?) But the temptation must be resisted. The properties in experience are properties*, which have no constitutive connection with the ordinary objectual properties they contingently represent. So something beyond experience itself is needed to establish representation relations between experience and the rest of the world.

One final thought. I have been assuming throughout this paper that most of the world that we represent in experience is mind-independent in a strong metaphysical sense (it would still have existed even if humans with perceiving minds had never evolved). An alternative would be to view the world itself as made of idealist materials, as some kind of construction with sensory constituents. In the context of this idealist alternative, the sharp distinction that I have drawn between sensory properties* and ordinary objectual properties would need re-examination. If lemons are made of the same fundamental material as minds, then perhaps they can possess just the same properties as experiences after all. And then perhaps sense experience could be shown to be constitutively representational, via the line of thought that I have been considering in this section. But that is all a topic for another paper. For now it will be enough if I have shown that, on any non-idealist metaphysics, sensory experience is not essentially representational.

Notes

1. I intend this term to cover not only views that *identify* the phenomenal properties of experiences (their 'what-it's-likeness') with their representational properties (their accuracy conditions), but also views that take phenomenal properties to ground *representational characters*, in David Kaplan's sense, which in turn yield accuracy conditions when combined with contexts. For further discussion of the latter option, see sections 6 and 7 below.
2. See Papineau 2006 for a survey of such theories.
3. See Soteriou 2000 for the problems facing attempts to read sense experiences as having general existential contents.
4. See also footnote 12 below.
5. 'Swampman' thought experiments are sometimes invoked to lend intuitive support to the thesis that the mental states of intrinsic identicals must have the same *representational* contents. In my view, they do very little to support this intuition. In the present context, however, the issue is rather whether intrinsic identicals must share *phenomenal* properties, and here intuition seems much more definite, for what that is worth.
6. I originally defended this non-relationist position in Papineau 2014.
7. Philosophers of physicalist inclinations are likely to start asking at this point whether the brain vehicle properties that fix phenomenal character are supposed to be strictly physical properties or (narrow) 'functionalist' ones. This is a serious question, but not one that we need answer here. The central point is that either way the relevant properties will intrinsic non-representational ones. Indeed

this central point could be agreed by a dualist who takes conscious states to be metaphysically independent of physical ones. (More generally, none of the arguments in this paper depends on physicalism.)
8. In Papineau 2014 I advocated this neo-Davidsonian way of formulating representational facts as a means of avoiding existential commitment to propositions as abstract set-theoretical objects. But since then I have been persuaded that propositions need not be thought of in this way, and in truth are no more ontologically objectionable than properties (indeed we can think of them as 0-adic properties of the world) (see Rumfitt 2014). In the present paper the point of portraying representational facts in neo-Davidsonian terms is merely to bring out their complex conditional nature.
9. Indeed it is doubtful that representing a property requires that the property *ever* be instantiated. Perhaps I am mistakenly representing the lemon to have a particular shade of yellow that no object has or will ever possessed. Of course, there are specific questions about how mental states can get to refer to such never-instantiated properties, but I take them to be answerable.
10. I haven't forgotten that representationalists take conscious sensory experience to represent 'gappily'. However this only makes the relationship between a subject and any sensorily represented property Q even more indirect: the subject houses a mental predicate which, if combined with a mental name of a particular, *would* yield a mental state which would be true iff p ... where p involves Q.
11. It is of course consistent with non-relationism that we normally refer to experiential properties indirectly, by invoking their contingent properties of representing certain objectual properties (as in 'an experience *of yellowness*'). Reference via contingent description is a common enough linguistic phenomenon.
12. It follows from the commitments of phenomenal intentionalism that the correctness conditions of sensory (and cognitive) states must be narrow. Phenomenal intentionalists thus face all the difficulties about specifying narrow contents raised in sections 6 and 8 above. It is not clear to me that these difficulties are always fully appreciated. Thus Horgan and Tienson (2002, 229), discussing states with the phenomenology of ordinary cat thoughts, suggest that 'You, your Twin Earth doppelganger, and your Cartesian duplicate all have phenomenally identical thoughts with the same narrow truth conditions. For all three of you, these thoughts are intentionally directed toward certain small, common furry critters that meow, rub legs, drink milk, etc.'. But of course the referential value of concepts of *furry, meowing, legs* and *milk* cannot themselves be assumed in this context. The familiar Newman-style objections to Ramsifications of scientific theories are relevant here.
13. Thus consider Horgan and Tienson (2002, 225, my italics): 'sensory-phenomenal states ... present an *apparent* world full of *apparent* objects that *apparently* instantiate a wide range of properties and relations ...'. Where do the 'apparents' come from here? There is nothing apparent about the property my experience possesses when I have an experience as of a yellow lemon. It is what it is. To see this property as 'apparent' is already to assume that it is the same property that a real lemon might or might not have.

Disclosure Statement

No potential conflict of interest was reported by the author.

References

Block, N. (1990) 'Inverted Earth', *Philosophical Perspectives* 4: 53–79.
Block, N. (2004). 'Mental Paint', in M. Hahn and B. Ramberg (eds) *Reflections and Replies: Essays on the Philosophy of Tyler Burge*, 165–200. Cambridge MA: MIT Press
Burge, T. (1979) 'Individualism and the Mental', *Midwest Studies in Philosophy* 4: 73–121.
Byrne, A., and M. Tye (2006) 'Qualia Ain't in the Head', *Noûs* 40: 241–255.
Dretske, F. (1995). *Naturalizing the Mind*. Cambridge MA: MIT Press
Dretske, F. (1996). 'Phenomenal Externalism, or If Meanings Ain't in the Head, Where Are Qualia?' in E. Villanueva(ed.) *Philosophical Issues 7 Perception*, 143–158. Atascadero CA: Ridgeview Publishing
Dretske (2003) 'Experience as Representation', *Philosophical Issues* 13: 67–82.
Farkas, K. (2013) 'Constructing a World for the Senses', in U. Kriegel (ed.), *Phenomenal Intentionality*, 99–115. Oxford: Oxford University Press.
Fodor, J. (1980) 'Methodological Solipsism Considered As a Research Strategy in Cognitive Psychology', *Behavioral and Brain Sciences* 3: 63–109.
Harman, G. (1990) 'The Intrinsic Quality of Experience', in E. Tomberlin (ed.) *Philosophical Perspectives 4 Action Theory and Philosophy of Mind*, 31–52. Atascadero CA: Ridgeview Publishing.
Horgan, T., and Tienson, J. (2002). 'The Intentionality of Phenomenology and the Phenomenology of Intentionality'. in D. Chalmers (ed.) *Philosophy of Mind: Classical and Contemporary Readings*, 520–533. Oxford: Oxford University Press
Kriegel, U. (2013). 'The Phenomenal Intentionality Research Program', in U. Kriegel (ed.) *Phenomenal Intentionality*, 1–26. Oxford: Oxford University Press.
Kripke, S. (1980) *Naming and Necessity*, Oxford: Basil Blackwell.
Lycan, W. (1996) *Consciousness and Experience*, Cambridge MA: MIT Press.
Lycan, W. (2001) 'The Case for Phenomenal Externalism', in J. Tomberlin (ed.) *Philosophical Perspectives 15 Metaphysics*, 17–35. Atascadero CA: Ridgeview Publishing.
Masrour, F. (2013). 'Phenomenal Objectivity and Phenomenal Intentionality', in U. Kriegel (ed.) *Phenomenal Intentionality*, 99–115. Oxford: Oxford University Press.
Papineau, D. (2006) 'Naturalist Theories of Meaning', in B. Smith and E. Lepore (eds) *Oxford Handbook of the Philosophy of Language*, 175–188. Oxford: Oxford University Press.
Papineau, D. (2014). 'Sensory Experience and Representational Properties', *Proceedings of the Aristotelian Society* 114: 1–33.
Peacocke, C. (1983) *Sense and Content: Experience, Thought, and Their Relations*, Oxford: Oxford University Press.
Peacocke, C. (2008) 'Sensational Properties: Theses to Accept and Theses to Reject', *Revue Internationale de Philosophie* 62: 7–24.
Putnam, H. (1975). 'The Meaning of 'Meaning'', in K. Keith Gunderson (ed.) *Minnesota Studies in the Philosophy of Science 7 Language, Mind and Knowledge*, 131–193. Minneapolis, MN: University of Minnesota Press
Rumfitt, I. (2014). 'Truth and Meaning', *Aristotelian Society Supplementary* 88: 21–55.
Segal, G. (2002). *A Slim Book About Narrow Content*, Cambridge MA: MIT Press
Soteriou, M. (2000). 'The Particularity of Visual Perception', *European Journal of Philosophy* 8: 173–189.
Tye. M. (1992) 'Visual Qualia and Visual Content' in T.Crane (ed.) *The Contents of Experience*, 158–176. Cambridge: Cambridge University Press.
Tye, M. (1995). *Ten Problems of Consciousness: A Representational Theory of the Phenomenal Mind*, Cambridge MA: MIT Press

Tye, M. (2002) 'Representationalism and the Transparency of Experience', *Nous* 36: 137–151.

Tye, M. (2014) 'What is the Content of a Hallucinatory Experience?', in B. Brogaard (ed.) *Does Perception have Content?*, 291–230. Oxford: Oxford University Press.

Deleuze and Naturalism

Paul Patton

University of New South Wales, Australia

ABSTRACT
Against the tendency to regard Deleuze as a materialist and a naturalistic thinker, I argue that his core philosophical writings involve commitments that are incompatible with contemporary scientific naturalism. He defends different versions of a distinction between philosophy and natural science that is inconsistent with methodological naturalism and with the scientific image of the world as a single causally interconnected system. He defends the existence of a virtual realm of entities that is irreconcilable with ontological naturalism. The difficulty of reconciling Deleuze's philosophy with ontological naturalism is especially apparent in his recurrent conception of pure events that are irreducible to their incarnation in bodies and states of affairs. In the last section of this essay, I canvass some of the ways in which Deleuze's thought might be reconciled with a more liberal, pluralist and ethical naturalism that he identified in an early essay on Lucretius.

The question whether or not Deleuze can be considered a naturalistic philosopher and if so in what sense of the term 'naturalist' is not one that has been widely discussed in the secondary literature. His repeated reference to and use of the natural sciences throughout his work, along with the proliferation of efforts to link his philosophy to recent developments in complexity theory, non-linear dynamics and 'new materialism', point towards a consensus that he is a naturalist thinker (DeLanda 2002; Protevi 2013; Dolphijn and van der Tuin 2012). Although what is means to be a naturalist thinker is a matter of dispute, the prevailing view in contemporary philosophy is that naturalism implies a commitment to a scientific conception of the world and to scientific method as the only reliable path to knowledge. Despite his recurrent use of the natural sciences, I will argue that there are good reasons to doubt that Deleuze was a thoroughgoing scientific naturalist.

PHENOMENOLOGY AND NATURALISM

There is a minority counter-view in support of a more liberal, non-reductive form of naturalism that would allow 'a more inclusive conception of nature than any provided by the natural sciences' (De Caro and Macarthur 2004, 1). While Deleuze's metaphysical pluralism has more in common with this contemporary liberal naturalism, it also departs from it in significant respects. In an essay on Lucretius and naturalism first published in 1961, Deleuze set out a number of principles of naturalism considered as both a speculative and a practical philosophy.[1] He also made it clear that, in his view, the importance of Lucretius' philosophy derived from the way in which it saw naturalism as a means to oppose all forms of mystification, sadness and human incapacity. Throughout his career, Deleuze aligned himself with the ethical and political orientation that he discerned in Epicurean naturalism and that he described in the following terms:

> From Lucretius to Nietzsche, the same end is pursued and attained. Naturalism makes of thought and sensibility an affirmation. It directs its attack against the prestige of the negative; it deprives the negative of all its power; it refuses to the spirit of the negative the right to speak in the name of philosophy ... Lucretius established for a long time to come the implications of naturalism: the positivity of Nature; Naturalism as the philosophy of affirmation; pluralism linked with multiple affirmation; sensualism connected with the joy of the diverse; and the practical critique of all mystifications. (Deleuze 1990, 279)

I return to this practical dimension of Deleuze's naturalism at the end of this paper, after outlining some of the ways in which his philosophy is incompatible with scientific naturalism.

There are two problems that arise at the outset of any consideration of whether or not Deleuze can be considered a naturalist philosopher. The first is what we mean by Deleuze's philosophy and the second is what we mean by naturalism. The question whether or not there is such a thing as Deleuze's philosophy, and if so what is the nature of this philosophy, is the subject of an ongoing debate among Deleuze scholars. This problem arises partly because of the way that so much of Deleuze's early work took the form of reconstruction of and commentary on the thought of others. The naturalism of some of the philosophers about whom he wrote, notably Kant, Bergson and Nietzsche, is subject to debate.[2] However, other philosophers with whom he engaged, notably Lucretius, Hume, and Spinoza, are widely regarded to be naturalist thinkers. In any case, Deleuze's reconstructions of these philosophers were idiosyncratic accounts that presented his own thought as much as that of the authors discussed. François Zourabichvili characterized this form of historical reconstruction as an unconventional use of the narrative technique of free indirect discourse in which Deleuze's own voice infiltrates the voice of the philosopher under discussion so that we cannot be sure whether what is presented is Deleuze's thought or that of Bergson, Hume, Kant, Nietzsche or Spinoza (Zourabichvili 2004, 42–43).[3]

PHENOMENOLOGY AND NATURALISM

The problem of identifying Deleuze's philosophy persists in his later works, whether written in his own name or jointly with Félix Guattari, but for other reasons. Here the issue is not so much the use of other philosophers as the fact that Deleuze's own language, concepts and philosophical ambitions change from one book to the next. For example, the aims of *A Thousand Plateaus* (1987 [1980]) are very different from those of *Difference and Repetition* (2011 [1968]) although not unrelated: the latter identified an overarching image of thought that Deleuze argued had dominated the philosophical tradition, while the former sought to develop a practice of thinking governed by a very different, rhizomatic or nomadic image of thought. We should take seriously these changes in philosophical method and vocabulary and approach Deleuze's successive works not as a single, coherent thought or system but as expressions of a practice of philosophy that is problem driven. Whatever he took from other philosophers was always for particular purposes and always in relation to a specific project. Even when he returns to the same thinker, the same problem, or the same concept, this is only to begin again so that we are confronted each time with a different thinker, a different problem, or a different concept. This kind of movement and discontinuity in his thinking from one series of problems to the next is apparent, for example, in the different versions of Nietzsche's philosophy presented in *Nietzsche and Philosophy* (1983 [1962]), then in 'Nomadic Thought' (2004 [1973]) and *A Thousand Plateaus*. The first is a rigorous and systematic thinker who constructed a philosophy of nature around the complex concept of will to power. The second is the inventor of an antisystematic thought defined by its essential relation to the outside, to intensity and to laughter. This Nietzsche barely belongs in philosophy at all (Deleuze 2004 [1973]).[4]

The implicit pragmatism of Deleuze's approach to philosophy is evident in *What is Philosophy?* when he defines philosophy as the invention of concepts. He suggests that concepts are always invented in response to problems and that they are to be assessed by their usefulness in enabling new ways of describing things, events and states of affairs. Philosophy, he writes,

> does not consist in knowing and is not inspired by truth. Rather, it is categories like Interesting, Remarkable, or Important that determine success or failure. (Deleuze and Guattari 1994, 82)

To the extent that he saw philosophy as a practice involving the invention of and experimentation with distinct vocabularies, there is reason to believe that his own thought cannot be reduced to or captured in any 'ultimate vocabulary', to adopt a term from Richard Rorty.[5] Taken together, Deleuze's method of philosophical free indirect discourse and his ongoing experimentation with new philosophical vocabularies make it difficult to identify something we can recognize as 'Deleuze's philosophy', much less a stable corpus of texts that express this philosophy. Nevertheless, I will take the following core texts as the basis for my exploration of Deleuze's relation to naturalism: *What is Philosophy?*, which is in many ways a retrospective account of philosophy as it is practised by Deleuze and Guattari in *Anti-Oedipus* and *A Thousand Plateaus*, as well as an account of some of the overlapping concerns and continuities between these and *The Logic of Sense* and *Difference and Repetition*.

The second problem that any exploration of Deleuze's relation to naturalism must confront is what we understand by 'naturalism'. It is common for discussions of naturalism in philosophy to begin by pointing out that the term has no precise meaning or that it is one of those empty signifiers like 'world peace' to which everyone swears allegiance while holding quite different views about what this requires: 'once you start specifying concretely exactly what it involves and how to achieve it, it becomes increasingly difficult to reach and to sustain a consistent and exclusive "naturalism"' (Stroud 2004, 22). Granted the indeterminacy of the precise boundaries of naturalism, there is nonetheless a degree of overlap among contemporary philosophers about the requirements of a naturalistic approach. It has become customary to distinguish between ontological and methodological dimensions of scientific naturalism. Ontological naturalism is focused on the contents of reality and the claim that these are confined to what natural science tells us there is: reality has no place for 'supernatural' or other 'spooky' kinds of entity (Papineau 2009, 2). Papineau points out that contemporary versions of ontological naturalism rely on the underlying principle of the 'causal closure' or completeness of the physical realm whereby physical states or events are caused only by physical states or events. In its strongest form, this amounts to the physicalist doctrine that 'the world contains nothing but the entities recognized by physics' (Armstrong 1980, 156). Weaker versions might allow the existence of non-physical states or events, on the condition that these do not have physical effects (Papineau 2009, 6–25).

By contrast, methodological naturalism is focused on the ways in which we come to know what there is. It generally involves acceptance that natural science is a privileged if not the only form of knowledge and that, to the extent that philosophy aims to produce knowledge, it is continuous with science: 'Methodological naturalists see philosophy and science as engaged in essentially the same enterprise' (Papineau 2009, 25). Weaker versions of methodological naturalism might allow for distinct philosophical knowledge and ways of knowing so long as these do not conflict with scientific knowledge (Leiter 2013). The general requirements of ontological and methodological naturalism are summed up in the formulation advanced by Loptson, according to which

> the world is a unitary causally interconnected system, without 'gods' or systemic 'purposes,' and best understood, or only rationally intelligible, by scientific means. (Loptson 2007, 116)

There is no doubt that Deleuze denied the existence of gods and systemic purposes. His commentaries on Lucretius, Spinoza and Nietzsche make it clear that he viewed ideas of god, the soul, the afterlife and even moral responsibility as illusions, however necessary these might have been. He opposed teleological conceptions of history and human flourishing. However, he was not committed to the idea of the world as a single causally interconnected system intelligible only by scientific means. On the one hand, he defended a conception of philosophy as distinct from science and characterized by its own distinctive aims, objects and method that is difficult to reconcile with even the weakest forms of methodological naturalism. On the other hand, he endorsed the existence of some decidedly 'spooky' entities such as pure events, abstract machines and other kinds of virtual reality that make it difficult to regard him as an ontological naturalist. In his commentaries on Epicurean and Stoic philosophy, he draws attention to the different ways in which they complicate the causal relation (Deleuz, 1961; 1990). In *The Logic of Sense* and *Difference and Repetition*, he postulated causal factors, ranging from the Lucretian *clinamen* to the differentials of virtual Ideas, that appear inconsistent with the modern scientific image of the world as a single, closed causally interconnected system.

Philosophy, science and the conditions of experience

Throughout his work, Deleuze made repeated reference to and use of scientific material, especially from the mathematical, physical and biological sciences. For example, in Chapter Four of *Difference and Repetition* he drew upon the history of differential calculus and eighteenth and nineteenth century interpretations of it by Salomon Maïmon, Hoëne Wronski and Jean Bordas-Demoulin in his elaboration of a concept of Ideas or structures as the virtual origins of particular domains of thought and empirical reality. In Chapter Five he drew upon a number of elements of physical and biological science, including thermodynamics, the theory of evolution, and embryology, to give an account of the complex processes by means of which virtual structures are actualized in spatio-temporal form. In each case, he made it clear that he used elements of natural science for explicitly philosophical purposes. Moreover, he used them in the course of outlining a Transcendental Empiricism that appears to be incompatible with both stronger and weaker forms of methodological naturalism.

Difference and Repetition proposes a structuralist metaphysics of difference, at the basis of which are Ideas conceived as problems or structures whose elements are completely determined by reciprocal differential relations. These problems or structures are presented as real but virtual multiplicities whose existence is importantly anterior to that of the actual domains to which they give rise: 'The reality of the virtual consists of the differential elements and relations along with the singular points which correspond to them. The reality of the virtual is structure' (Deleuze 2011, 260). In the terms of this Deleuzian metaphysics, Ideas are what determine distinct regions of natural, social, linguistic or psychic reality. In other words, the characteristics of the actual are 'determined' by the differential features of the relevant Idea or structure, where the determination in question is structural rather than linear.[6] Models for this kind of determination include the way in which linguistic structures 'determine' the distinctive features of a particular language or the way in which the specification of a mathematical problem 'determines' the distinctive features of its solution. Deleuze suggests that particular structures have their own 'purely logical, ideal or dialectical time', which in turn determines a 'time of differenciation, or rather rhythms or different times of actualisation which correspond to the relations and singularities of the structure and, for their part, measure the passage from virtual to actual' (2011, 262). Deleuze does not dwell on the causal interconnection of the world as a whole, but it seems clear that the causality with which natural science is concerned applies only within the extended and temporal world that is the outcome of the process of actualization. Here, as in his early essay on Lucretius, Deleuze (1990, 268) seems happy to accept a 'highly structured principle of causality' that allows for distinct realms and distinct kinds of causal interconnection.

Difference and Repetition outlines a metaphysical conception of the world that is incompatible with the naturalistic conception of a single causally interconnected world. This is a world that is divided into two parts: an internal or virtual part defined in terms of structures and an external or actual part defined as the outcome of a process of actualization by means of which the ideal relations and differences of the virtual are expressed or translated into kinds, species and individual things with their characteristic spatiotemporal properties. The process by which virtual Ideas are actualized is what Deleuze calls different/ciation, a neologism that combines mathematical differentiation with biological or physical differenciation:

> Whereas differentiation determines the virtual content of the idea as problem, differenciation expresses the actualisation of this virtual and the constitution of solutions (by local integrations). Differenciation is like the second part of difference, and in order to designate the integrity or the integrality of the object we require the complex notion of different/ciation. (Deleuze 2011, 261)

In the Preface to the English translation he was careful to point out that this was a matter of making use of scientific functions for overtly philosophical purposes and in no way intended to advance the scientific domains involved (Deleuze 2011, xiv). Philosophy has no privileged status in this relationship: if anything, the preeminent field of thought is the science on which philosophy draws in the creation and exposition of its own concepts. In this sense, he suggests, that he

> tried to constitute a philosophical concept from the mathematical function of differentiation and the biological function of differenciation, in asking whether or not there was a statable relation between these two concepts which could not appear at the level of their respective objects. (Deleuze 2011, xiv)

A Thousand Plateaus is even more replete with material from the social as well as the natural sciences, used in both the construction and exposition of novel concepts such as those of assemblages, abstract machines, strata and smooth and striated spaces. Ansell-Pearson and Protevi argue that Deleuze and Guattari's machinic materialism is compatible with weaker forms of ontological naturalism, suggesting that their '"machinism" denotes the creative self-organization of material systems' (Ansell-Pearson and Protevi, 2016). However, there are features of this machinic ontology that suggest that *A Thousand Plateaus* is no more compatible with ontological naturalism than *Difference and Repetition*. For example, a version of the distinction between an inner virtual world and its external actualizations reappears in the form of a distinction between absolute and relative deterritorialization, where the former is the underlying condition of all forms of relative deterritorialization. 'Absolute deterritorialization' is Deleuze and Guattari's concept of an abstract, nonorganic, and creative life that is expressed both in the deterritorialization of existing assemblages and the connection of deterritorialized elements and their reconfiguration into new assemblages. It is the immanent source of transformation, the reserve of freedom or movement in reality that is activated whenever relative deterritorialization occurs. Deleuze and Guattari describe it as

> an Absolute, but one that is neither undifferentiated nor transcendent ... The deeper movement for conjugating matter and function – absolute deterritorialization, identical to the earth itself – appears only in the form of respective territorialities, negative or relative deterritorializations, and complementary reterritorializations. (Deleuze and Guattari 1987, 142–143)

The concept of assemblage also reproduces some features of the relationship between Ideas or structures and their fields of actualization found in *Difference and Repetition*. Assemblages are more or less concrete arrangements of material things and immaterial statements, but they are 'directed' by the virtual or abstract machine that they embody. Deleuze and Guattari distinguish this directive power of abstract machines from other models of causal interaction in a manner that appears, prima facie, inconsistent with the idea of a single causally interconnected world.[7]

The world outlined in *A Thousand Plateaus* is no more compatible with methodological than with ontological naturalism. Deleuze reaffirms the methodological difference between philosophy and science when he insists in an interview that *A Thousand Plateaus* is a work of philosophy, nothing but philosophy (Deleuze 2007, 176, trans. modified). Among the precedents for this distinction between philosophy and science, Kant is perhaps the most important. In *Difference and Repetition*, philosophy was presented in the overtly Kantian terms of an account of the Ideas or problems, in the sense that Kant described Transcendental Ideas as problems for which there is no solution. These were, as he put it, both immanent in and transcendent to knowledge of the relevant field (Deleuze 2011, 215, 225–227, 237). Deleuze followed Kant in distinguishing between the empirical knowledge of objects in space and time provided by the science, and the a priori 'knowledge' of the conditions of such empirical knowledge provided by philosophy. Unlike Kant, however, he did not argue for a unique set of pure concepts implicit in the reason of a transcendental subject and that form the intellectual conditions of all knowledge. Instead he argued for an open-ended series of Ideas or problems located in an a-subjective transcendental field, the details of which remain to be thought by means of a 'Transcendental Empiricism'.[8] In this sense, for Deleuze, the task of philosophy is not so much to discover as to produce the transcendental conditions of knowledge and experience.

François Zourabichvili takes up this a-subjective transcendental reading of Deleuze's conception of philosophy and applies it to *A Thousand Plateaus* in arguing that the concepts invented by Deleuze and Guattari should be considered local or regional conditions of experience. Kant thought that the pure concepts of the understanding needed to be supplemented by a priori concepts applicable to the world in general before these in turn were filled out by the empirical concepts of natural science. Similarly, the concepts created in *A Thousand Plateaus* by Deleuze and Guattari can be understood to apply only to restricted fields of experience. They amount to fragments of a philosophy of nature that provide conditions of experience limited to certain aspects of the natural and social world. For example, strange though it may be to affirm that a human life is made up of lines, we have no idea of what a life is apart from relations of this kind. We are used to thinking of lives in terms of natural processes, progressions or the movement from beginning to end and so on. Thinking of lives in terms of molar and molecular lines and lines of flight thus implies another way of understanding or another *experience* of human life (Zourabichvili 2011, 71).

Philosophy and science in *what is philosophy?*

What is Philosophy? develops a more comprehensive account of the differences between philosophy, science, and art by considering them as distinct modes of intellectual production, each with its own distinctive aims, methods, raw materials and products. Philosophy and only philosophy produces concepts, while science produces mathematical or propositional functions. Philosophy is like science in that it fulfils a cognitive rather than an affective function, but like art, especially modern art, in that it does not seek to refer or to represent independently existing objects or states of affairs. Deleuze and Guattari equivocate between suggesting that philosophy is not concerned with knowledge and suggesting that it does provide a kind of knowledge but one that is different from the knowledge provided by science. Whereas science provides knowledge of empirical processes and states of affairs, philosophy provides knowledge of pure events by means of concepts: 'The following definition of philosophy can be taken as being decisive: knowledge through pure concepts' (Deleuze and Guattari 1994, 7).

The difference between philosophy and science is in the first instance a difference between the kinds of thought objects produced. Science produces functions on a plane of reference. The history of science involves the construction of such planes of reference and the specification of relevant co-ordinates in terms of which functions may be determined. By contrast, philosophy produces concepts understood as a certain kind of intensional object produced on what Deleuze and Guattari call a 'plane of immanence', by which they mean a certain conception of the nature of thought. Concepts are complex in the sense that they involve components that are themselves conceptual. These components of concepts are neither constants nor variables but 'pure and simple *variations* ordered according to their neighbourhood' (Deleuze and Guattari 1994, 20). Concepts are always produced in relation to a particular problem: what is thinking? What is political or civil society? They are defined by the internal relations between their components and by their external relations to other concepts. Thus, for example, Descartes' *Cogito* is a complex concept with three components: I (who doubts) think, and therefore I am (a thinking being). The three components of this concept – the doubting I, the thinking I and the existent I – are like so many intensive ordinates 'arranged in zones of neighbourhood or indiscernibility that produce passages from one to the other and constitute their inseparability'. (Deleuze and Guattari 1994, 24–25).

In addition to the formal differences between philosophical concepts and scientific functions, *What is Philosophy?* argues that they have a different relation to their respective objects. Philosophical concepts *express* pure events, which are the undetermined events that we describe using the infinitive verb and that are actualized in determinate forms: to think, to speak, to walk, to become-animal, to deterritorialize and so on. The relation between the philosophical concept and the event expressed is internal to the concept. For this reason, Deleuze and Guattari claim that 'the concept ... has no reference: it is self-referential, [in the sense that] it posits itself and its object at the same time as it is created' (Deleuze and Guattari 1994, 22). By contrast, scientific functions *refer* to states of affairs, things or bodies supposed to exist independently of the functions concerned. Propositional functions and formalized sentences of ordinary language exemplify this referential relation. In this case, the independence of the objects that constitute the extension of the concept is given by their being considered the referents of the singular terms that serve as arguments. The independence of the co-ordinates or variables is essential to the manner in which science specifies the nature of things or states of affairs that 'actualize the virtual on a plane of reference', whereas philosophical concepts 'express an event that gives consistency to the virtual on a plane of immanence' (Deleuze and Guattari 1994, 133).

Deleuze and Guattari provide a striking illustration of the difference between the objects of philosophical concepts and scientific functions when they contrast the scientific characterization of a bird, which refers to species and genus and distinguishing features, with a philosophical concept that comprises 'the composition of its postures, colours and songs' (Deleuze and Guattari 1994, 20). This contrast parallels the contrast drawn in *A Thousand Plateaus* between two modes of individuation of things: a differentiation of bodies by genus and species and their differentiation by affects and the relative motions of their parts. The latter is the mode of individuation of haecceities or events, and it is a thesis of this book that, for philosophy, individuation of this type is primary. The bird as it is expressed in the philosophical concept is a singular assemblage of movement, sound and colour, in other words the bird as haecceity or event.

Events and ontological naturalism

As we saw in the preliminary definition of naturalism at the outset, a core idea is that of the world as a single causally interconnected system: 'What is key to naturalism is the idea of a single unitary world, with a single set of nomological principles underscoring that unity' (Loptson 2007, 125). Throughout his work, Deleuze writes about the nature of events in a manner that is difficult to reconcile with ontological naturalism. He draws a distinction between 'pure' and actual events that, like his concepts of virtual Ideas or abstract machines, seems to imply a nomologically divided world. Coupled with the methodological distinction he draws between philosophy and science, the theses that he advances about the nature of pure events make it difficult to consider him a thoroughgoing naturalist.

Deleuze's interest in the nature of events relates to his preference for a philosophy of process or becoming rather than of substance or being. In a 1988 interview, he suggested that he had always been concerned with the nature of events, in part because he saw the philosophical concept of the event as 'the only one capable of ousting the verb "to be" and its attributes' (Deleuze 1995, 141). Variations on the distinction between being and becoming occur throughout his work, for example in the distinction between absolute and relative deterritorialization, or the distinction between a virtual realm of becoming and an actual realm of embodied historical events. In a 1990 interview with Antonio Negri, Deleuze comments that he had become 'more and more aware of the possibility of distinguishing between becoming and history' (Deleuze 1995, 170). In *What Is Philosophy?* this distinction took the form of a contrast between an ahistorical realm of pure events and a historical realm in which events are actualized in bodies and states of affairs.

This distinction between pure events and their incarnation in bodies and states of affairs may be traced back to *The Logic of Sense*, which provides one of the most detailed accounts of the incorporeal realm of becoming and the event to be found anywhere in Deleuze. This is an avowedly experimental book organized into series or short chapters and concerned among other things with the nature of sense or meaning. As well as a commentary on Lewis Carroll, structuralism, psychoanalysis and language, it can also be read as an essay in defence of the ontological priority of events (Bowden 2011). Deleuze draws on Stoic philosophy to formulate a concept of events as incorporeal entities expressed in propositions and attributed to bodies and states of affairs. The Stoics drew a fundamental distinction between a material or physical realm of bodies and states of affairs and a nonphysical realm of incorporeal entities that includes time, place, and the sense, or the 'what is expressed' (*Lekta*) in statements. They took the sense of a statement to be identical with the event expressed in it: 'Sense, *the expressed of the proposition*, is an incorporeal, complex and irreducible entity, at the surface of things, a pure event which inheres or subsists in the proposition' (Deleuze 1990, 19).

This implies that events are a different order of being to bodies and states of affairs: 'The event subsists in language, but it happens to things' (Deleuze 1990, 24). On Deleuze's account of this Stoic metaphysics, events are singular but incorporeal entities, different in kind from physical bodies but capable of being expressed in particular configurations and movements of bodies. In this way, for example, an actual battle is made up of the movements of certain bodies and pieces of equipment at a particular place and a particular time, but the event of battle is not confined to these elements because it can recur on other occasions when it would be expressed in entirely different elements. The event is expressed in these particular elements while nevertheless remaining irreducible to them: in any flesh and blood battle, 'the event hovers over its own field, being neutral in relation to all of its temporal actualizations' (Deleuze 1990, 100).

Deleuze's distinction between the event and its actualization in particular circumstances is further reinforced by the distinction drawn in *The Logic of Sense* between a historical time within which actual events occur (*Chronos*) and a 'time of the event' (*Aion*) that cannot be reduced to the former time. This distinction provides further support for the view that events proper in some sense 'escape History'. The opening paragraph of *The Logic of Sense* takes an example from Lewis Carroll to show that events imply contradictory properties of a thing in a manner inconceivable within linear time. When we say that Alice grew (she became taller), this implies that she became taller than she was before. By the same token, however, she also became shorter than she is now (assuming that she continued to grow). Although it makes no sense to say that she is taller and shorter at the same time, we can say that she *becomes* taller and shorter at the same time, thereby exhibiting 'the simultaneity of a becoming whose characteristic is to elude the present' (Deleuze 1990, 1). A further reason for drawing a distinction between 'event time' and 'linear time' involves the paradox involved in identifying, in historical time, the precise moment at which events occur. Suppose we take a time before the event and a time after: the infinite divisibility of the series of moments implies that there are two converging series on either side of the event but no point at which these series meet. Thus, from the perspective of historical time, there is no present moment at which the event takes place. As Deleuze (1990, 63) expresses this point in *The Logic of Sense*: 'The agonizing aspect of the pure event is that it is always and at the same time something which has just happened and something about to happen; never something which is happening.'

This distinction between ordinary historical time and the time of the event is one of the more puzzling aspects of Deleuze's Stoicism. It raises the question whether events understood in this manner can be considered compatible with the naturalistic conception of a single causally interconnected world. In the case of the Stoics, Deleuze argues that the duality between bodies and states of affairs, on the one hand, and incorporeal events or effects on the other, implies a 'dismemberment' of the causal relation whereby bodily things are causes to one another while incorporeal events are only attributes or effects of bodies (Deleuze 1990, 6). He cites the commentary of Emile Bréhier on examples from Sextus Empiricus, suggesting that bodies act on one another to produce effects that are not themselves bodies but incorporeal attributes expressed in propositions:

> when the scalpel cuts through the flesh, the first body produces upon the second not a new property but a new attribute, that of being cut. The attribute does not designate any real quality ... it is, to the contrary, always expressed by the verb, which means that it is not a being but a way of being. (Deleuze 1990, 5)

At the same time, events stand in 'quasi-causal' relations to other events, which are not simply relations of logical dependence but of harmony or conflict, compatibility or incompatibility. Even though events are effects of bodily causes the relations between them 'cannot be derived from the thoroughly deterministic causal order' (Bowden 2011, 37). For the Stoics, events are a means to knowledge of the world, which is achieved when a person acquires a comprehensive rational representation of their interrelations at a given moment.

Returning to Deleuze's conception of philosophy as the creation of concepts that express pure events: there is no doubt that the description of actual events and states of affairs in the terms of a given philosophical concept has causal effects. Controversies in history and political science are made of this. Consider the event of colonization in a particular country: in its purest form, does this amount to the capture of territory, peoples, and resources by a technologically superior power, or is it rather an encounter between different peoples that might have taken very different forms to those that it took historically? How we answer these questions makes a difference to how we might address the present consequences of past colonial events. But these are philosophical questions, not to be answered by examining the historical facts, in the way that we suppose scientists proceed in reconstructing the virtual origins of material processes.

But what of the events themselves? How do the events that are expressed in philosophical concepts stand in relation to ontological naturalism? Do they form part of the causal order of the natural world? One reason to think they do is provided by Deleuze's reluctance to allow that events are transcendent to the states of affairs in which they are actualized and his insistence that they are immanent. This is one of the significant changes in his thinking alongside his growing commitment to the distinction between becoming and history. In *Difference and Repetition* he was happy to treat virtual Ideas or problems as both immanent and transcendent and to attribute to the ideal series of events 'the double property of transcendence and immanence in relation to the real' (Deleuze 2011, 237). By contrast, *What Is Philosophy?* describes transcendence as one of the illusions that arise in relation to the plane of immanence on which philosophical concepts are created (Deleuze and Guattari 1994, 49–50). It denies that pure events are transcendent and insists that they are 'pure immanence of what is not actualized or of what remains indifferent to actualization' in states of affairs (Deleuze and Guattari 1994, 156).

This might lead us to suppose that pure events and more generally Deleuze's later version of the distinction between an inner, virtual and outer, actual world is compatible with science, even if it does imply a particularly complex picture of nature. Unfortunately this interpretation is ruled out by the fact that he also insists that it is not the same virtual that is actualized in scientific functions and that is expressed in philosophical concepts (Deleuze and Guattari 1994, 156). We do not descend from virtuals to actuals and ascend from states of affairs to virtuals on the same line: 'actualisation and counter-effectuation are not two segments of the same line but rather different lines' (Deleuze and Guattari 1994, 160). If the virtual that science begins with in order to retrace the paths of actualization is not the same virtual as the one that philosophy produces in counter-actualizing actual events and states of affairs, then we are left with a methodologically and substantively divided world that is incompatible with naturalism.

Deleuze and ethical naturalism

While Deleuze's philosophy does not respect the constraints of contemporary scientific naturalism, it does accord with some aspects of a more liberal and pluralist naturalism. For example, in his early essay on Lucretius and naturalism, he set out a number of principles of naturalism considered as a speculative philosophy that implied an ontological pluralism as well as an acceptance of forms of philosophical knowledge that go beyond natural science. He argued that it is with the Epicureans that 'the real noble acts of philosophical pluralism begin' (Deleuze 1990, 267). In Lucretius, this took the form of a conception of nature not simply as diverse but as the ongoing production of diversity. According to this conception, nature is not a collection or a totality but an open-ended distribution of things in time. It follows that there is 'no combination capable of encompassing all the elements of nature at once, there is no unique world or total universe' (Deleuze 1990, 267). It is not governed by the logic of identity and contradiction but that of conjunction and disjunction, resemblance and difference, composition and decomposition. In Lucretius's world 'everything is formed out of connections, densities, shocks, encounters, concurrences, and motions' (Deleuze 1990, 268).[9] Throughout his writings, Deleuze explicitly aligned himself not only with the broad outlines of this conception of the world as the generative power that produces diversity but also with the practical orientation that he saw as primary, namely to distinguish what is nature from what is mythological, where the latter involves mere illusions of the mind that enslave humans through fear and superstition. What linked Lucretius, Hume, Spinoza, Nietzsche and, we might add, Deleuze was 'their critique of negativity, their cultivation of joy, the hatred of interiority, the externality of forces and relations, the denunciation of power ... and so on' (Deleuze 1995, 6).

The conception of philosophy outlined in *What is Philosophy?* restates the priority of practical alongside speculative concerns in the terms of Deleuze's appropriation of the Stoic conception of pure events. The suggestion that the concepts produced by philosophy express pure events implies that the realm of sense, meaning or pure events is irreducible to the spatial and temporal world described by the sciences. For the Stoics, the pure events that are expressed in language were bound up with a moral imperative that Deleuze glosses in terms of 'willing the event', where this is not so much a matter of willing what occurs 'but something in that which occurs, something yet to come which would be consistent with what occurs' (Deleuze 1990, 149). In these terms, the event is what must be thought and willed in order to live freely in the terms of the naturalistic ethic that he finds in Stoic philosophy. Deleuze retains something of this ethic when he suggests that the task of philosophy is to counter-actualize the events that condition and shape our lives, and that

> There is a dignity of the event that has always been inseparable from philosophy as *amor fati*: being equal to the event, or becoming the offspring of one's own events ... Philosophy's sole aim is to become worthy of the event... (Deleuze and Guattari 1994, 159–160)

What it means to become worthy of the event must be assessed in tandem with the utopian vocation that Deleuze attributes to philosophy, and that he defines in terms of its manner of engaging with the present. Philosophy helps us to make sense of what is happening around us by creating concepts that express pure events. To think philosophically about the present is to counter-effectuate the pure events expressed in concepts by using these to describe historical events and processes. To describe current events in terms of such philosophical concepts is to relate them back to the pure events of which they appear only as one particular determination. In this manner, we can dissociate the pure event from the particular form in which it has been actualized and point to the possibility of other determinate actualizations: another justice, a different democracy, or a colonial encounter that did not take the form of the legal, political, economic or cultural capture of one people by another. Philosophy understood as the creation of concepts does not extract just any event from things but 'untimely' events that are forever new or renewable, such as justice, unconditional hospitality or the pure event of a democracy to come, or we might add smooth and striated spaces, nomadic war-machines or absolute deterritorialization. In this way, philosophy creates concepts that enable us to break with established or self-evident forms of understanding and description. For Deleuze, philosophy is not continuous with science but above all a form of practical reason that provides new forms of description and, as a consequence, new possibilities for thought and action.

Notes

1. Recent discussions of Deleuze's relation to ancient Greek naturalism include Hayden (2008), Holmes (2012) and Ansell-Pearson (2014).
2. See for example Zammito (2008) on Kant and naturalism, Leiter (2013) on Nietzsche, and Ansell-Pearson and Protevi (2016) on Bergson.
3. Joe Hughes (2012, 6) describes this practice of philosophizing through the voice of others as a kind of 'philosophical ventriloquism'. See also his extended discussion of Deleuze's practice of free indirect discourse in *Difference and Repetition* in Hughes 2009, 14–17.
4. Brooke Holmes discerns a similar pattern in Deleuze's recurrent presentations of Lucretius over the course of his career, suggesting that 'he came back time and again to Lucretius, producing ever shifting images of his philosophical pluralism' (2012, 341).
5. For discussion of Deleuze's relation to Rorty and to pragmatism and neo-pragmatism in general, see chapters by Allen and Patton in Bowden, Bignall, and Patton 2015.
6. In *Difference and Repetition*, Deleuze endorsed the concept of structural causality in terms of which Althusser and his collaborators sought to make sense of Marx's thesis of economic determination, suggesting that 'this structure never acts transitively, following the order of succession in time; rather, it acts by incarnating its varieties in diverse societies and by accounting for the simultaneity of all the relations and terms which, each time and in each case, constitute the present: that is why "the economic" is never given properly speaking, but rather designates a differential virtuality to be interpreted, always covered over by its forms of actualisation' (Deleuze, 2011, 234–235).
7. 'There is no doubt that an assemblage never contains a causal infrastructure. It does have, however, and to the highest degree, an abstract line of creative or specific causality, its *line of flight or deterritorialization*; this line can be effectuated only in connection with general causalities of another nature' (Deleuze and Guattari 1987, 283).
8. On the differences between Kant's and Deleuze's conception of the transcendental field, see Voss 2013.
9. Deleuze is quoting here from the first book of *De Rerum Natura*.

Disclosure Statement

No potential conflict of interest was reported by the author.

References

Ansell-Pearson, Keith. (2014) 'Affirmative Naturalism: Deleuze and Epicureanism', *Cosmos and History: The Journal of Natural and Social Philosophy* 10(2): 121–137.

Ansell-Pearson, Keith, and John Protevi (2016) 'Naturalism in the Continental Tradition', in Kelly James Clark (ed.) *The Blackwell Companion to Naturalism*, 34–48, Hoboken, NJ: Wiley-Blackwell.

Armstrong, David M. (1980) 'Naturalism, Materialism and First Philosophy', *The Nature of Mind and Other Essays*, 149–165, St. Lucia: University of Queensland Press.

Bowden, Sean (2011) *The Priority of Events: Deleuze's Logic of Sense*, Edinburgh: Edinburgh University Press.

Bowden, Sean, Simone Bignall, and Paul Patton (eds) (2015) *Deleuze and Pragmatism*, London and New York: Routledge.

De Caro, Mario, and David Macarthur (2004) 'Introduction: The Nature of Naturalism', in De Caro and Macarthur (eds) *Naturalism in Question*, 1–17, London and Cambridge, Mass: Harvard University Press.

DeLanda, Manuel (2002) *Intensive Science & Virtual Philosophy*, London: Continuum.

Deleuze, Gilles (1961) 'Lucrèce et le naturalisme' [Lucretius and Naturalism], *Les Études philosophiques*, Nouvelle Série, 16(1): 19–29. [Revised version translated as 'Lucretius and the Simulacrum' and published as an appendix to The Logic of Sense, 266–279]

Deleuze, Gilles (1983 [1962]) *Nietzsche and Philosophy*, trans. Hugh Tomlinson, London: Athone Press.

Deleuze, Gilles (1990 [1969]) *The Logic of Sense*, trans. Mark Lester with Charles Stivale, (ed.) Constantin Boundas, New York, NY: Columbia University Press.

Deleuze, Gilles (1995 [1990]) *Negotiations 1972–1990*, trans. Martin Joughin, New York, NY: Columbia University Press.

Deleuze, Gilles (2004 [1973]) 'Nomadic Thought' in *Desert Islands and Other Texts 1953–1974*, translated by Michael Taormina and edited by David Lapoujade, 252–261, New York, NY: Semiotext(e). Originally published in *Nietzsche aujourd'hui? Tome 1: Intensités* [Nietzsche Today? Volume 1: Intensities], 159–174, Paris: UGE 10/18.

Deleuze, Gilles (2007 [2003]) *Two Regimes of Madness: Texts and Interviews 1975–1995*, trans. Ames Hodges and Mike Taormina, New York, NY: Semiotext(e) [Revised Edition].

Deleuze, Gilles (2011 [1968]) *Difference and Repetition*, trans. Paul Patton, London: Continuum (Corrected edition).

Deleuze, Gilles, and Guattari, Felix (1987 [1980]). *A Thousand Plateaus: Capitalism and Schizophrenia*, trans. Brian Massumi, Minneapolis, MN: University of Minnesota Press.

Deleuze, Gilles, and Felix Guattari (1994 [1991]) *What Is Philosophy?*, trans. Hugh Tomlinson and Graham Burchell, New York, NY: Columbia University Press.

Dolphijn, Rick, and Iris van der Tuin (2012) *New Materialism: Interviews & Cartographies*. London: Open Humanities Press.

Hayden, Patrick (2008) 'Gilles Deleuze and Naturalism: A Convergence with Ecological Theory and Politics', in Bernd Herzogenrath (ed.) *An [Un]likely Alliance: Thinking Environment[s] with Deleuze|Guattari*, 23–45, Newcastle Upon Tyne: Cambridge Scholars Publishing.

Holmes, Brooke (2012) 'Deleuze, Lucretius and the Simulacrum of Naturalism,' in Brook Holmes and W.H.Shearin (eds) *Dynamic Reading: Studies in the Reception of Epicureanism*, 316–343, Oxford: Oxford University Press.

Hughes, Joe (2009) *Deleuze's Difference and Repetition: A Reader's Guide*, London: Continuum.

Hughes, Joe (2012) *Philosophy After Deleuze*, London: Bloomsbury.
Leiter, Brian (2013) 'Nietzsche's Naturalism Reconsidered', in Ken Gemes and John Richardson (eds) *The Oxford Handbook to Nietzsche*, 576–598. New York, NY: Oxford University Press.
Loptson, Peter (2007) 'Naturalism', in Constantin V. Boundas (ed.) *The Edinburgh Companion to Twentieth-Century Philosophies*, 116–127, Edinburgh: Edinburgh University Press.
Papineau, David (2009) 'Naturalism', *Stanford Encyclopedia of Philosophy*. http://plato.stanford.edu/archives/spr2009/entries/naturalism/
Protevi, John (2013) *Life, War, Earth: Deleuze and the Sciences*. Minneapolis, MN: University of Minnesota Press.
Stroud, Barry (2004) 'The Charm of Naturalism', in M.De Caro and D.Macarthur (eds) *Naturalism in Question*, 21–35, London and Cambridge, MA: Harvard University Press.
Voss, Daniela (2013) *Conditions of Thought: Deleuze and Transcendental Ideas*, Edinburgh: Edinburgh University Press.
Zammito, John H. (2008) 'Kant and Naturalism Reconsidered', *Inquiry* 51(5): 532–558.
Zourabichvili, François (2004) *Deleuze: A Philosophy of The Event*, Edinburgh: Edinburgh University Press.
Zourabichvili, François (2011) *La littéralité et autres essais sur l'art* [Literality and Other Essays on Art], Paris: PUF.

Exile and return: from phenomenology to naturalism (and back again)

David R. Cerbone

Department of Philosophy, West Virginia University, USA

ABSTRACT
Naturalism in twentieth century philosophy is founded on the rejection of 'first philosophy', as can be seen in Quine's rejection of what he calls 'cosmic exile'. Husserl's transcendental phenomenology falls within the scope of what naturalism rejects, but I argue that the opposition between phenomenology and naturalism is less straightforward than it appears. This is so not because transcendental phenomenology does not involve a problematic form of exile, but because naturalism, in its recoil from transcendental philosophy, creates a new form of exile, what I call in the paper 'exile from within'. These different forms of exile are the result of shared epistemological aspirations, which, if set aside, leave open the possibility of phenomenology without exile. In the conclusion of the paper, I appeal to Merleau-Ponty as an example of what phenomenology without epistemology might look like.

If the synthesis could be genuine and my experience formed a closed system, if the thing and the world could be defined once and for all, if the spatio-temporal horizons could, even theoretically, be made explicit and the world conceived from no point of view, then nothing would exist; I should hover above the world, so that all times and places, far from becoming simultaneously real, would become unreal, because I should live in none of them and would be involved nowhere. (Merleau-Ponty 1962, 331–32)

1. Introduction: on exile

I want to start with a bit of philosophical melodrama, two moments from very different perspectives in twentieth-century philosophy. One is an expression of philosophy's longing for a privileged standpoint, the other a resounding denial of any such possibility. The denial comes from the final paragraph of Quine's

Word and Object, wherein he summarizes the naturalistic view of language, mind, and meaning articulated throughout the book:

> The philosopher's task differs from the others', then, in detail; but in no such drastic way as those suppose who imagine for the philosopher a vantage point outside the conceptual scheme that he takes in charge. There is no such cosmic exile. He cannot study and revise the fundamental conceptual scheme of science and common sense without having some conceptual scheme, whether the same or another no less in need of philosophical scrutiny, in which to work. (Quine 1960, 275–76)

Quine's prohibition on what he refers to as 'cosmic exile' is a restatement of what he elsewhere refers to as the inevitability of philosophy's (and, really, any form of serious inquiry's) always 'working from within' (Quine 1976, 252). There is, for Quine, no getting 'outside' when it comes to our 'conceptual scheme', which comprises both common sense and the natural sciences. Any attempt to make sense of that scheme, as philosophy aspires to do, must make use of – and so operate 'within' – that ongoing scheme: 'No inquiry being possible without some conceptual scheme, we may as well retain and use the best one we know – right down to the latest detail of quantum mechanics, if we know it and it matters.' Quine continues: 'Analyze theory-building how we will, we all must start in the middle' (Quine 1960, 4).

Contrast Quine's killjoy pronouncements with the earlier, and far more exuberant, words of Eugen Fink, from near the end of his *Sixth Cartesian Meditation*, which was written as a recapitulation and critical extension of Husserl's transcendental phenomenology. Here, Fink reports the feeling of awe upon achieving just the kind of 'exile' whose possibility Quine would later deny:

> The *world* as the total unity of the really existent, boundlessly open in space and time, with the whole immensity of nature filling it, with all the planets, Milky Ways, and solar systems; with the multiplicity of existents such as stones, plants, animals, and humans; as soil and living space for human cultures, for their rise and fall in the turn of history; as locale for final ethical and religious decisions; the world in this manifoldness of its existence – in a word, *being* – *is only a moment of the Absolute*. The awful tremor everyone experiences who actually passes through the phenomenological reduction has its basis in the dismaying recognition that the inconceivably great, boundless, vast world has the *sense of a constitutive result*, that therefore in the *universe of constitution* it represents only a *relative "totality."* (Fink and Husserl 1995, 143–44)

For Fink, everything making up our conceptual scheme in Quine's sense can ultimately be viewed from a position entirely apart from it, whereby it can be understood as a 'constitutive result' of an entirely different set of processes. Once seen in this way – as a result – what we take to be the case from within our ordinary (and scientific) conceptual scheme is seen to be only *relative*.

The opposition dramatically expressed in these passages encapsulates the standard opposition between phenomenology and naturalism. On this standard view, phenomenology can be understood as something of a 'last stand' for the kind of first philosophy naturalism rejects. That rejection is fueled in large part by a healthy dose of skepticism concerning the idea that we can make sense of our 'conceptual scheme' from a vantage point entirely external to it, such that we can see the former as a 'result' of whatever is going on with respect to the latter. What phenomenology refers to as *constitution* is just the kind of thing a prohibition on cosmic exile would exclude. Although Quine is referring primarily to Carnap and his project in the *Aufbau* when he asks, 'But why all this creative reconstruction, all this make-believe?' (Quine 1969, 75) the question pertains equally to Husserl's ambitions.

There is, I think, reason to be suspicious of the idea of constitution, even before it reaches the heights of Fink's grandiose rhetoric. I will try to develop some of those suspicions shortly. But I want to claim, more surprisingly,[1] that Quine's own naturalism falls under the purview of these suspicions as well. For all his importuning against 'cosmic exile', Quine is nonetheless tempted by it, in that he still hopes to achieve an understanding of our conceptual scheme – or large stretches of it, at least – as a *result* of something less than what our scheme – or those stretches – purport to be about. This hope creates a kind of exile from within that faces many of the same difficulties as we find in the Husserlian conception of constitution.

Documenting these different forms of exile will be the work of the next two sections. That naturalism's recoil from the kind of cosmic exile Husserlian phenomenology aspires to results in exile once again suggests that the standard opposition between phenomenology and naturalism is not as straightforward as it may initially appear. Rather than simply opposed positions, they are instead two sides of the same coin, whose currency is used to purchase a very special form of epistemological explanation. If we get out of the business of epistemology altogether, then new possibilities for phenomenology emerge. This is especially evident in the case of Merleau-Ponty, whose conception of phenomenology self-consciously forswears any kind of philosophical (or scientific) exile.

2. Transcendental exile

What is it about the notion of constitution that seems to require – or prompt a desire for – cosmic exile? Consider a question Husserl raises in 'Philosophy as Rigorous Science.' There, he asks, 'How can experience as consciousness give or contact an object?' (Husserl 1965, 87). Husserl regards this and related questions as central to the very idea of epistemology: asking and answering such questions is necessary to understanding how knowledge is possible. Immediately after raising this question, Husserl dismisses the idea that it can be adequately addressed (or even addressed at all) by the natural sciences, including empirical psychology:

> It requires only a rigorous consistency in maintaining the level of this problematic (a consistency missing, it is true, in all theories of knowledge up to the present) to see clearly the absurdity of a theory of knowledge based on natural science, and thus, too, of any psychological theory of knowledge. (Husserl 1965, 88)

The central questions of epistemology are 'riddles', which arise from reflection on the natural sciences. Since these riddles are inherent to the sciences – indeed, to the natural attitude in its entirety – Husserl thinks 'it is self-evident that the solution of these riddles according to premises and conclusions in principle transcends natural science' (Husserl 1965, 88). To think otherwise is to become ensnared in fallacious reasoning:

> To expect from natural science itself the solution of any one of the problems inherent in it as such – thus inhering through and through, from beginning to end – or even merely to suppose that it could contribute to the solution of such a problem any premises whatsoever, is to be involved in a vicious circle. (Husserl 1965, 88–89)

The how-possible questions raised by epistemology cannot be addressed by the natural sciences without engendering a vicious circularity because any premises the natural sciences might contribute already appeal to the kinds of objects for which the possibility of contact is at issue. Typically, such premises would appeal to objects and events that serve as *causes* for the experience we enjoy. These would include the distal objects our experience purports to be about, as well as the proximate links in the causal chain involving various parts of our bodies ranging from perceptual organs to the interior workings of our nervous systems. It is clear that any such premises presuppose that contact of the kind Husserl asks after has been made and that means, for Husserl, that no such premises can be genuinely explanatory. Any proper explanans must be free of the commitments that inform the explanandum, since otherwise it will not be made clear just how those commitments are really possible, let alone legitimate. Since the 'solution of these riddles … transcends natural science', epistemology requires a perspective equally transcendent, a perspective purged of any and all assumptions and commitments regarding 'contact' between consciousness and its objects.

Husserl's phenomenological reduction can be understood as aspiring to provide just such a transcendent perspective, as the performance of the reduction involves – indeed consists in – suspending or 'bracketing' any and all such commitments to objects beyond consciousness. In this way, phenomenology can answer the kinds of how-possible questions raised within epistemology that are beyond the reach of any kind of natural scientific account. It should be noted that Husserl's claims regarding the limits of natural scientific inquiry are not in any way a rejection of the natural sciences in general, but they are a rejection of *naturalism*, which holds that all genuine questions are natural scientific questions.

What, according to Husserl, does the performance of the reduction reveal and how does it afford insights regarding how-possible questions that are not available otherwise? To answer this last question, let us consider a sketch Husserl offers in a lecture from 1917 that is meant to provide an introduction to transcendental phenomenology. Remarking on the subject matter of phenomenology, Husserl notes that even though that subject matter is, for each phenomenological investigator, his or her own experience (at least to begin with), what phenomenology reveals is entirely 'invisible to naturally oriented points of view' (Husserl 1981, 10). What becomes visible from the reduced, reflective standpoint of phenomenology are precisely *phenomena*, which are to be sharply contrasted with the *objects* our experience is ordinarily directed toward in the natural attitude:

> Within this widest concept of object, and specifically within the concept of individual object, *Objects* and *phenomena* stand in contrast with each other. Objects [*Objekte*], all natural objects, for example, are objects foreign to consciousness. Consciousness does, indeed, objectivate them and posit them as actual, yet the consciousness that experiences them and takes cognizance of them is so singularly astonishing that it bestows upon its own phenomena the sense of being appearances of Objects foreign to consciousness and knows these 'extrinsic' Objects through processes that take cognizance of their sense. Those objects that are neither conscious processes nor immanent constituents of conscious processes we therefore call Objects in the pregnant sense of the word. (Husserl 1981, 13)

To unpack this passage a bit, let us start with a simple example. When I work at my desk, I typically have a cup of coffee positioned to the left of my keyboard. I will occasionally look away from the screen of my computer toward my cup and then reach toward it, either to take a sip of coffee or check to see if I need to head downstairs for more. Throughout any such episode, I see my coffee cup as a singular, continuously existing entity with stable, more or less constant properties (color and shape are constant, while the warmth of the cup is experienced as variable in relation to how much coffee is in the cup and how recently it was poured). While I understand myself in episodes of this kind as *seeing* the cup, as *smelling* the coffee, as *reaching out* to *touch* the cup, and so on, I do not take myself to be *doing anything* such that my experience is directed toward – is of or about – my coffee cup. I may, in more deliberate fashion, choose or decide to look at my coffee cup rather than something else, but I don't in any way make *that* looking have the coffee cup as its object; I just look that way and the coffee cup comes into view. This is part of what it means to say that the cup is *given* in my experience. But if I shift my attention in the manner Husserl describes here, things change dramatically. If I attend not to the cup, but to my *seeing* (and touching, and so on) of the cup, the singularity and constancy characteristic of my straightforward experience of the cup is exchanged for what Husserl refers to as 'multiform conscious processes', and these processes have 'constantly changing immanent constituents'. What I ordinarily perceive simply as my coffee cup I now recognize as being presented via partial and continuously changing 'looks', in that I see just this bit of the coffee cup, now that bit, and so on. The shape of the coffee cup is 'perspectivally silhouetted in definite ways', in that the looks I get are systematically interrelated (if I'm looking at *this* side of the cup, then turning it *this* way will show me *that* side).

I can similarly note the way the color of the cup – a quality I see as constant – is given through sensuously altering shadings. What I take to be one stable object with stable properties is given through 'continuously flowing aspects' (Husserl 1981, 13). If I begin to inspect each of these 'aspects' as though they are snapshots, I will see how different in appearance they are: the stable and uniform color of the cup is presented through appearances that are by no means uniform, but involve numerous variations in shading, replete with highlights, glare, shadows, and color shifts caused by, among other things, variations in illumination and reflections of other neighboring surfaces.

What Husserl finds 'singularly astonishing' here are the ways in which consciousness manages to impose unity and stability upon this ever-shifting flow of phenomena. None of these phenomena *is* the coffee cup, but the phenomena are 'construed referentially' such that consciousness 'posits' or 'objectivates' the cup. More generally, consciousness 'bestows upon its own phenomena the sense of being appearances of Objects foreign to consciousness'. The astonishment Husserl records here owes at least in part to the kind of invisibility mentioned previously. All of this bestowing, construal, positing, and objectivating happens 'behind the scenes' even though all of these various acts are 'excecuted' by or within one's own consciousness:

> The bestowing of each of these senses is carried out in consciousness and by virtue of definite series of flowing processes. A person in the natural attitude, however, knows nothing of this. He executes the acts of experiencing, referring, combining; but, while he is executing them, he is looking not toward them but rather in the direction of the objects he is conscious of. (Husserl 1981, 13)

Husserl's sharp distinction between phenomena and objects, between what is immanent to consciousness and what is foreign to it, allows him to address the how-possible questions that are fundamental to epistemology without landing in the kind of vicious circularity a natural scientific approach would encounter. When Husserl asks, 'How can experience as consciousness give or contact an object?' the answer in short is that consciousness does so by construing its immanent phenomena so as to be of or about objects. Objects foreign to consciousness are *constituted* within consciousness, not in the sense that they are literally made out of conscious stuff (whatever that would mean), but the *sense* 'object foreign to consciousness' is consciousness's own achievement. What Husserl describes in *Cartesian Meditations* as the 'marvelous work of "constituting" identical objects' (Husserl 1973, 48) – an echo of what he finds 'singularly astonishing' in the lectures I've been citing – avoids the threat of circularity remaining within the natural attitude faces. Phenomena can be discerned and studied free of any commitment to external or transcendent objects. Such objects, Husserl claims, are in no way presupposed, but instead can be understood as the *result* of something that can be seen to be available and intelligible apart from them. (This understanding, reached via reflection on my experience of my coffee cup, might occasion a small quiver on the way to the 'awful tremor' reported by Fink.)

I want to interrupt my exposition of Husserl at this point and ask after the merits of this last claim. My worry here is whether Husserl, via the phenomenological reduction, really has managed to break free of the commitments of the natural attitude or, if he has, whether what remains can do the kind of explanatory work he envisions. That there are 'processes' that are 'invisible' when we enjoy, for example, perceptual experience is by itself not a particularly startling idea. All of the causal processes that Husserl brackets count as such. I know, for example, that my *seeing* my coffee cup involves light reflecting off the surface of the cup and reaching the surface of my eyes, which is only the beginning of a long series of further processes that enable me to be aware of the cup at all. But in seeing the cup, I cannot be said to see any of these processes, crucial though they are to my perceptual experience. Not only do I not see these processes, seeing them is not something I am even *able* to do. No matter which way or how hard I look, I will not make visible any of these processes, at least not while I am still looking at the coffee cup. There are special instruments that might help to bring these processes into view, but that just shows that it takes more than a shift in attention to do so. The processes that Husserl appeals to, by contrast, *can* be made visible by just such a shift. By reflectively regarding my own experience in the special way Husserl describes, I can thereby *see* these 'multiform conscious processes' and recognize them as having 'constantly changing immanent constituents', and in doing so, I will appreciate how they have been operative throughout the straightforward experience I had been enjoying prior to reflection.

There is certainly something right in the idea that I can distinguish between what I see – my cup on the desk, to the left of my computer – and my seeing of it. Moreover, it sounds right to say that my experience can be understood as changing even while the cup is not. My visual field is not constant. My looking at things is a dynamic process: I look at things while *looking around*, and so what comes into view – and the way things come into view – changes continually, even if undramatically. But I can introduce a bit more drama: if I take my glasses off while I am looking at the cup, the way it looks changes in a sudden and striking manner, even though I don't for a moment take the cup itself to have changed at all. It is not clear, however, that distinguishing between what I experience and my experience of it in this manner is sufficient for Husserl's purposes. That is, the distinction has to be such that one side of the divide can provide the resources for answering the special kind of how-possible questions that serve to found epistemology. To do so, those resources have to be understandable without presupposing any 'contact' with objects. Only then will I be able to appreciate how sense is 'bestowed' on those processes such that contact with objects is thereby explained.

Consider again Husserl's claim that when, for example, I am looking at my coffee cup, its shape is 'perspectivally silhouetted in definite ways'. What this suggests is that when I reflect on my experience of the cup, I discern more clearly how I see the cup from one side or another (and never all of it all at once). Even if we allow Husserl the idea that these perspectival 'looks' are 'immanent constituents' of consciousness, in contrast to the 'foreign' coffee cup, any and all such constituents still make reference to the cup. If I attend to my experience as it unfolds over time, I notice that I am perceptually aware of the cup *now from this side, now from that side*, but in noticing this, I have not revealed something in my experience entirely independent of the cup. We need to be careful here in terms of what this talk of independence comes to in this context. It is true – or at least I think Husserl thinks it is true – that we can make out the idea of my experience having just these constituents – perspectivally silhouetted appearances – even without (or at least without weighing in on) the real existence of the coffee cup. I can suspend the question of whether there really is a coffee cup out there on my desk while still examining my experience. Let us grant Husserl the intelligibility of this kind of bracketing. Even so, it does not follow that the experience I have left over to examine is thereby purged of everything pertaining to the coffee cup, since my principal way of identifying and tracking the moments of that experience is via their being an ongoing presentation of the *cup* (cup from this side, cup from that side, color of the cup shaded this way, color of the cup shaded that way), whether or not the cup actually exists 'out there'. Without this kind of reference to the cup, it is not clear what I have left to examine.

The point I am trying to make here might be put like this. Husserl's appeal to conscious processes faces something of a dilemma: either such processes make reference to objects such as my coffee cup or they do not. The first horn of the dilemma is clearly unacceptable, given Husserl's transcendental aspirations. If such processes are identified and tracked with reference to the objects they purport to be about, then we are still presupposing the kind of 'contact' with, or 'givenness' of, objects Husserl's investigations were meant to explain. To say that consciousness of my coffee cup is possible via a series of *coffee cup presentations* does not sound especially explanatory, at least not in the special way Husserl envisions: since all such presentations are available only as already being about the coffee cup, they cannot serve to explain how such aboutness is possible in the first place.[2] To give the kind of special explanations Husserl is after, those presentations have to be identifiable independently of any reference to coffee cups and the like, in order to discern some activity on the part of consciousness of bestowing the sense 'coffee cup' upon that flow of experience.[3] Hence, the second alternative is the only one to which Husserl can really appeal. Even if we leave aside the issue of whether we really can make out anything about our own experience that is not already object-involving, it would be entirely unclear how an objective sense gets bestowed upon *that*. What is it about those 'multiform conscious processes' that motivates – let alone justifies – their having the sense 'enduring object foreign to consciousness' bestowed upon them? If the processes are from the start understood as partial presentations of such objects, then there is no problem of motivation, but then we are also back to the first horn of the dilemma. But if such processes are something *less* than that, any such 'bestowal' would appear to be a shot in the dark. As Quine (1976, 251) notes: 'The positing of physical objects must be seen not as an *ex post facto* systematization of data, but as a move prior to which no appreciable data would be available to systematize.' What Quine's remark suggests is that there is no perspective free from 'the positing of physical objects' that we can take up so as to bear witness to the kind of 'marvelous work' that so enchants Husserl. Any such 'work' has always already been done, so that there is no getting back behind it to catch it in the act, and this tells against the possibility of the special kind of explanations Husserl's phenomenology is meant to provide. That is, Husserlian phenomenology will not be able to answer the question of *how* it is possible for experience to contact an object in a way that does not presuppose some kind of contact already having been made.

Although I have appealed to Quine at the conclusion to underscore this point, whether Quine always pays it sufficient heed to his own insight is another matter. Perhaps what Husserl found to be 'marvelous' and 'singularly astonishing' still holds some allure, even for the likes of Quine.

3. Exiled from within: Quine's naturalized epistemology

For Husserl, the fundamental questions of epistemology are entirely beyond the reach of the natural attitude, including even the most sophisticated of the natural sciences. Transcendental phenomenology's methods are structured so as to address these fundamental questions in a way Husserl thinks science cannot. By bracketing any commitment to – or any positing of – transcendent objects, Husserl thinks phenomenology can address the kind of how-possible questions that science is unable to answer. These aspirations are defeated, however, if it turns out that the 'immanent data', which serve as the basis for the activity of 'sense bestowal', can only be identified and made sense of with reference to the very objects that were allegedly bracketed in the first place.

For Quine, the lesson of this defeat is that epistemology has for too long deprived itself of resources to which it was in fact entitled. In 'coping' with the problems raised within epistemology, he insists that 'we are free to use scientific knowledge' (Quine 1973, 3). For Quine, the 'old epistemologist failed to realize the strength of his position' (1973, 3). Consider again the example of my perceptual experience of my coffee cup. A natural scientific investigation of that experience will not deprive itself of any appeal to the coffee cup, nor will it exclude any reference to various additional causal factors; on the contrary, it will make 'free use' of any and all such data in order to tell a long and complicated story about how the interaction between something in my environment (the coffee cup) and the subject (me) is such that I come to perceive, as well as think and talk about, that environment as including the coffee cup (and lots of other objects like it). While Quine notes the Husserlian worry that the 'appeal to physical sense organs in the statement of the problem would have seemed circular', he is unmoved by such considerations: 'This fear of circularity is a case of needless logical timidity' (1973, 2). It is little wonder that Quine (1973, 3) declares this new approach to be 'a far cry ... from old epistemology', but he maintains that it is 'no gratuitous change of subject matter, but an enlightened persistence in the original epistemological problem'.

Quine thinks that the 'original epistemological problem' remains in view because of the findings of that very natural scientific investigation. Although an investigation of my experience of the coffee cup might begin by understanding it as arising through an interaction between me and the coffee cup, as that investigation becomes more detailed and nuanced, a long and complex causal chain can be discerned and delineated. After all, the presence of the coffee cup in my vicinity is not sufficient to account for my experiencing the presence of that cup. If my eyes are closed or my head is turned, I will not see the cup, nor will I see it if the cup is screened off by something else in my environment or there is no illumination of any kind. Whatever begins at the surface of the cup has to reach the surface of my 'sensory receptors', and the stimulation of my receptors marks the beginning of a long inward journey through my nervous system. Reflection on this long and complex process, even if only sketched out in this crude manner, allows for a restatement of the 'original epistemological problem'. That problem concerns our entitlement to, or warrant for, thinking of the world as containing things like my coffee cup. Although the scientific restatement of the problem appeals to 'things' like sensory receptors and whatever it is that stimulates their surfaces, my thinking that my environment includes the coffee cup can be seen to be underdetermined by these stimulations. As Quine (1973, 2) notes:

> Science itself teaches that there is no clairvoyance; that the only information that can reach our sensory surfaces from external objects must be limited to two-dimensional optical projections and various impacts of airwaves on the eardrums and some gaseous reactions in the nasal passages and a few kindred odds and ends.

What 'science itself teaches' gives rise to the following question: 'How, the challenge proceeds, could one hope to find out about that external world from such meager traces?' (Quine 1973, 2). In other words, what science teaches is that an entirely different causal chain that nonetheless terminated at my sensory surfaces in just the same way would produce in me the same experience, but insofar as that experience involves a belief that the coffee cup is present, that experience is mistaken. Indeed, we do not even have to appeal to there being something 'out there' that initiates the causal chain; any such sequence of causes could simply begin at the surfaces of my sensory receptors or perhaps even further in. Although it appeared that the coffee cup itself was one crucial datum in the natural scientific investigation of my experience, the upshot of that investigation reveals it to be a 'posit' or 'projection' based upon a set of data that does not include the cup or really anything like it.

For Quine, the subject whose experience (or, in more starkly Quinean terms, dispositions and verbal behavior) is to be explained is revealed through the 'free use' of the resources of the natural sciences to be fundamentally limited or restricted. As he puts it in 'Epistemology Naturalized', the epistemological project is one of 'studying how the human study of our subject posits bodies and projects his physics from his data', where that data is seen to be a 'meager' set of stimuli, in contrast to the 'torrential output' of all that 'positing' (Quine 1969, 83). Despite that meagerness, the epistemological investigator may still be able to understand and explain how his subject's 'output' amounts to *knowledge* (or at least true belief) by comparing that output with the environment in which the subject is situated. The investigator can see that my positing of the coffee cup involves a series of causes that involve the coffee cup itself, so that when I say, 'Ah, there's my coffee cup', the investigator can discern both that and how I've managed to say something true. At the same time, the investigator can make sense of the possibility of that utterance occurring even when there is no coffee cup in my vicinity, in which case the utterance is false. The 'free use' to which Quine thinks the epistemologist is entitled would thus appear to involve both the sophisticated findings of the natural sciences about causal chains and sensory surfaces, as well as the humbler, more commonsensical notions regarding the gross physical objects that populate our environment.

By means of such free use, Quine's enlightened epistemologist would appear to be equipped to explain how the subject of his investigation comes to have true beliefs (and possibly knowledge) of the world in some cases, while coming to have false beliefs in others. In offering such explanations, the epistemologist will characterize that subject as only positing or projecting what those beliefs are about, based upon meager input, which is the only evidence the subject can be said to have. That by itself does not threaten the epistemologist's project of explaining how at least some of the subject's output amounts to knowledge, as long as the investigator continues to make free use of the knowledge whose possibility for his subject he wants to explain. If, however, that continued free use is itself called into question, the project *is* threatened in a more thoroughgoing way. Consider the fuller passage from 'Epistemology Naturalized' that I quoted part of above:

> The old epistemology aspired to contain, in a sense, natural science; it would construct it somehow from sense data. Epistemology in its new setting, conversely, is contained in natural science, as a chapter of psychology. But the old containment remains valid too, in its way. We are studying how the human subject of our study posits bodies and projects his physics, and *we appreciate that our position*

in the world is just like his. Our very epistemological enterprise, therefore, and the psychology wherein it is a component chapter, and the whole of natural science wherein psychology is a component book – *all of this is our own construction or projection from stimulations like those we are meting out to our epistemological subject.* (Quine 1969, 83 – emphases mine)

The difficulty here lies in following through on the kind of appreciation Quine asserts here.[4] Can the epistemologist still make sense of and explain his subject's beliefs while at the same time appreciating that he is in just the same position as the subject? After all, what emerges from that investigation is the unbridgeable gap between input and output: the epistemological subject has only meager data, information, or evidence,[5] on the basis of which he posits bodies. He is, in a word, confined to something far less than what his posits purport to be about, as what is posited is a world of objects well beyond the confines of his sensory surfaces (although even his sensory surfaces are something he posits based on their stimulation). If the epistemologist maintains a privileged position in relation to that subject, so as to correlate sensory stimulations with the farther-flung goings on in the world, then he can explain how, despite that meager input, the subject manages to have true beliefs. Absent that privilege, however, the explanatory prospects quickly dissipate: if the epistemologist sees himself as likewise confined to a meager set of data, such that everything he takes to be true is only a posit or projection of that data, then he will have no way to understand how his subject (who must also, of course, be regarded only as a posit based on meager data) comes to have true beliefs about the world. In order to understand that, he has to understand himself as in touch with the world, so as to be able to differentiate between his subject's coming to have true beliefs in some cases and false beliefs in others. An epistemological project that cannot differentiate between the two has little hope of explaining how knowledge is possible. Rather than 'an enlightened persistence in the original epistemological problem', Quine's naturalism looks instead to be a disappointing surrender.

4. At Home in the world: phenomenology without epistemology

Although the rejection of the idea of 'first philosophy' is a cornerstone of Quine's view, I have tried to argue that even Quine's naturalized epistemology remains enamored with the questions and problems that concern a philosopher like Husserl. Quine's recoil from the difficulties and confusions of Husserl's attempt at 'cosmic exile' via the phenomenological reduction and the ensuing idea of constitution nonetheless retains enough of Husserl's explanatory ambitions to create a new form of exile with no clear path home.

That two otherwise diametrically opposed positions nonetheless face analogous difficulties marks the starting point of Merleau-Ponty's *Phenomenology of Perception*. What unites the two is a shared commitment to what he calls *objective thought* and the kind of explanatory task that comes with that commitment.

Merleau-Ponty's generic *empiricist* endeavors to explain the subjective in terms of the objective, whereby the experience of objects is to be understood in terms of sensations or stimulations mechanically combined through a series of psychological mechanisms, while the *intellectualist* seeks to account for the objective in terms of the subjective, whereby the agency of consciousness imposes meanings on what are otherwise meaningless sensations. Both Husserl's 'multiform conscious processes' and Quine's 'sensory irritations' instantiate these generic prejudices, and each plays a crucial role in the attempt each of them makes 'to build up the shape of the world' (Merleau-Ponty 1962, 23). Both of them, in other words, are engaged in a kind of reconstructive project, using what are offered as a privileged set of materials. In contrast to this sort of project and its many pitfalls, Merleau-Ponty insists that 'the real has to be described, not constructed or formed' (Merleau-Ponty 1962, x). Describing the real requires resisting the temptation to account for it from a perspective that does not already have it in view. 'The world is there before any possible analysis of mine', and so it is

> artificial to make it the outcome of a series of syntheses which link, in the first place sensations, then aspects of the object corresponding to different perspectives, when both are nothing but products of analysis, with no sort of prior reality. (x)

Phenomenology, for Merleau-Ponty (1962), must not pretend that 'the perceiving subject approaches the world as the scientist approaches his experiments' (24), nor that it has discovered a 'constituting power' (x) within the depths of consciousness.

Consider again our running example and what is revealed by describing rather than explaining. When I look to the left of my computer and see my coffee cup, I see it as *there, in reach* for me to grasp should I desire a sip of coffee or wonder whether I'm in need of a refill. I can also reach out for it for no particular reason, to fidget or distract myself while I rest my eyes. My experience is throughout directed toward – and gears into – the cup and is indescribable without it:

> In the action of the hand which is raised towards an object is contained a reference to the object, not as an object represented, but as that highly specific thing towards which we project ourselves, near which we are, in anticipation, and which we haunt. (Merleau-Ponty 1962, 138)

When I reach for the cup, my hand is already poised to grasp it around the middle without my thinking about just how – and how much – to curve my hand. If I were asked to show just how to shape my hand in order to grasp the cup in the absence of it, I could not provide a demonstration with any kind of confidence; present me with the cup and my self-assurance is restored. Although it might be difficult for me to reach for it properly with my eyes closed, I do not need to pay much attention to the cup as I look toward it and reach out my arm. I do not *represent* the cup prior to or while reaching out for it, and while I may in some sense 'zero in' on the cup, both with my gaze and my reach, I continually perceive the cup and myself as situated in a broader milieu: my study, the upstairs of my house, and so on. I experience the cup as *available*, since it is 'in my vicinity' (Merleau-Ponty 1964, 14)[6]. My seeing it and my being able to reach for it are intertwined with one another, and both of these are in turn embedded in my broader orientation toward the world.

Merleau-Ponty refers to the human world 'as the seat and as it were the *homeland* of our thoughts'. Referred back to this homeland, 'the perceiving subject ceases to be an "acosmic" thinking subject, and action, feeling and will remain to be explored as original ways of positing an object' (Merleau-Ponty 1962, 24). While the appearance of *positing* suggests a kind of activity that can be discovered and understood prior to the object's manifestation, that 'action, feeling and will' are the 'original ways' undermines that conceit, as all of these only come into play in response to the objects whose positing is at issue. My reaching in the particular way I do, with my hand opened just so, is a way of making sense of the world as containing things like coffee cups, but such a gesture makes little sense without them. Whatever kind of positing is at issue here, it is not the work of an '"acosmic" thinking subject', detached from the world yet somehow able to constitute it, nor is it the activity of a Quinean subject, a body bombarded by particles so as to project just such a world of constant irritants.

As we saw above, the invitation to exile is extended by means of Husserl's question in 'Philosophy as Rigorous Science': 'How can experience as consciousness give or contact an object?' The best answer to that question is one that refuses the terms in which the question is posed, i.e. that refuses to pretend that consciousness is intelligible prior to, or apart from, 'its' objects. If we return to the perspective of the subject as an acting, feeling, and willing – in short as a *worldly* – agent, then the best answer is one that refuses the restrictions Husserl imposes: there is no answer that does not already involve the thing that summons the bodily agent to act in relation to it. At the same time, such an answer is a refusal of epistemology, as it denies that we can make sense of the kind of generality to which the epistemologist aspires. Saying how perception is possible would require a kind of knowledge that managed to operate *beyond* those horizons, but any such attempt to get a grip on perception 'from the outside' lapses into distortions and confusion:

> The philosopher describes sensations and their substratum as one might describe the fauna of a distant land – without being aware that he himself perceives, that he is the perceiving subject and that perception as he lives it belies everything that he says of perception in general. For, seen from the inside, perception owes nothing to what we know in other ways about the world, about *stimuli* as physics describes them and about the sense organs as described by biology. (Merleau-Ponty 1962, 207)

Since 'all knowledge takes its place within the horizons opened up by perception, it would be a mistake to describe 'perception itself as one of the facts thrown up in the world'. As a result, 'we can never fill up, in the picture of the world, that gap which we ourselves are, and by which it comes into existence for someone, since perception is the "flaw" in the "great diamond"' (Merleau-Ponty 1962, 207).

Ultimately, to forego epistemology is to acknowledge that 'the thing and the world are mysterious', to which Merleau-Ponty adds:

> They are indeed, when we do not limit ourselves to their objective aspect, but put them back into the setting of subjectivity. They are even an absolute mystery, not amenable to elucidation, and this through no provisional gap in our knowledge, for in that case it would fall back to the status of a mere problem, but because it is not of the order of objective thought in which there are solutions. (Merleau-Ponty 1962, 333)

Phenomenology freed of epistemological demands releases us from exile (or, more accurately, our longing for exile), but leaves us at home in a world that is nonetheless mysterious. That this is so may help us in understanding why we wanted to leave in the first place.

Notes

1. The claim will be less surprising to those familiar with Barry Stroud's writings on Quine, upon which I will be drawing heavily in the discussion to follow. See especially Chapter VI ('Naturalized Epistemology') of Stroud 1984, as well as Stroud 2000a and Stroud 2000b. While I have learned a great deal from all these sources, my discussion in Section 3 below will make most use of the first.
2. Recall Husserl's fundamental question in 'Philosophy as Rigorous Science.' There Husserl asks: 'How can experience as consciousness give or contact an object?' Husserl might be understood as sketching an answer to that question in § 49 of Husserl (1982) when he writes: 'A something transcendent is *given* by virtue of certain concatenations of experience. As given directly and with increasing perfection in perceptual continua which show themselves to be harmonious and in certain and methodical forms of thinking based on experience, a something transcendent acquires, more or less immediately, its insightful, continually progressive determination' (110). The dilemma I am posing in this paragraph concerns this appeal to 'concatenations of experience'. If such concatenations are understood from the start as being of or about transcendent objects, then they do not provide a non-circular answer to Husserl's question. But if they are not so understood, then it is entirely unclear how they ever come to be about anything at all. In other words, the dilemma is meant to expose the difficulties inherent in Husserl's talk in this section about the so-called annihilation of the world.
3. This appeal to *activity* alludes in a very compressed way to what Husserl calls 'noesis'. What I am questioning here is the ability of this 'process' to provide any kind of genuine explanation, as it would appear to presuppose precisely what it is meant to explain.
4. See Stroud 1984, 242–45 for a fuller discussion of the ramifications of this moment of appreciation in Quine's naturalized epistemology.

5. Quine uses these three notions interchangeably. All of them are problematic insofar as Quine's naturalized epistemology is meant to make any kind of headway against traditional forms of skepticism.
6. Merleau-Ponty uses this phrase in the course of making sense of the way the perceived object is always presented such that there is *more to it* to perceive. To say the object is present as 'in my vicinity' is part of an account of the way the object engages me in a bodily way, rather than primarily as an object of thought. As he notes, the givenness of the object is a 'practical synthesis', rather than an intellectual one.

Disclosure statement

No potential conflict of interest was reported by the author.

References

Fink, Eugen, and Edmund Husserl. (1995) *Sixth Cartesian Meditation: The Idea of a Transcendental Theory of Method*, trans. Ronald Bruzina, Bloomington: Indiana University Press.
Husserl, Edmund. (1965) 'Philosophy as Rigorous Science', in Quentin Lauer trans. *Phenomenology and the Crisis of Philosophy*, New York: Harper and Row.
Husserl, Edmund. (1973) *Cartesian Meditations*, trans. Dorion Cairns. The Hague: Martinus Nijhoff.
Husserl, Edmund (1981) 'Husserl's Inaugural Lecture at Freiburg im Breisgau (1917)', in Peter McCormick and Frederick Elliston (eds.) *Husserl: Shorter Works*, 9–17, Notre Dame: University of Notre Dame Press.
Husserl, Edmund (1982) *Ideas Pertaining to a Pure Phenomenology and to a Phenomenological PhilosophyFirst Book*, trans. F. Kersten, Dordrecht: Kluwer Academic Publishers.
Merleau-Ponty, Maurice (1962) *Phenomenology of Perception*, trans. Colin Smith, London: Routledge.
Merleau-Ponty, Maurice (1964) 'The Primacy of Perception', in James M. Edie (ed.) *The Primacy of Perception and Other Essays on Phenomenological Psychology, the Philosophy of Art, History and Politics*, 12–42, Evanston: Northwestern University Press.
Quine, W. V. O. (1960) *Word and Object*, Cambridge: The MIT Press.
Quine, W. V. O. (1969) 'Epistemology Naturalized' in *Ontological Relativity and Other Essays*, 69–90. New York: Columbia University Press.
Quine, W. V. O. (1973) *The Roots of Reference*, La Salle: Open Court.
Quine, W. V. O. (1976) 'Posits and Reality', Chap. 23 in *The Ways of Paradox and Other Essays*, 246–54, Cambridge: Harvard University Press.
Stroud, Barry (1984) *The Significance of Philosophical Scepticism*, Oxford: Oxford University Press.
Stroud, Barry (2000a) 'Quine on Exile and Acquiescence' , Chap. 10 in *Meaning, Understanding, and Practice: Philosophical Essays*, 151–69, Oxford: Oxford University Press.
Stroud, Barry (2000b) 'Quine's Physicalism', Chap. 7 in *Meaning, Understanding, and Practice: Philosophical Essays*, 95–112, Oxford: Oxford University Press.

Return to Nature

John Sallis

Department of Philosophy, Boston College, USA

ABSTRACT
This essay explores the various ways in which in the history of philosophy the imperative to return to nature has been understood. Against this background, it takes up the question as to how the concept of nature is to be determined in contemporary thought.

What is to be Heard in the Phrase 'Return to Nature'?

Taken most directly, the phrase expresses an imperative. Suppose that it is addressed to someone or even that in solitude one addresses it to oneself. On those to whom it is addressed it imposes the demand that they return to nature. As the condition of its pertinence, the imperative presupposes that its addressees either have themselves retreated from nature or have somehow been withdrawn from it, so that in either case they are separated or at least distanced from nature. The imperative enjoins them to return across this distance, to close the space of separation, so as to come again into proximity to nature, so as to arrive once more at the place where they would once have been, even if in a past that would never quite have been present.

And yet, in completing such an odyssey, they would come to occupy this place differently. Once immediacy has been disrupted, even if always already, the situation is never again the same as it would have been. Once, having been set apart, they return to nature, they will have reinstalled themselves therein with a certain deliberateness; they will perdure within the compass of nature only through resolve and thus always with a certain residual detachment. The trajectory through which they will have passed will always have left its trace in their comportment.

PHENOMENOLOGY AND NATURALISM

The imperative to return to nature has been repeatedly sounded in the history of philosophy, and the heterogeneity of its sources is indicative of the manifold senses borne by the phrase. It is voiced already in antiquity. It receives one of its most direct expressions in the contrast that Diogenes of Sinope drew between convention and nature and in his insistence that happiness depends on acting in accordance with nature (see Bréhier 1965, 13–16). The human in search of happiness is thus enjoined to measure his actions by reference to nature, by turning – or returning – to nature as his guide. According to ancient testimony, both Chrysippus and Diogenes of Babylon declared that choice, as in selecting some things and rejecting others, should be exercised in accordance with nature, that is, again, by turning – or returning – to nature as guide (Long and Sedley 1987, vol. 1: 356–57). Reporting the precepts of the Stoics, Stobaeus writes: 'All things in accordance with nature are to-be-taken, and all things contrary to nature are not-to-be-taken.' And again: 'All things in accordance with nature have worth, and all things contrary to nature are unworthy' (Long and Sedley 1987, vol. 1: 355, trans. modified; Greek text, vol. 2: 350–51). The theme is pervasive from the early Cynics throughout much of Stoicism: the measure of actions, of things, and of their worth is to be found by turning – or returning – to nature, by determining whether they are in accordance with nature (κατὰ φύσιν).

Thus, the return to nature may be carried out in order to secure a proper measure; actions and dealings with things will then be executed in accord with nature, will be fitted to its measure. Yet the very concept of measure, the differentiation between what provides the measure and what is measured by it, indicates that these instances of human comportment retain a residual detachment from nature itself. They are to be measured by nature, not assimilated to it.

The return to nature, as demanded in the imperative, may be carried out in other ways, that is, with other ends in view and in various registers. In the mid-eighteenth century the imperative was sounded in a form unheard-of in antiquity. In his *Discourse on the Origin and Basis of Inequality among Men* – the so-called *Second Discourse* – Rousseau undertook to return descriptively to the human as it existed in its original – that is, savage – stage, in what Rousseau calls the state of nature (*l'état de nature*). In recovering and describing the human in the state of nature, his intent is to show how, once humans left this state and the development of society commenced, human inequality and hence oppression and injustice came about. Here, then, the return to nature is theoretical; it is a matter, not of modern men again becoming savages, but only of describing that original state. The description of the state of nature is meant, in turn, to serve a political end, or at least to enable an analysis of modern social-political conditions, of the means by which the inequality in modern society came about. Yet, in turn, this analysis identifies the customs, laws, and institutions that would need to be dissolved or at least radically transformed in order to eliminate inequality and establish a society in which, as was the case with humans in the state of nature, all are equal. Thus, Rousseau's descriptive return to nature opens the way to a condition that, though not that of the savage, would, in a way accordant with modern life, approximate the state of nature.

Yet within the scope of this return to nature, Rousseau also carries out other, more specific modes of return, returning to nature in other registers. One such register is that of the origin of language. In Rousseau's description of the human condition in the state of nature, it becomes evident that as long as humans were living in such proximity to nature, they had little or no need for language. Only at the threshold of the break with the state of nature did incipient speech first appear, namely, as what Rousseau calls 'the cry of nature [*le cri de la nature*]', which was uttered only in situations of great danger or violent pain (Rousseau 2008 [1755], 87). Later, other sounds besides the mere cry were added: the inflections of the voice were multiplied and combined with gestures. Still later, in order to overcome the limitation of gestures, our progenitors introduced articulate vocal sounds, and language in the proper sense thus began to develop. Hence, through his descriptive return to nature, to humans in the state of nature, Rousseau provides the basis for his account of the origin and development of language.

Another register in which Rousseau carries out the return to nature is that of music. In his *Essay on the Origin of Languages*, which in its full title bears the further designation 'In Which Melody and Musical Imitation are Treated', Rousseau focuses on another phase in the development of language. It is a phase that he presents by depicting a kind of primal scene at a fountain or a festival where the passions of lovers-to-be are aroused and speech first flourishes, first comes fully into its own. According to Rousseau, it was here, along the way from the state of nature, that music was born. As it arose, it consisted solely of melody and was bound closely to speech. This was, as it were, music's state of nature.[1] What came later was, perhaps even more than in society at large, a matter of degeneration: with the rationalization of language, separation ensued between speech and song; then, as harmony became dominant, melody – and hence song – was impaired, so that finally there resulted an expressionless music forgetful of the voice. Need it be said that through this analysis Rousseau is proposing a return by which music would come into proximity to its state of nature? Then melody would again become primary, harmony serving only for its enhancement; and song, thus restored, would again follow the accents of speech. This is a proposal that Rousseau not only declared but also, as composer, sought to carry out, as in his celebrated opera *Le Devin du Village*.

In some instances a return to nature is broached within a highly determined register and within a larger context committed contrariwise to separation from nature. Consider the case of Kant. Although the *Critique of Pure Reason* begins by acknowledging the dependence of knowledge on experience, the primary movement enacted in the critical project consists in a regress from experience – primarily from the experience of nature – to the a priori conditions of such experience, conditions that lie not in nature but in the subject. This directionality expresses the very sense of Kant's so-called Copernican Revolution. The movement counter to nature is even more pronounced in Kant's practical philosophy: morality itself lies in self-determination that, utterly detached from natural inclination, is carried out in accordance with the moral law.

It is only in the *Critique of Judgment* that an exception is found, one that is all the more striking in that it occurs within a context in which, even as the beauty of natural things is discussed, there remain moments of retreat from nature. The relevant passage is that in which Kant affirms the contemplation of nature, or, more precisely, intellectual interest in the beautiful in nature. Such interest attests, according to Kant, to a mental attunement to moral feeling; for a person so attuned will always take an interest in any trace that nature provides of its harmony with our own spirit and its law. It is precisely such a trace that nature offers in the purposiveness of its beauty. On this basis Kant declares natural beauty superior to the beauty of art. The return to nature, as the turn from art to nature, he then expresses in a single, very remarkable sentence depicting the scene of such a return:

> A man who has taste enough to judge the products of fine art with the greatest correctness and refinement may still be glad to leave a room in which he finds those beauties that minister to vanity and perhaps to social joys, and to turn instead to the beautiful in nature, in order to find there, as it were, a voluptuousness for his spirit in a train of thought that he can never fully lay out. (Kant 1968a, vol. 5, 299–300)

That the trace of spirit is to be found in nature, through the return to nature, is a theme that resonates throughout post-Kantian thought, not only in the absolute form it assumes with Schelling and Hegel, but also in a quite different mode and tone with the New England transcendentalists. Emerson (1940a [1836], 7, 14, 35) writes incessantly of nature, that 'nature always wears the colors of the spirit', that 'nature is the symbol of spirit', and, still more succinctly, that 'behind nature, throughout nature, spirit is present'. Or again, clearly echoing Kant, he writes: 'The moral law lies at the center of nature and radiates to the circumference' (23). Thus it is that the human spirit is expanded and enhanced by coming into proximity to nature, by returning from the detachment from nature enforced and inculcated by city life. In the poem that Emerson places at the head of his essay entitled 'Nature', he writes:

Spirit that Lurks Each Form Within

Beckons to spirit of its kin.

In the essay itself he describes the return from the city to nature:

> At the gates of the forest, the surprised man of the world is forced to leave his city estimates of great and small, wise and foolish. The knapsack of custom falls off his back with the first step he takes into these precincts. Here is sanctity which shames our religions, and reality which discredits our heroes. Here we find Nature

> to be the circumstance which dwarfs every other circumstance, and judges like a god all men that come to her. (Emerson, [1844] 1940b, p. 406)[2]

Thoreau also writes of nature in such a way, though in a more exclamatory style, as near the beginning of *Walden*: 'To anticipate, not the sunrise and the dawn merely, but, if possible, Nature herself!' (Thoreau 1965 [1854], 15). Yet what is most distinctive in the case of Thoreau is that he enacted the return, living alone for two years in the woods on the shore of Walden Pond and transcribing that enactment in his book *Walden*.

In all these instances the force of the imperative to return to nature is based on the capacity of nature to set before human sensibility a trace of spirit or to offer a recovery of the originary. It is imperative that one return to nature because it is in and from nature that one is displayed to oneself in some specific manner: as submitted to measure, as spirit, or in the originary form that characterized the human in the state of nature. The return to nature is less for the sake of experiencing nature itself than for the sake of discovering in it something more originary that is reflected back from nature to oneself. If such reflective self-discovery is taken to be definitive of the human, then the imperative 'Return to nature', addressed to a person, is an absolute imperative and one to which a person will always already have responded, regardless of whether the imperative has actually been addressed to that person. One will always already have been engaged, as we say, by one's very nature, in the return to nature, and the imperative by which one is addressed serves only to redouble the engagement.

In German Idealism the reflection from nature back to the spiritual and originary comes to be thought in an absolutely decisive manner and in all its consequences. Thus, in delimiting the concept of nature at the outset of the *Philosophy of Nature*, Hegel writes: 'Nature has arisen as the idea in the form of otherness [*Form des Andersseins*]'. Still further, he writes that the idea is precisely this: 'to disclose itself, to posit this other [i.e., nature] outside itself and to take it back again into itself in order to be subjectivity and spirit' (Hegel 1970, §247). Much more succinctly, Schelling (1967, 380) declares that nature is visible spirit and affirms 'the absolute identity of spirit *within* us and nature *outside* us'. Nature thus comes to be thought as the originary, the idea, in its otherness, in an externality – indeed as externality itself – to be cancelled as spirit emerges in its self-disclosure. The return to nature occurs only for the sake of the return, in turn, from nature back to spirit; in this ultimate return nature is cancelled as mere nature, is relieved of its nature, and is brought back to spirit, raised to the level of spirit. Here Hegel's speculative word *Aufhebung* has its broadest extension.

The determination of nature as both other than spirit and yet none other than spirit is reflected in the double sense born by the word. For one speaks not only of nature but also of the nature of things, even of the nature of nature. On the one side, the word designates the domain of natural things – mountains and rivers, trees and flowers – which is regarded as quite apart from the spiritual, but, on the other side, it designates what something essentially is, its essence, which in modern thought is intrinsically allied with subjectivity or spirit. Yet, this double sense of nature extends back to Greek antiquity: already in the Platonic dialogues the word φύσις is commonly used in both senses. In its broader application, the word signifies, on the one side, the domain or origin of natural things and, on the other side, the εἴδη that define all such things, that determine them to be what they are, thus constituting the answer to the question: τί ἐστι? As correlative to νόησις, the εἴδη are designated as νοητά, as what comes to be called the intelligible; and the intelligible is then distinguished from the αἰσθητά, the sensible. The dyad of intelligible and sensible that is thus designated comes, therefore, to encompass in its span the entire range of being, and as such it provides the founding distinction of what comes to be called metaphysics. In its double sense nature enjoys the same gigantic span. Nothing lies outside this span, neither beyond it nor before it. Nothing lies outside of nature. Hence, the return to nature will always be also a return within nature.

And yet, both in classical antiquity and in our time, this ontological configuration has been disrupted. This disruption of the intelligible/sensible dyad involves, though in very different ways, the emergence of another sense of nature.

In classical antiquity this disruption occurs, in its most manifest form, in Plato's *Timaeus*. In the account given of how the godly δημιουργός formed the cosmos, the dyad of intelligible and sensible is affirmed and indeed is woven into the entire first discourse that Timaeus delivers. And yet, precisely at the point where the discourse focuses most intently on the order in the heaven, a certain disordering begins to announce itself. As a result Timaeus interrupts his discourse and proposes to begin again from the beginning. In the second discourse, which then follows, this interruption proves to have been the interruption of the intelligible/sensible dyad. Not that Timaeus rejects the dyad or in any way puts it aside; rather, along with these two kinds, the intelligible and the sensible, he introduces a third kind. Thereby he both demonstrates that the dyad is not comprehensive, that it does not encompass the entire range of being, and that its very possibility is based on the third kind.

The third kind is named in numerous ways, all of which – even the designation 'third kind' – are necessarily consigned to what Timaeus terms bastard discourse. Timaeus declares it to be like gold that can be molded into all possible shapes. He also calls it by the name ἐκμαγεῖον, which designates a mass of wax or other soft material on which the imprint of a seal can be stamped. He calls it also ὑποδοχή, commonly translated as 'receptacle', and, most insistently, by the name χώρα. These different designations are cast in such a way that they clash and utterly resist being brought together into a single image of a certain kind. For what is being named – in a necessarily bastardly way – is neither a kind, that is, an intelligible εἶδος, nor an image of a kind, that is, a sensible thing.

The word φύσις is scattered throughout the *Timaeus* and is used in several different senses. Early in the dialogue Timaeus is described as one who has made it his task to know 'about the nature of the all [περὶ φύσεως τοῦ παντός]' (*Timaeus* 27a). Much later, when Timaeus actually enumerates the three kinds, he refers to the offspring, that is, the sensible, as the φύσις between the other two (50d). But among the many usages of the word, there are two that are especially significant in the present context. One is exemplified when Timaeus speaks 'about the nature that receives all bodies [περὶ τῆς τὰ πάντα δεχομένης σώματα φύσεως]' (50b). In this phrase it is the third kind that is designated as nature, as a nature other than the nature that Timaeus described in his first discourse. The other usage occurs when, as he proposes to begin again, Timaeus enjoins his interlocutors that 'We must bring into view the nature itself [φύσιν ... αὐτήν] of fire and water, and air and earth, before the birth of the heaven' (48b). The reference is to what will prove to be, not the elements themselves, but rather the elements as not yet themselves, as mere traces (ἴχνοι) held in the χώρα. This entire scene lies before the birth of the heaven; it is a nature that preceded nature, a nature older than sensible nature.

Let me pass over the renewal and development that such a concept of nature underwent with Schelling, who called it *die alte Natur* (see Sallis 1999, 155–67), in order now to address the way in which in our time, that is, from Nietzsche on, the classical ontological configuration is disrupted. This disruption is encapsulated in a single sentence in the Prologue to *Thus Spoke Zarathustra*. It is a performative utterance that borders on issuing an imperative. It reads: 'I beseech you, my brothers, *remain true to the earth* [*bleibt der Erde treu*], and do not believe those who speak to you of otherworldly hopes!' (Nietzsche 1968, 9). Here the earth represents the things of the earth, that is, the sensible; and the otherworld represents the intelligible, now that, in Nietzsche's idiom, this allegedly true world, the otherworldly, has finally become a fable. What the sentence announces is thus an inversion of the classical configuration, an inversion by which the sensible is now to be regarded as the true world, while the intelligible is allowed to drift away into oblivion, that is, is abolished. There remains – so it seems – only the sensible, only nature in the sense of the sensible. It is to this nature, the only nature, that Nietzsche implores his brothers to return. To philosophize after Nietzsche would require a return to nature in which there are mountains and rivers, trees and flowers.

And yet, in Nietzsche's celebrated account of how the true world finally became a fable, the abolition of the intelligible constitutes only the penultimate stage. What follows in the final stage thoroughly disrupts the direct and seemingly self-evident return to nature that would seem to be prescribed. Here is Nietzsche's account of the final stage: 'The true world we have abolished. What world has remained? The apparent one perhaps? But no! *With the true world we have also abolished the apparent one*' (Nietzsche 1969, 75). Yet, what is the sense of this final graphic deed, this claim to have abolished the apparent

– that is, the sensible – world? For most certainly the sensible world is not, in its actuality, abolished; it is not done away with. We open our eyes or attune our ears, and – behold! – the things of sense are there before us. While it may be that the intelligible, since it was never more than a specter, has vanished completely and has only to be put out of our minds, erased from our memory, the sensible stubbornly persists in its perceptibility and in its support of and resistance to our endeavors.

What is it, then, about the sensible that has been abolished? It is only – and precisely – its character as apparent, as *scheinbar*, as appearance (*Erscheinung*) of something beyond it, namely, of the intelligible. Because since classical antiquity the sensible has always been understood by reference to the intelligible, the abolition of the intelligible deprives the sensible of the determination it has borne throughout the history of metaphysics. Now that it can no longer be understood as imaging the intelligible, the sensible is utterly lacking in determination. Now that it stands alone, there is no telling what it is, not at least in a discourse that continues to be governed by the conceptuality of metaphysics. Now that there remains only the nature in which there are mountains and rivers, trees and flowers, the very sense of nature must be determined anew. Now we must – like Timaeus – begin again from the beginning.

A beginning can be discerned in certain directions taken in the development of phenomenology from Heidegger on. Responding to the Nietzschean injunction, *Being and Time* sets sensible beings free of the intelligible. No longer are they determined as imaging a remote intelligible set beyond them nor as grounded in the pure concepts of a transcendental subject or of spirit. Rather, they are taken as determined by their insertion in a world, by their placement within the referential structures that constitute a world. The world itself is nothing set beyond the sensible beings within it. Without itself being a sensible being, it belongs nonetheless to the domain of the sensible; it is *of* the sensible even though not itself a sensible being. Though in Heidegger's early thought the world is intrinsically bound to the human, this bond is not a grounding, nor is the human taken as a transcendental subject or as spirit. In the development of Heidegger's thought that begins in *Contributions to Philosophy*, even this bond is broken, and whatever affinity there might have been with the metaphysics of the subject is eliminated. Merleau-Ponty's conception of the invisible, as that which, without itself being visible, belongs to and indeed renders possible the visible, extends and develops the redetermination of the sensible that frees it from governance by an intelligible beyond.

But what does this beginning ventured in phenomenology entail with regard to the determination of the sense of nature? Is nature to be regarded simply as the totality of sensible beings? Most certainly it was not so regarded by the ancients. Even in Aristotle the distinction persists between nature and natural things, between φύσις and τὰ φύσει ὄντα; nature itself Aristotle defines as an inner ἀρχή that governs the origination and growth of natural things. While the *Timaeus* does sometimes employ the word φύσις in reference to sensible beings, it also applies the word to other kinds such as the χώρα that are rigorously distinguished from sensible beings. Kant, too, avoids simply identifying nature with the totality of sensible beings. In a highly significant footnote in the *Critique of Pure Reason*, he distinguishes between a formal or adjectival sense of nature and a material or substantive sense. Nature in the latter sense he identifies as 'the sum of appearances insofar as ... they are thoroughly interconnected.' These are, says Kant, 'the things of nature', while nature itself is 'a subsisting whole [*ein bestehendes Ganzes*]'. He distinguishes this sense of nature from the formal sense, according to which nature designates 'the connection of the determinations of a thing according to an inner principle of causality'. Hence, nature in the formal sense is not a totality of beings but rather the connection (*Zusammenhang*) between their determinations. Nature in this sense consists, not of beings, but of the connection by which they are determined as what they are. It is because of its bearing on *what* things are that Kant links nature in this sense to such expressions as 'the nature of fluid matter, of fire, etc.' (Kant 1968b, vol. 3, A419/B446).

In view of these historical indications, the question needs to be addressed as to whether there are discernible moments or entities that, while intrinsically related to sensible beings, nonetheless are distinct from them. Is it possible, beyond the structure of world and the conception of the invisible, to discern and determine moments, configurations, or even entities that go beyond – that exceed – the domain of sensible beings, that lie outside it, such that, if nature is to include these, it cannot be identified simply as the totality of sensible beings?

There are at least two such moments or kinds of entities that can be discerned. Each has the effect of rendering nature as something in excess of the mere totality of sensible beings. One has come to light very recently; the other is to be retrieved from very ancient sources.

The first corresponds to the discovery in recent astrophysics of beings that are not sensible, that by their very nature cannot be presented to sense. Among the several instances of such beings, the most obtrusively excessive are black holes. Such beings have a structure that in no way corresponds to that of a terrestrial thing, of a being having sensibly perceptible properties. A black hole is centered in a singularity, which is an intense concentration of very large mass (at least several times that of our sun) that converges asymptotically toward a point. Consequently, it has such enormous density that its gravity prevents even light from escaping; that is, the escape velocity is greater than the speed of light. As distance from a singularity increases, the escape velocity decreases, and at a certain distance it is equal to the speed of light. This distance defines the extent of the black hole. The imaginary sphere described by this radius constitutes what is called the event horizon. This is the place of no return for light. In its vicinity a shower of particles is produced, and it is only the presence of this peculiarly configured array of particles that allows the event horizon, itself entirely invisible, to be detected. Light – and everything else – that reaches the event horizon will disappear into the black hole. Since no light can escape it, the black hole is entirely invisible – not really black as a thing can be black, which would still be visible, but absolutely invisible (see Sallis 2012a, 152–62; 2012b, ch. 7).

The invisibility of a black hole is a kind of invisibility hitherto unknown, indeed virtually inconceivable. It is not an invisibility that can be breached and converted in degree or manner into visibility as with the unseen other side of an object or as with a perceptual horizon; neither is its invisibility comparable at all to that ascribed by metaphysics to the intelligible, for it belongs, not apart from sensible things, but in their very midst. A black hole is a being that, by virtue of what it is, cannot in any manner be present to sense; it is a being that is not a sensible being. Yet, as set among such things, it presumably belongs to nature. This belonging expands the concept of nature beyond that of the totality of sensible beings.

The second of the moments or entities by which nature exceeds the mere totality of sensible beings can be discerned by taking up the connection drawn in the *Timaeus* between nature, especially in the sense of the χώρα, and the traces of the elements. This connection points back to the elemental thinking of early Greek philosophers such as Anaximenes, Heraclitus, and especially Empedocles; for all these figures, thinking is, as such, directed to φύσις, and φύσις is thought primarily as the gathering of the elements. Engagement with these ancient sources prompts a renewal of the sense of element, of element in the sense still heard when we speak of being exposed to the elements. Even the elements named by the ancients, in names barely translatable as fire, air, water, and earth, open toward senses that resist appropriation by metaphysics: elements such as light and sky, wind and rain, the sea, the earth. These expand the sense of nature, not – as with black holes – by being nonsensible, not by remaining withdrawn from sense. On the contrary, the elements surround us and are eminently displayed before our senses – in the blue of the sky, the brilliance of the light, the coolness of the wind, the sound of the falling rain. What is decisive is that the elements are encompassing, that they are not determinately bounded but rather display a certain indefiniteness not to be found in things, that they betoken also a depth unlike the profile-determined depth of things. By elaborating these and other features, a rigorous distinction can be drawn between elements, on the one side, and things or objects, on the other (see Sallis 2000, ch. 6). By including also the elements, nature exceeds the mere sum of sensible things.

There remains still the question as to whether, granted these moments of excess, the extent of nature is to be limited or whether nature is to be determined as including all that is, hence as coextensive with being. Would it be possible, for the sake of accord with what Emerson calls the common sense of nature, to distinguish it from the cosmos at large? Could such a distinction be drawn without simply reinstating in another guise the Ptolemaic distinction – long since refuted – between the sublunary world and the incorruptible heaven? One possibility would be to regard the sky as the limit separating nature from the cosmos, for, like any genuine limit, the sky displays a peculiar relation to each of the regions it would distinguish. From within nature and to the senses naturally employed, the sky appears as a uniform dome that, together with the earth, encloses the enchorial space in which the things that concern humans come to pass. But when the senses are supplemented, as by powerful telescopes, so that humans can look beyond the surface appearance that is the sky, the sky as such dissolves and becomes an opening onto the cosmos.

If such a distinction between nature and cosmos were to be elaborated, then while extraterrestrial entities such as black holes would be regarded as beyond nature, they could nonetheless be taken as attesting to the limit of the sensible. For such entities do not present themselves to the senses. If, in the wake of the Nietzschean inversion, there is presentation *only* to the senses, then it follows that such entities do not present themselves at all. Recognition of such entities would require, then, that the very sense of being as presence be suspended.

Yet within nature, presence would remain decisive, at least in connection with the elements. It is in this regard that one could begin to elaborate a sense of the imperative beyond the range of the Nietzschean inversion. For, quite apart from theoretical reflections on nature, humans share a capacity to be entranced by elemental nature. When we stand motionless and silent with our gaze fixed upon a towering mountain peak or an expanse of sea stretching to the horizon, our interest is neither in seeing what a mountain or sea looks like nor in coming to know what its essence is. Rather, standing in the presence of the elemental, we simply abide with it and let our senses be absorbed by it. In giving ourselves over to it, we at the same time enhance our sense of belonging to the elemental – in a sense of sense irreducible to mere perception and to essential cognition. By engaging such an elemental sense, a path can perhaps be opened for rethinking the return to nature in a manner that, at once, advances beyond mere inversion while also returning to the beginnings of Western philosophy.

Notes

1. It is only by analogy that one can ascribe a state of nature to music. For Rousseau regards music as intrinsically distanced from nature. Thus, contrasting it with painting, he writes: 'One sees from this that painting is closer to nature and that music depends more on human art' (Rousseau 1970, ch. 16, 537. The final version of this text dates from 1762, though it was not published until after Rousseau's death. It was originally a fragment from the *Second Discourse*, which Rousseau omitted as too long and out of place).
2. This essay belongs to the Second Series, which was first published in 1844.

Acknowledgments

This paper originally appeared as chapter 3 of the author's book *The Return of Nature*. Reprinted here with permission of Indiana University Press.

Disclosure Statement

No potential conflict of interest was reported by the author.

References

Bréhier, Émile. (1965) *The Hellenistic and Roman Age*, trans. Wade Baskin, Chicago: University of Chicago Press.
Emerson, Ralph Waldo. ((1836) 1940a) 'Nature', in Brooks Atkinson (ed.) *The Selected Writings of Ralph Waldo Emerson*, New York, NY: Random House.
Emerson, Ralph Waldo. ((1844) 1940b) 'Nature', in Brooks Atkinson (ed.) *The Selected Writings of Ralph Waldo Emerson*, New York, NY: Random House.
Hegel, G. W. F. (1970) *Enzyklopädie der philosophischen Wissenschaften im Grundrisse (1830), Zweiter Teil: Die Naturphilosophie* [Encyclopedia of the Philosophical Sciences in Outline (1830), Second Part: The Philosophy of Nature]. Vol. 9 of *Werke*. Frankfurt: Suhrkamp.
Kant, Immanuel. (1968a) *Kritik der Urteilskraft* [Critique of Judgment]. In vol. 5 of *Werke: Akademie Textausgabe*. Berlin: Walter de Gruyter.
Kant, Immanuel. (1968b) *Kritik der reinen Vernunft* [Critique of Pure Reason]. Vol. 3 of *Werke: Akademie Textausgabe*. Berlin: Walter de Gruyter.
Long, A. A., and D. N. Sedley (ed.), (trans.), and commentators. (1987) *The Helenistic Philosophers*. 2 vols. Cambridge: Cambridge University Press.
Nietzsche, Friedrich. 1968. *Also Sprach Zarathustra* [Thus Spoke Zarathustra]. Vol. VI/1 of *Werke: Kritische Gesamtausgabe*. Berlin: Walter de Gruyter.
Nietzsche, Friedrich. (1969) *Götzen-Dämmerung* [Twilight of the Idols]. *In vol. VI/3 of Werke: Kritische Gesamtausgabe*. Berlin: Walter de Gruyter.
Rousseau, Jean-Jacques. ((1755) 2008) *Discours sur L'Origine et les Fondements de L'Inégalité parmi les Hommes* [Discourse on the Origin and Foundations of Inequality among Men]. Paris: Flammarion.
Rousseau, Jean-Jacques. (1970) *Essai sur l'origine des langues* [Essay on the Origin of Languages]. Paris: La Bibliothèque du Graphe.
Sallis, John. (1999) *Chorology: On Beginning in Plato's "Timaeus"*. Bloomington: Indiana University Press.
Sallis, John. (2000) *Force of Imagination: The Sense of the Elemental*. Bloomington: Indiana University Press.
Sallis, John. (2012a) 'The Cosmological Turn', *Journal of Speculative Philosophy* 26(2): 152–162.
Sallis, John. (2012b) *Logic of Imagination: The Expanse of the Elemental*. Bloomington: Indiana University Press.
Schelling, F. W. J. (1967) 'Ideen zu einer Philosophie der Natur', in *Schriften von 1794-1798*. Darmstadt: Wissenschaftliche Buchgesellschaft.
Thoreau, Henry David. ((1854) 1965) *Walden*. Brooks Atkinson (ed.), New York: Random House.

Phenomenology and naturalism: a hybrid and heretical proposal

Jack Reynolds

Deakin University, Australia

ABSTRACT

In this paper I aim to develop a largely non-empirical case for the compatibility of phenomenology and naturalism. To do so, I will criticise what I take to be the standard construal of the relationship between transcendental phenomenology and naturalism, and defend a 'minimal' version of phenomenology that is compatible with liberal naturalism in the ontological register (but incompatible with scientific naturalism) and with weak forms of methodological naturalism, the latter of which is understood as advocating 'results continuity', over the long haul, with the relevant empirical sciences. Far from such a trajectory amounting to a Faustian pact in which phenomenology sacrifices its soul, I contend that insofar as phenomenologists care about reigning in the excesses of reductive versions of naturalism, the only viable way for this to be done is via the impure and hybrid account of phenomenology I outline here.

Two of the dominant philosophical forces since the beginning of the twentieth century have been naturalism and phenomenology, albeit reaching their respective zeniths at differing ends of that century. We will consider some of the main varieties of philosophical naturalism throughout, but on the standard construal philosophy and science are said to be continuous, and any form of 'first philosophy' that aims to autonomously secure its own epistemic credentials, or to establish significant ampliative truths on the basis of a priori argument alone, is thought to be suspect. It is usually also said to involve: an ontological commitment (that the furniture of the world is just those entities postulated by our best sciences); and an epistemic or methodological claim (that the only veridical/reliable way of garnering knowledge is through scientific methods). Phenomenology, by contrast, began with Husserl's protestations against psychologism in the Prolegomena to the *Logical Investigations*, and thereafter naturalism more generally became his target, especially as the phenomenological method was developed in a transcendental direction. Notwithstanding the various metamorphoses that phenomenology has undergone since, the orthodox view remains that phenomenology is an anti-naturalism (Moran 2013; Glendinning 2007), concerned with understanding experience on its own terms rather than presupposing the truth of any causal or explanatory theories.

In more recent times, however, there have been increasing amounts of scholarship on naturalising phenomenology (e.g. Varela et al. 1991; Petitot et al. 2000; Gallagher 2005, 2013; Thompson 2007; Zahavi 2010, 2013). Much of this literature focuses upon how phenomenology might be of use to empirical science as a supplement in empirical and experimental contexts, or it remains at the meta-philosophical level and offers a negative assessment of the methodological proximity of phenomenology and naturalism (it is possible to do both). In this paper, however, I develop a largely non-empirical case for the compatibility of phenomenology and naturalism. To do so, I criticise one standard construal of the relationship between transcendental phenomenology and naturalism, and defend a 'minimal' version of phenomenology that does not preserve a self-sufficient domain that is distinct from empirical science, either methodologically or substantively. This minimal phenomenology is shown to be compatible with liberal naturalism in the ontological register (but incompatible with scientific naturalism) and with weak forms of methodological naturalism, understood as advocating 'results continuity' with the relevant empirical sciences over the long haul, albeit not necessarily deference to the current best findings of science. I will contend that such a trajectory does not amount to a Faustian pact in which phenomenology sacrifices its soul, since one can still coherently defend some core phenomenological commitments. Moreover, insofar as phenomenologists care about reigning in the excesses of reductive versions of naturalism, I contend that the only viable way to do so is via this sort of bastard or hybrid account of phenomenology.

Précis

One way of motivating the potential compatibility of phenomenology and naturalism is to start by laying my philosophical cards on the table, a sort of abridged account of the argument and central claims.[1] They are:

Claim 1: The idea of the strict autonomy of transcendental phenomenology, and the explanatory neutrality of phenomenological description, are insufficiently justified. If there are good grounds for thinking that phenomenology cannot be self-sufficient, phenomenology will either be circular in a potentially vicious way, or it will need to derive some of its justification from its engagement with 'non-phenomenology'. Insofar as phenomenology makes claims concerning the mind, agency, time-experience, embodiment, etc., this will need to include substantial and systematic interaction with the relevant empirical sciences.

Claim 2: The idea of an objective and neutral scientific method that might do without the first-person perspective is insufficiently justified, both methodologically and ontologically. If there are good grounds for thinking that scientific naturalism of this kind cannot be self-sufficient (e.g. they will presuppose phenomenology and a robust first-person perspective), then it will need to derive some of its justification from its capacity to account for the evidences of first-person experience, including meaning, morality, mentality, and normativity.

I hope to show, then, that these two dominant philosophical trajectories are insufficient on their own, and bound to 'fail' if they aspire to be all-encompassing. Moreover, in their 'failure' they necessarily presuppose and come into relation with each other. Presented in such an abstract fashion this via *negativa* is unlikely to convince anyone sceptical, but if any genuine persuasion is to take place it will require a 'work of words' (Glendinning 2007) to show that this compatibilist thesis, this admittedly revisionist reorientation of phenomenology and naturalism, is not simply stipulative or trivial.

Phenomenological and naturalism: methodological incompatibilism

Although phenomenology is a tradition of heresies as Ricoeur observed, there is a standard line (with some variations) about the relationship between phenomenology and naturalism, and, perhaps to a lesser extent, about the appropriate way to conceive of the relationship between phenomenology and empirical science. All of the canonical European phenomenologists, and most contemporary phenomenologists, express misgivings about naturalism, notwithstanding that the term is often imprecisely defined. Husserl, of course, is especially clear about his opposition to naturalism, describing it as the 'original sin' (Moran 2013, p. 92). As Zahavi (2013, p. 33) puts it, for Husserl 'a phenomenologist who embraced naturalism would in effect have ceased being a philosopher'. While Husserl's complaints against naturalism initially develop in parallel with his complaints against psychologism – the claim that psychological and natural facts explain human cognition and the ideal laws of logic and mathematics – his basic contention throughout his oeuvre is that the sciences cannot ground or legitimate themselves without untenable circularity, and hence are in need of phenomenology to act as a sort of meta-science to secure their claims (philosophical naturalism is not up to the job). Crucially, however, phenomenology is not in need of engagement with such empirical sciences, remaining independent and autonomous. It stands on nothing other than itself, resting on intuitive self-givenness and the famous 'principle of all principles': 'that every originary presentive intuition is a legitimising source of cognition' (Husserl 1982, §24). The claims of others, be they scientists, metaphysicians, the folk, and even other trained phenomenologists, are strictly empty until fulfilled by my first-personal evidence, which is alone capable of apodicticity. While this conclusion can be mitigated by noting that it is *possible* rather than *actual* fulfilment in a presentive intuition that is required by Husserl, phenomenological and scientific inquiry are still envisaged as radically different in kind, and there is a strong asymmetry between them such that science needs phenomenology but the reverse does not hold. On such a view, phenomenology is unable to be falsified on empirical grounds; indeed, it appears to be unable to even learn from empirical studies, *qua* transcendental phenomenology, at all. It is this kind of irenic separatism that a naturalist is unlikely to accept, even more 'liberal' varieties.

While Husserl's commitment to the autonomy of transcendental philosophy, and the neutrality of phenomenological description, is weakened in the work of many of those who follow him, variations of this story perdure. The phenomenological ambition of 'returning to the things themselves' is characterised as involving a perspectival shift that brackets the putative successes of natural science (e.g. planes stay in the air, modern medicine allows us to live much longer, etc.) and asks after their presuppositions, conditions, and 'grounds' (understood non-empirically). Moreover, this sort of phenomenological 'seeing', accompanied by thorough description, is not progressivist, inductive, causally explanatory, etc. The sort of inferential modes of reasoning that play a central role within the empirical sciences are ruled out of the phenomenological tool box, primarily because they are not sufficiently transcendental, and do not bracket the natural attitude: that is, they presuppose the reality of the objects that are being examined, rather than looking at how such objects are constituted as objects for us, and hence have meaning for us. They are, for Husserl, rigidifications of the natural attitude that he calls the 'naturalistic attitude' in 'Philosophy as Rigorous Science' (1965) and *Ideas II* (see Moran 2008, 403). If both scientists and philosophical naturalists (who offer theoretical reconstructions of science) partake in the natural attitude, and if the natural attitude is precisely what phenomenology is meant to bracket, then phenomenology and naturalism seem to be either direct philosophical opponents, or they are concerned with radically different domains. In short, transcendental phenomenology cannot validly appeal to any explanatory theories from the empirical sciences without giving up its transcendental status, and the associated idea of explanatorily neutral description. This sort of methodological separatism remains the phenomenological orthodoxy today, expressed by some of the best contemporary phenomenologists (see Crowell 2013, 28), and philosophers who are centrally involved in naturalising projects.

Indeed, while Dan Zahavi and Shaun Gallagher have done some of the most important work on the question of the relationship between phenomenological and empirical inquiry, they also *sometimes* adopt a methodological separatist/incompatibilist position. While Gallagher's own single authored texts are more inclined to emphasise something like the position I will ultimately endorse here, in their co-authored works they sometimes invoke a move of philosophical quarantine in which phenomenology and empirical science are each allocated a separate space or job description, such that there is no potential for conflict. This is apparent in their response to Jonathan Cole's review of their 2008 book, *The Phenomenological Mind* (Zahavi and Gallagher 2008, 88), and in reply to Dan Hutto's paper where they strictly differentiate transcendental phenomenology from any sort of inference to the best explanation (2008, 90–91). Of course, the relationship that Zahavi and Gallagher envisage between phenomenological *psychology*, and the empirical sciences that deal with data of relevance to the first-person, is quite different. Phenomenological psychology refers to forms of phenomenology that have not yet become fully transcendental but instead work within the natural attitude. Borrowing the phrase from Merleau-Ponty, Gallagher suggests that this kind of phenomenology explores the 'shadow of the transcendental', and he fruitfully develops a dialectical relationship between phenomenological psychology and empirical science in which each transforms and challenges the other (see Gallagher 2005, 2013). Zahavi is also happy to sign up to this kind of naturalising of phenomenology, at least insofar as it concerns phenomenological psychology: it is not, however, relevant to the goals of transcendental phenomenology (Zahavi 2013). Zahavi generally holds that transcendental phenomenology proper is simply on a different level than empirical science of any sort, hence not able to be either a prolegomena for such studies, nor potentially falsified, corrected, or improved, by what is revealed by such studies. To think that it might be is to commit a category mistake, as he notes in more than one place (Zahavi 2013, 23–42; Zahavi 2001, 9, 108, 127). For Zahavi (2013, 34):

> Phenomenology is basically, to repeat, a transcendental philosophical endeavor, and although one might ease the way for its naturalization by abandoning the transcendental dimension, one would not retain that which makes phenomenology a distinct philosophical discipline, strategy, and method.

Phenomenological over-bidding – against methodological incompatibilism

Although many phenomenologists have held this view, I think there are some problems with it. Firstly, it is based on particular understandings of naturalism that have an eliminative or reductive ambition, which neither exhaust the field nor take full account of the distinction between ontological and methodological claims. It is also based on an understanding of transcendental phenomenology in which it has autonomy from other forms of philosophical and theoretical enquiry on account of its explanatorily neutral description, as well as its transcendental privilege in enumerating the conditions of possibility for particular kinds of experiences. I want to challenge this view in three ways here: (1) an argument via authority (i.e. historico-hermeneutically); (2) a deconstructive style argument concerning the necessity of phenomenology appealing to meta-philosophy in a manner that breaches its own principles (especially in regard to science), and (3) a more direct philosophical argument about the insufficiencies of methodological separatism.

1. One way to motivate my critique of what Dominique Janicaud (2000, 89–106) aptly calls 'phenomenological overbidding' is via recourse to countervailing forces within the phenomenological tradition that challenge this understanding. While this is tacitly an argument via authority, and thus ultimately insufficient, it is worth briefly sketching it in order to show that my proposal retains enough overlap with the phenomenological tradition so as to merit the continued invocation of the name 'phenomenology'. In particular, it might be legitimately claimed that there is at least some support for claim 1 in the précis within *existential* phenomenology. That is so, even if Heidegger, Sartre, Merleau-Ponty, etc., do not pursue it as far as I will ultimately advocate, and are, with the exception of Merleau-Ponty, cautious to explore its potential implications for the relationship between philosophy and empirical science. In this vein, one might cite Merleau-Ponty's famous remarks concerning the incompletability of the reduction in the 'Preface' to *Phenomenology of Perception* (1958), and argue that hermeneutic phenomenology challenges Husserl's methodological separatism/incompatibilism by partly relativising the transcendental (see Wheeler 2013), notwithstanding that there is typically still a strong hermeneutic distinction drawn between understanding and explanation. While I think there is something to such a story, especially in regard to Merleau-Ponty (cf. Reynolds 2017), this sort of appeal to the tradition of phenomenology as itself authorising (if only tacitly) this trajectory is not especially compelling, since these interpretations of Merleau-Ponty and Heidegger, for example, remain contested. Moreover, whatever verdict is reached on that question does not show that the neo-Husserlian position is wrong: it remains open to the transcendental phenomenologist of this ilk to claim that Husserl alone is a properly transcendental phenomenologist, or that a properly transcendental phenomenology that fully abides by Husserlian principles is a task that is still to be performed.

2. A more promising strategy is to show that claim 1 is attested to in the work of phenomenological philosophers, even where they expressly deny or disavow it. The persistence of such infelicities would provide some inductive evidence that the opposition between phenomenology and science, and between phenomenology and naturalism, is not as stark as many phenomenologists maintain. This would involve a deconstruction of phenomenology as concerns the ostensible purity of the method and its reliance upon a strict transcendental-empirical distinction, but by extending it to look at the role of empirical science within phenomenology, and the role of meta-philosophy within phenomenology. Without doing the labour of showing this in engagement with classical phenomenological texts (but cf. Derrida 2000, 1974), my basic claim is a simple one: implicitly or explicitly, phenomenology is always called upon to justify itself in regard to other ways of theorising and philosophising (this

will also involve a dialogue with that which is ostensibly non-phenomenology, non-philosophy, and includes art, science, common sense, the history of philosophy, etc.). Moreover, it cannot do so strictly within the terms of the principle of all principles alone, notwithstanding various programmatic statements to that effect. It is not difficult to show that cultural and social presuppositions perdure within extant phenomenological theorising (e.g. Husserl or Heidegger's various Judeo-Christian commitments), and that cultural and social matters (including the advent of new technologies) condition and constrain cognition (cf. Woelert 2012), perhaps even in regard to the structure of time-consciousness itself, a justly famed and fundamental aspect of phenomenology (see Thompson 2007, 357). Moreover, it is often ignored just how much phenomenology itself depends upon science, not just for inspiration as with Heidegger's controversial appropriation of Jacob Von Uexkull's biological work on animals and the *umwelt*, but implicitly, even in terms of the very conception of phenomenological philosophy as a rigorous science. Can science (as well as the history of metaphysics) really be kept in principle apart, or do certain theoretical and cultural ways of thinking become part of our life-world in such a way that the epoché is a useful tool, perhaps even an indispensable tool for certain philosophical purposes, but not a presuppositionless and autonomous attitude?

It is clear that phenomenology cannot simply *oppose* (or negate, refute, etc.) the natural attitude, and it cannot simply oppose (or negate, refute, etc.) science, which is considered a theoretically sophisticated version of the natural attitude. It is too strong to say that the natural attitude is an error or mistake. Firstly, no phenomenology is possible without the background that is the natural attitude, and even on its traditional formulation the technique of bracketing does not entail the rejection, elimination, negation, or refutation, of that which is bracketed (it is an agnosticism of sorts). Secondly, despite persistent phenomenological critiques of scientism it is important to ask on what grounds any putative opposition to science, and/or its philosophical reconstructions (e.g. scientific naturalism) might be proffered? What establishes that phenomenological method(s) are to be preferred, say, to the scientific methods(s) generalised to all things, as with, say, scientism? It cannot be on methodological grounds that derive from phenomenological reflection alone, since that would be to beg the question against those other methods. Insisting that only phenomenology can properly understand consciousness, as if that were akin to an analytic truth, presupposes precisely what is in question in the contrast with naturalism (as does scientism when it rules out the evidences of the first-person perspective). Common sense also cannot legitimately (i.e. non-dogmatically) be appealed to as a tie-breaker, since that is part of what phenomenology ostensibly brackets. Moreover, if the privileging of phenomenology were to be justified explicitly on metaphysical grounds (say the conviction that mind, meaning and morality are ultimately more real than neurons, since able to be directly experienced in accord with the 'principle of all principles'), that would also beg the question, either methodologically, or by revealing phenomenology to not be metaphysically neutral as it is (sometimes) proclaimed to be. Indeed, it is no coincidence that at a pivotal point in *Ideas I* (Husserl 1982, §49), and subsequently repeated in *Ideas II*, Husserl has recourse to an infamous thought experiment invoking the annihilation of the world with consciousness remaining. Although there are many interpretations of this thought experiment, Husserl appears to invoke a metaphysics to justify the need for a unique method to investigate consciousness, as is also the case when he tightly connects the phenomenological method with idealism in *Cartesian Meditations* (Husserl 1950). This legitimation of phenomenology is, it seems, extra-phenomenological.

How then, can phenomenology be validly opposed to scientism and some major forms of philosophical naturalism (but not all) without begging the question? It must involve an account of salient phenomenological matters (e.g. the irreducibility of the first-person perspective 'for us'), *and* an immanent critique of the manner in which philosophical construals of science surreptitiously presuppose the first-person perspective while aiming to eliminate or reduce it. In those respects, then, phenomenology can validly oppose versions of naturalism that over-reach, over-bid, and fail by their own lights, but that depends on an engagement between phenomenology and non-phenomenology, and seeing that something like a dialectic must obtain between such considerations. It also means that phenomenology does not rest on itself and that strategies of methodological incompatibilism cannot succeed in preserving a domain, attitude, or transcendental 'region', that is proper to phenomenology alone. Phenomenology is contaminated by non-phenomenology, and it is meta-philosophy that occasions such contamination. Might we purge phenomenology of these meta-philosophical and metaphysical infelicities, and thus better perform the reduction and attend strictly to the 'things themselves'?[2] Perhaps, but the history of phenomenology in the twentieth century gives us reason to be rather less sanguine about such hopes.

3. There are also more direct objections to phenomenologically-grounded assertions of methodological incompatibilism and their one-way character (i.e. the claim that science needs phenomenology, but the reverse does not hold). In particular, we need a good answer as to how and why science needs phenomenology as a grounding meta-science, without that answer compromising the separatist/incompatibilist thesis. Given the confines of space, however, I would like to focus here just on the status of phenomenological transcendental 'arguments'.[3] Such arguments generally take as their first premise some subject-involving experience (e.g. the experience of shame), and use that to establish what we must be like in order for the said experience to be as it is. It is important to note, however, that such arguments are not strictly a priori, and they open the door to empirical matters. For example, even if the phenomenological claim to necessity concerns merely the relationship between different kinds of subject-involving experiences,

empirical data seems to be directly relevant here, including in regard to pathological and anomalous experiences. We might think, for example, of the phenomena of thought-insertion in schizophrenic patients. It complicates, but does not necessarily simply refute, phenomenological claims about the 'mineness' of experience, in particular claims to the effect that such self-identification is immune from the possibility of error (Romdenh-Romluc 2013; Gallagher 2012, 135). It does not refute them, because there is some evidence that even in schizophrenic episodes individuals will reportedly still say 'my body has been moved', thus again suggesting the persistence of some basic 'mineness' about experience (Gallagher 2012, 135; Parnas et al. 2005). Likewise, if a philosophical argument concerning bodily motility, and the proprioceptive sense of one's own body, is directly challenged by a pathological case (e.g. Schneider's war injuries that prevent him from pointing to his nose despite being able to grasp it), the phenomenological philosopher will need to be prepared to revise their claims, and to consider whether their phenomenological account has been missing something or is impoverished in some way. Our descriptions of intentional action and embodied motility may well be prejudiced in particular ways – we cannot through eidetic variation imagine all possibilities – and the consideration of pathological cases, as well as the causal/explanatory dimensions of such cases, can help to force the phenomenologist to clarify, revise, and adjust their position. Not only might they provide a more filled out thought experiment than phenomenological reflection alone can provide, and hence act as a spur to deeper phenomenological reflection, but they can challenge what has been taken for granted in a given phenomenological account, perhaps even causing it to be abandoned (cf. Bermudez 1995, 391), but it does not have to entail (and, in fact, rarely does) direct falsification. Much of the work done within empirically-minded phenomenology either explicitly or implicitly concedes this point, even in regard to the famed Husserlian and post-Husserlian analyses of internal time-consciousness. Evan Thompson makes this explicit when he suggests that while Husserl's anti-naturalism is committed to the synthesis of consciousness necessarily being different from any external combination of natural elements, neuro-phenomenology shows that the formal structure of time-consciousness has an analogue in the dynamic structure of neural processes. Thompson thus contends that, 'the kind of phenomenological anti-naturalism' espoused by Husserl has been 'outstripped by science' (2007, 357).

Does the conjunction of these claims force us to give up on the kind of methodological separatism characteristic of classical transcendental phenomenology? I think they should. The idea of a transcendental dimension to phenomenology that rests on nothing other than itself, and the idea of an autonomous and explanatorily neutral description, are counsels to perfection rather than something that is ever actually achieved.

Minimal phenomenology

What remains of phenomenology on such a heretical construal? Dermot Moran suggests that phenomenology is 'an inquiry into the normative conditions for the possibility of intentional meaning that *respects* the first-person starting-point' (Moran 2014). This definition is arguably not sufficient, since it might be protested that phenomenology is not restricted to the first-person perspective but elaborates consciousness' involvement in the world, and through the eidetic reduction seeks to elaborate essential structures that are third-personal (cf. Drummond 2007). Nonetheless, I think Moran is right that this lived experience, given predominantly in the first-person perspective, is the 'starting point', and what I call 'minimal phenomenology' remains within this admittedly broad definition. In addition, I can endorse Crowell's (2013, 44) recent claim that the lived body, the person, being-in-the-world, etc., do not show up if we are labouring under a certain externalist conception of 'nature', a conception that remains strong in some forms of philosophical naturalism that presuppose a mechanistic conception of nature as *partes extra partes*. That does not show, however, that such analyses are *ipso facto* autonomous, nor that respecting the first-person perspective, and its normative conditions, means privileging either as the grounds for apodictic knowledge. While a case can be made for a special sort of immunity against error in the first-person perspective as concerns the basic 'mineness' of experience (Romdenh-Romlec 2013; Gallagher 2012, 135), the broader epistemic consequences of this are minimal, and in general minimal phenomenology provides something closer to what Tyler Burge (2010) calls a priori *warrants for belief* rather than a priori *truths*. It is a fallibilist rather than foundationalist epistemology, and acknowledges that as embodied agents there will be a complex intertwining between a posteriori matters and a priori ones. But we are entitled to these first-personal convictions, even if they cannot be justified from a neutral or third-person perspective. They are an ineliminable part of any epistemic investigation, but, and here is the core of my challenge to the phenomenological orthodoxy, they can be justified only in interaction with that which is ostensibly not part of phenomenology (including, notably, science, but also art, common sense, psychoanalysis, etc.), and also partly in terms of what they do in any such juxtaposition, including for future epistemological and scientific enquiry.

Minimal phenomenology hence requires a double move of justification: phenomenological description and analysis (but this is not autonomous or presuppositionless); and something like an inference to the best explanation in relation to other theories and their problems, which may be both empirical and conceptual/theoretical. Minimal phenomenology abandons the idea that phenomenological and transcendental methods are alone sufficient, since they involve claims to necessity (understood as necessity 'for us', and not meant to hold for all possible worlds and all possible cognising beings) that can and should be amenable to empirical data, and inferential reasoning regarding how these levels might interact. But it keeps attentiveness to experience as one sort of evidence that will need to be accommodated as a cornerstone of the theory in question. The reduction, for example, remains a useful heuristic tool to access dimensions of first-personal experience that are often overlooked, and it emphasises the value in attempting to understand such experiences while minimising one's other theoretical commitments, thus helping to ensure vigilance regarding the over-reaching of philosophical naturalism insofar as it prejudges and imposes a metaphysics (say, of simulations, representations) or a scientific explanation (say, of simulations, representations) come what may. Phenomenology, then, will need to engage in two strategies, pulling in different directions, but not necessarily incompatible. As Evan Thompson (2014) puts a related point:

> One approach, known as the 'naturalizing phenomenology' project, seeks to absorb phenomenological analyses of consciousness into some kind of naturalistic framework. Another approach, 'phenomenologizing nature,' uses phenomenology to enrich our understanding of nature, especially living being and the body, in order to do justice to consciousness as a natural phenomenon. Ultimately, both strategies are necessary and must be pursued in a complementary and mutually supporting way, if phenomenology is not to be reduced to or eliminated in favor of scientific naturalism, and if naturalism is not to be rejected in favor of metaphysically dualist or idealist forms of phenomenology.

The overbidding of philosophical naturalism: against ontological and scientific naturalism

Naturalism is the 'default and restraining presupposition' of contemporary analytic philosophy today (Gardner 2007, 26), and it involves more than merely the somewhat platitudinous desire to avoid the postulating of supernatural entities in the metaphysical register, or modes of knowing and understanding that are premised on 'papal infallibility' (Dennett 1991). As Lynne Baker (2012, xvi) suggests, the scientific naturalist advocates two strong claims: '1. at bottom, reality is what natural science says it is and nothing more; and 2. our beliefs are ultimately only justifiable by the methods of science.' Both views are suspicious of any philosophy that is focused on first-person description. Ontological naturalists aim to either eliminate the first-person perspective from an account of what ultimately there is, or to replace first-person involving descriptions and beliefs with items that are admissible to science and are framed from the third-person perspective. But just as the phenomenological orthodoxy tends to be committed to methodological incompatibilism, so too is the scientific naturalist orthodoxy, seeking to discredit first-person modes of knowing and understanding, whether that be in terms of phenomenology, introspection, empathic understanding, intentional explanation, etc. The scientific naturalist contends, instead, that 'there is only one way of knowing, the empirical way that is the basis of science' (Devitt 1996, 2), which understands the methods of science fairly narrowly, with physics, chemistry, and the biological sciences being privileged. Without being able to settle this here, I will briefly outline some prima facie reasons to doubt the claims of ontological and scientific naturalism. These reasons also suggest that phenomenology is the most appropriate dialectical counterpoint for the sort of hybrid middle-way position that I will endorse in subsequent sections.

1. Firstly, the scientific naturalist's attempted reductions and eliminations seem to inevitably presuppose, or smuggle in, a robust first-person perspective (this is the accusation of 'hypocrisy', or 'naivety'). I think this has been convincingly shown by various phenomenologists in their engagement with Dennett's conception of hetero-phenomenology, especially by Zahavi (2007, 39) who powerfully argues that

> Dennett's hetero-phenomenology must be criticized not only for simply presupposing the availability of the third-person perspective without reflecting on and articulating its conditions of possibility, but also for failing to realize to what extent its own endeavor tacitly presupposes an intact first-person perspective.

Some related arguments have been put forward outside of phenomenological circles by Baker (2012, 78–79) in her engagement with Dennett and Metzinger, amongst others. The core claim, in both cases, is that the atheism or agnosticism regarding the first-person perspective (whether epistemically or ontologically construed) is performatively undermined within the terms of their own discourse and/or in a given scientific practice. Of course, even if this were true of Dennett and Metzinger, and even if it were held to be the case for all current ontological and scientific naturalists, that does not prove that all eliminativist and reductionist programs must fail. Nonetheless, if Baker and Zahavi are right, and I think they are, we have a prima facie reason to: (a) sit on the fence; (b) take issue with the core claim of ontological naturalism that all that exists is what science says there is; or (c) consider a more pluralistic conception of ontological naturalism, since it might be claimed that the first-person perspective plays an ineliminable and functional role within science, and hence should be counted as part of what exists. This would be to consider naturalism as lending support to ontological pluralism rather than physicalist monism, and hence to countenance more liberal versions of naturalism.

2. As is well known, scientific naturalism faces various difficulties concerning what Huw Price has called the 4Ms – Meaning, Mentality, Morality, and Modality (cf. Price 2004) – and whether these can be adequately accounted for within such a philosophical framework. While some take the project of attempting to reduce such aspects of experience to their empirical conditions to be an ongoing research program, and one in which headway is being made, others conclude that the 4Ms remain a significant hurdle. While strong naturalists might bite the bullet, and simply reject worries about the 4Ms and the first-person perspective, and say that 'everything must go' in the manner

of Ladyman and Ross (2007), this move is counter-intuitive in two ways: it rules out resources central to both our own self-understanding *and* to contemporary scientific practice, which relieves heavily upon mathematics and also first-person phenomenological dimensions in regard to observation. Moreover, in psychology and the cognitive sciences, at least, such factors are also the explanandum, and it is arguable that to put the explanans before the explanandum is to put the cart before the horse (cf. Pigden 2010, 179), and to prosecute a philosophical agenda that has left the scientific practice behind. Scientific naturalism of this kind looms as itself a form of *prima philosophia*. While supplements to orthodox naturalism that might better accommodate the 4Ms can be provided in many alternative ways, including in the manner characteristic of the 'Canberra Plan' as well as renewals of German Idealism and classical pragmatism, it seems to me that phenomenologically-inspired accounts are best-placed to elucidate these objections to scientific and ontological naturalism in a plausible and metaphysically modest (albeit not presuppositionless) manner. That is because it looks plausible to hold that each of the 4Ms (even modality, as Arthur Prior's work on tense shows) depends on the first-person perspective and its place or role, and this is something that has been a central concern of phenomenology throughout, and in the minimal conception proffered here.

3. Finally, we have the first-person evidences themselves, including the basic pre-reflective 'mineness' of experience that Baker (2012, 64) highlights in discussing the difference between seeing an unkempt person in the window of a bus and coming to realise that one is that unkempt person. Short of a convincing debunking that does not performatively undermine or contradict itself, it seems to me that the first-person evidences of phenomenology should be taken as ontologically and epistemically significant, if not the last word or 'The Datum' as Baker calls it, notwithstanding the various 'user-illusions' that psychology and cognitive science have shown we are prone to.

While all of these issues with naturalism have been raised within the phenomenological tradition, the classical critique overbids when it claims to establish that, necessarily, an adequate scientific explanation of a given phenomena cannot be come by, or that such analyses (whatever their empirical value) are strictly irrelevant to transcendental phenomenology. There are more pragmatic and modest versions of closely related arguments that are not so necessitarian and modally committed in character. Instead, they refer to the insufficiency of existing attempts at reduction or elimination, and that also note our first-personal commitments to norms, agency, and the like, and conclude inferentially that the best current explanation is that the first-person level – the 'here' and 'now' – is ontologically irreducible and required for understanding normativity and other subject-involving phenomena. While the evidentiary force of our experience counts, it cannot by itself rule out eliminativist counter-proposals without begging the question, but a probabilistic case for the irreducibility of the first-person perspective is provided when juxtaposed with the ongoing failures of attempted reductions and eliminations. Rather than this irreducibility being autonomously 'proven' by phenomenology itself, such a view makes essential reference to non-phenomenology. The justification is two-pronged, given in first-person phenomenological analysis (and the accounts of other phenomenologists of a related experiential datum), but also in dialogue with non-phenomenology (including empirical science), and here inferences to the best explanation play a significant role.

Minimal phenomenology as compatible with liberal naturalism

Sceptical about the over-reaching of scientific naturalism, philosophers like John McDowell and Hilary Putnam have developed a trajectory that has come to be called liberal naturalism. Without being able to address their work here, Mario De Caro and David Macarthur note in their framing introduction that liberal naturalism involves two key conditions:

(a) 'A necessary condition for a view's being a version of Liberal Naturalism is that it rejects Scientific Naturalism' – the latter of which encompasses both the ontological doctrine and its epistemic variety.
(b) 'Respect for the findings and methods of the natural sciences'. (De Caro and Macarthur 2010, 9)

It is clear that minimal phenomenology meets the first necessary condition. It rejects scientific naturalism partly on the grounds of the 'location problem' that the liberal naturalist perceives at the heart of scientific naturalism in regard to the 4Ms (Cf. Price 2004), especially in regard to meaning and normativity. But liberal naturalism would be incoherent if its identity consisted in nothing more than the rejection of scientific naturalism, indistinguishable from fully-fledged idealism, along with first philosophies and the irenic position about the relationship between phenomenology and science that I have criticised here. The more critical question, then, is whether my account of minimal phenomenology meets other conditions for admission to any putative liberal naturalist camp, and then whether those conditions are themselves sufficient to really warrant the label 'naturalist' or instead amount to a form of non-naturalism in disguise (cf. Neta 2007). In this regard, De Caro and Macarthur rely on the idea of 'appropriate *respect* for the findings and methods of the natural sciences' as their key positive condition for avoiding non-naturalism. Recall that Moran also explicates the phenomenological method using similar terms, suggesting that phenomenology is 'an inquiry into the normative conditions for the possibility of intentional meaning that *respects* the first-person starting-point' (Moran 2014). Of course, in both cases these statements are rather vague and a lot hangs on the word 'respect'. After all, one philosophers respect is another's disrespect and what is at issue is whether we can simultaneously respect both of these injunctions or are confronted by a forced choice such that respect for the one precludes respect for the other. While views on that will differ (cf.

Kornblith 2014), what I am calling minimal phenomenology appears to meet the liberal naturalist standard for this respect. Phenomenological descriptions and reflections are not only capable of being challenged by scientific findings, but they also require engagement with non-phenomenology (including empirical science and theoretical accounts of it) in order to be justified. This is unlikely to satisfy the scientific naturalist, but it suggests that a unity ticket between liberalism naturalism and minimal phenomenology is plausible.

Minimal phenomenology as compatible with weak methodological naturalism

The relationship between methodological naturalism and phenomenology is complex. On the one hand, it is clear that no version of phenomenology will agree that philosophy ought to be reduced to (or ought to emulate) certain selected methods from privileged natural sciences in the manner advocated by strong versions of methodological naturalism. On the other hand, there are weaker forms of methodological naturalism that are less disagreeable to phenomenology, in particular those which emphasise a relationship of 'mutual constraint' or 'results continuity' between philosophy and science, but do not take that to entail that philosophy is nothing but an abstract branch of science. What, then, might be the minimal condition to be a methodological naturalist?

Brian Leiter suggests that all versions of methodological naturalism are committed to emphasising some relationship of continuity between philosophy and science, and that they all repudiate first philosophy (Leiter 2002, 3, cf. Devitt 1996, 49). While first philosophy is difficult to define, Husserl explicitly embraces the idea in various places and I have argued that the orthodox construal of the relationship between transcendental phenomenology and empirical science remains a form of *prima philosophia*. But on the minimal version of phenomenology that I have advocated, empirical evidence is able to pressure ostensibly non-empirical philosophical arguments, as we saw earlier in the brief discussion of proprioception and embodied motility. This point generalises to many other areas where phenomenological experience and empirical inquiry intersect, including in regard to the relationship between phenomenological reflections on inter-subjectivity and debates about social cognition in psychology and cognitive science (cf. Gallagher 2005, 2013). Minimal phenomenology hence seems sufficiently invested in empirical matters not to count as a form of first philosophy.

It is also sometimes held that another condition to be a methodological naturalist is to accept that philosophical *results* ought to be continuous with those of the sciences, in the sense of meaningfully constrained by them (cf. Leiter 2002, 3, cf. Kornblith 2002, 27). A lot hinges upon precisely how to understand this continuity, but Leiter has proposed that a speculative and more traditionally philosophical dimension might be retained within such a form of naturalism, insofar as philosophy might help to prompt revolution in science in times of crisis, and its efficacy is indexed to the future results of such sciences. If so, this account is closely related to the view that I have outlined here, in which minimal phenomenology is not methodologically autonomous, which would be a problem for a methodological naturalist. Insofar as phenomenological experience and reflection remains a 'starting point' it is not because it is epistemically incorrigible, but because it is inevitable and will be part of any given philosophy or science, and it can be done better than it usually is done, especially by those not trained in phenomenology.

On the local level, of course, phenomenological claims will often still be in tension with many of the findings stemming from empirical science, and any genuine methodological naturalist cannot always side with philosophy over science in such situations. That would not indicate a relationship of respect and mutual constraint. Nonetheless, direct contradictions between the evidences of phenomenology and those of empirical science are rarer than one might think. That is partly because they focus upon different aspects, and because faced with an apparent contradiction, the philosopher may be inclined to adjust their description or theory. While such a gesture is antithetical to traditional phenomenology on the methodological separatist construal, and while it is also antithetical to positivism and Popperianism, many will today agree that it is both an inevitable and desirable part of scientific and philosophical practice, a consequence of the over and under-determination of theory by evidence. While stronger versions of methodological naturalism will not allow philosophical reflection to ever trump evidence derived from well-established sciences, there are reasons we might places our bets with philosophy that remain within the ambit of weak versions of methodological naturalism. For example, the empirical evidence may be ambiguous and contested, as it is often is, or we may elect to stick with the phenomenological account in the expectation that future transformations in the sciences will come to justify this decision (e.g. Leiter's speculative methodological naturalism). Not only might an experimental anomaly create a space for philosophical reflection, but philosophy may arrive at conclusions that are suggestive of further possible lines of empirical inquiry (cf. Bermudez 1995, 380). Phenomenological description and reflection can provide reasons for thinking that any science labouring under a certain conception of nature (i.e. nature as mechanistic, *partes extra partes*, made up of mutually external parts) will struggle with experience, normativity, etc., and be unable to countenance emergence. Likewise, phenomenological description and reflection can highlight that various contemporary approaches (notably 'theory theory' and simulation theory) to explaining social cognition take a third-personal stance that blinds them to other important aspects of our understanding of others that seem indispensable to our own self-understanding and also to be presupposed by psychology (Gallagher 2012). As Rouse (2005) puts it, phenomenology can thus combat the normalising tendency of science. In cases like these, however, the critical remarks about the presuppositions of certain sciences stand and fall for what they can do in the future for knowledge, and how they can help those sciences be more self-critical, and develop alternative and more accurate interpretations of the data. In both cases, this indicates a 'results continuity' thesis, in which the results from philosophy and science ramify upon and constrain each other.

Conclusion

It seems to me, then, that phenomenology and naturalism need each other, albeit in a manner that troubles the standard acceptations of each, as well as the standard understandings of the lines of demarcation between philosophy and science. It suggests, for example, that there is an a posteriori arm chair (Nolan 2015) and an a priori lab. In regard to the latter claim, it has long been acknowledged (starting with Frege and Husserl) that mathematics and logic are fundamental to the natural sciences and present a problem for the 'bald' naturalist, but the philosophical interpretation of data – e.g. theory-ladenness – can never entirely eliminate incipient forms of phenomenological reflection grounded in one's embodied and temporal situation, including most minimally the very capacity to identify one's experiences as one's own. However, acknowledging the encroachment between an a priori lab and an a posteriori arm chair does not necessarily mean that there is only one way of knowing. There are differences between philosophy and science, but they are differences in degree rather than in kind, and the best philosophical view will be able to navigate between each, in something akin to Sellars' stereoscopic view. This is a dialectical or 'mutual constraint' model, in which neither philosophy nor any given empirical science has methodological priority, and in which the methodological autonomy of each is placed in question and allows for encroachment between each, but not the reduction of one into the other, nor the neat preservation of separate domains for each. We could call this impure or bastard phenomenology, and it is compatible with weak methodological naturalism and liberal naturalism.

Notes

1. While beginning with a thesis in this manner is not a very phenomenological way of doing philosophy, it does at least partly derive from my own prior phenomenological work and is consistent with the hybrid view I will ultimately advocate, in which we are always *in media res*. Speaking of which, it is appropriate here to acknowledge Ricky Sebold for his detailed feedback on this paper and his more general provocations on this theme, the referees for IJPS, audiences at Johannesburg, Melbourne and Canberra where versions of this paper have been given, and to Rafael Winkler for putting the conference on in Johannesburg that first prompted these reflections.

2. Is it a mistake, or phenomenological infelicity, for Sartre to prepare his account of being-for-others by outlining the problems in the history of philosophy regarding the 'reef of solipsism', and thus motivating his account for a better explanation, which includes adequacy to phenomenological experience, but also internal coherence? Is Merleau-Ponty wrong to motivate his account of embodiment via his critique of intellectualism and empiricism and their insufficiencies?
3. It is sometimes said phenomenologists do not argue, but describe or transcendentally reflect (cf. Crowell 1999, 32). I think this opposition is a little exaggerated, however. Phenomenologists regularly maintain that various modes of experience exhibit a hierarchical structure with certain conscious acts claimed to be more or less 'basic', and an argument to this effect can be assembled (cf. Russell and Reynolds 2011, 301–302).

Disclosure Statement

No potential conflict of interest was reported by the author.

References

Baker, L. (2012) *Naturalism and the first-person perspective*, Oxford: Oxford University Press.

Bermudez, J. (1995) 'Transcendental Arguments and Psychology: The Example of O'Shaughnessy on Intentional Action', *Metaphilosophy* 26(4): 379–401.

Burge, T. (2010) *Origins of Objectivity*, Oxford: Oxford University Press.

Crowell, S. (1999) 'The Project of Ultimate Grounding and the Appeal to Intersubjectivity in Recent Transcendental Philosophy', *International Journal of Philosophical Studies* 7(1): 31–54.

Crowell, S. (2013) 'Transcendental Phenomenology and the Seductions of Naturalism: Subjectivity, Consciousness and Meaning', in *Oxford Companion to Contemporary Phenomenology*, edited by D. Zahavi, 25–47, Oxford: Oxford University Press.

DeCaro, M., and D. Macarthur (eds) (2010) *Naturalism and Normativity*, New York, NY: Columbia University Press.

Dennett, D. (1991) *Consciousness Explained*, New York, NY: Little Brown.

Derrida, J. (1974) *Speech and Phenomena*, Evanston: Northwestern University Press.

Derrida, J. (2000) *Aporias*, Palo Alto, CA: Stanford University Press.

Devitt, M. (1996) *Coming to Our Senses: A Naturalistic Program for Semantic Localism*, Cambridge: Cambridge University Press.

Drummond, J (2007) 'Personal Perspectives', *The Southern Journal of Philosophy* 45, 28–44.

Gallagher, S. (2005) *How the Body Shapes the Mind*, Oxford: Oxford University Press.

Gallagher, S. (2012) *Phenomenology*, New York, NY: Palgrave.

Gallagher, S. (2013) 'On the Possibility of Naturalizing Phenomenology', In *Oxford Handbook of Contemporary Phenomenology*, edited by D. Zahavi, 70–93, Oxford: Oxford University Press.

Gallagher, S., and D. Zahavi (2008) *The Phenomenological Mind*, London: Routledge.
Gardner, S. (2007) 'The Limits of Naturalism and the Metaphysics of German Idealism', in *German Idealism: Contemporary Perspectives*, edited by E. Hammer, 19–49, London: Routledge.
Glendinning, S. (2007) *In the Name of Phenomenology*, London: Routledge.
Husserl, E. (1950) *Cartesian Meditations: An Introduction to Phenomenology*, translated by D. Cairns, Dordrecht: Martinus Nijhoff.
Husserl, E. (1965) 'Philosophy as Rigorous Science', in *Phenomenology and the Crisis of Philosophy*, translated by Q. Lauer, New York, NY: Harper.
Husserl, E. (1982) *Ideas Pertaining to a Pure Phenomenology and to a Phenomenological Philosophy*, vol. I, translated by F. Kersten, The Hague: Nijhoff.
Janicaud, D. (2000) 'Toward a Minimalist Phenomenology', *Research in Phenomenology* 30(1): 89–106.
Kornblith, H. (2002) *Knowledge and its Place in Nature*, Oxford: Clarendon Press.
Kornblith, H (2014) *A Naturalistic Epistemology: Selected Papers*, Oxford University Press.
Ladyman, J., and D. Ross (2007) *Everything Must Go*, Oxford: Oxford University Press.
Leiter, B. (2002) *Nietzsche on Morality*, London: Routledge.
Merleau-Ponty, M. (1958) *Phenomenology of Perception*, translated by C. Smith, London: Routledge.
Moran, D. (2008) 'Husserl's transcendental philosophy and the critique of naturalism', *Continental Philosophy Review* 41: 401–425.
Moran, D. (2013) "Let's Look at it Objectively': Why Phenomenology Cannot be Naturalised', *Royal Institute of Philosophy Supplement* 72: 89–115.
Moran, D. (2014) 'Review of S. Crowell, Normativity and Phenomenology in Husserl and Heidegger', *Notre Dame Journal of Philosophical Reviews*. https://ndpr.nd.edu/news/46384-normativity-and-phenomenology-in-husserl-and-heidegger/.
Neta, R. (2007) 'Review of De Caro and Macarthur's *Naturalism in Question*', *Philosophical Review* 116: 662.
Nolan, D. (2015) 'The a Posteriori Armchair', *Australasian Journal of Philosophy* 93(2): 211–231.
Parnas, J., P. Møller, T. Kircher, J. Thalbitzer, L. Jansson, P. Handest, and D. Zahavi (2005) 'EASE: Examination of Anomalous Self-Experience', *Psychopathology* 38(5): 236–258.
Petitot, J., F. Varela, B. Pachoud, and J. Roy (2000) *Naturalising Phenomenology*, CA, Palo Alto: Stanford University Press.
Pigden, C. (2010) 'Coercive Theories of Meaning or Why Language Shouldn't Matter (So Much) to Philosophy', *Logique & Analyse* 210: 151–184.
Price, H. (2004) 'Naturalism without representationalism', in *Naturalism in Question*, edited by M. De Caro and D. Macarthur, 71–98, Cambridge, MA: Harvard University Press.
Reynolds, J (2017) *Phenomenology, Naturalism and Science: A Hybrid and Heretical Proposal*. Forthcoming, London: Routledge.
Romdenh-Romluc, K. (2013) 'First-Person Awareness of Intentions and Immunity to Error through Misidentification', *International Journal of Philosophical Studies* 21(4): 493–514.
Rouse, J. (2005) 'Heidegger on Science and Naturalism', in *Continental Philosophy of Science*, edited by G. Gutting, 123–141, London: Blackwell.
Russell, M., and J. Reynolds (2011) 'Transcendental Arguments about Other Minds', *Philosophy Compass* 6(5): 300–311.
Thompson, E. (2007) *Mind in Life*, Cambridge, MA: Harvard University Press.

Thompson, E. (2014) 'Review of Havi Carel and Darian Meacham (eds.), Phenomenology and Naturalism: Examining the Relationship between Human Experience and Nature, *Notre Dame Philosophical Reviews*. https://ndpr.nd.edu/news/49272-phenomenology-and-naturalism-examining-the-relationship-between-human-experience-and-nature/.

Varela, F., E. Thompson, and E. Rosch (1991) *The Embodied Mind*, Cambridge, MA: MIT Press.

Wheeler, M. (2013) 'Science Friction: Phenomenology, Naturalism and Cognitive Science', *Royal Institute of Philosophy Supplement* 72: 135–167.

Woelert, P. (2012) 'Idealization and external symbolic storage: the epistemic and technical dimensions of theoretic cognition', *Phenomenology and the Cognitive Sciences*. 11(3): 335–366.

Zahavi, D. (2001) *Husserl's Phenomenology*, CA, Palo Alto: Stanford University Press.

Zahavi, D. (2007) 'Killing the Strawman: Dennett and Phenomenology', *Phenomenology and the Cognitive Sciences* 6(1-2): 21–43.

Zahavi, D. (2010) "Naturalized Phenomenology", *Handbook of Phenomenology and Cognitive Science*, 3–20, New York, NY: Springer.

Zahavi, D. (2013) 'Naturalising Phenomenology: A Desideratum or a Category Mistake', *Royal Institute of Philosophy Supplement* 72.

Zahavi, D., and S. Gallagher (2008) 'Reply: A Phenomenology with Legs and Brains', *Abstracta* 2: 86–100.

Two Facets of Belief

Bernhard Weiss

University of Cape Town, South Africa

ABSTRACT
I begin by contrasting two facets of belief: that belief is a response to a sufficiency of evidence and that belief plays a role in one's representation of reality. I claim that these conceptions of belief are in tension because whilst the latter – Representationalism – requires Logical Coherence of belief the former – Thresholdism – conflicts with Logical Coherence. Thus we need to choose between conceptions. Many have argued that the Preface Paradox supports Thresholdism. In contrast I argue that Representationalism has a more plausible response to the paradox.

Here are two plausible facets of our everyday conception of belief. On the one hand beliefs ought to be formed in response to evidence. When the evidence in favour of a proposition is sufficiently strong one should endorse it by forming the appropriate belief. Depending on one's other views one may or may not build into the picture a claim that what counts as sufficient strength varies from context to context. Let's say that when one's level of credence in a proposition,[1] as warranted by the evidence available for it, exceeds a certain (perhaps contextually determined) threshold the proposition is then and only then properly believed. And let's call such views of belief 'Threshold Views'.

On the other hand, a believer forms beliefs as part of an enterprise of representing the world as it is. Loosely we might say that a believer's beliefs form – or ought to form[2] – her description or story of reality. Since the beliefs form a description of *reality* they ought to be *true*; and since they form a *description* of reality they ought to hang together, to cohere in a variety of ways: plausibly they ought, *inter alia*, to be logically coherent, to have explanatory power and/or to make narrative sense.[3] One ought to be able to cite some of one's beliefs in explanation of others; and, if the world's being a certain way follows from its being a way one believes it to be, then one ought to believe it is that certain way. Call such views of belief 'Representational Views'.[4]

A marked difference between Representational and Threshold views might seem to be that the former, as a consequence of thinking that reality exhibits certain coherences, emphasises relations between beliefs whereas the latter highlights each belief's relations to the available evidence. But, despite this apparent difference, there seemingly need not be a sharp conflict between the views. Since Representational views require that beliefs ought to be true and since the only way of securing truth is through sensitivity to the available evidence, Representational Views *seem* to incorporate the Threshold conception. And since Threshold views can allow that the evidence for a belief is mediated by other beliefs and that the evidential status of sets of beliefs are often linked in a variety of ways, the relations between beliefs emphasised by Representationalism *appear* to be accommodated by Thresholdism.

Indeed it seems quite clear that routinely the two sorts of view march in step. Most of our mundane beliefs are both well-supported by our evidence and play their roles in forming narratives, explanatory theories or other descriptions of reality. Despite this the two sorts of view are arguably quite clearly incompatible.

Let the Logical Coherence of belief be the claim that an agent's belief set ought to be Consistent and Closed under logical consequence, where these are characterised as follows:

$\{B1...Bn\}$ is Consistent iff it is not the case that $\{B1...Bn\} \vdash Q \wedge \neg Q$.

S is Closed under logical consequence iff, if $\{B1...Bn\} \subseteq S$ and $\{B1...Bn\} \vdash C$ then $C \in S$.

I'll now argue that Representationalism and Thresholdism are incompatible because Thresholdism entails denial of Logical Coherence whereas Representationalism entails Logical Coherence[5].

1. Thresholdism and Logical Coherence

If $\{B1...Bn\} \vdash C$ then the credence levels of B1 to Bn set a minimum on the credence level of C: $Cr(C) \geq 1-(1-Cr(B1))-...-(1-Cr(Bn))$. But since this credence level may be below the lowest credence level of B1 to Bn, we may have a situation in which Thresholdism requires belief in B1 to Bn but precludes proper belief in C, violating Closure. Likewise we can take C to be $Q \wedge \neg Q$, in which case each of B1...Bn might be properly believed, even though $\{B1...Bn\} \vdash Q \wedge \neg Q$. Thus Logical Coherence is violated on the Threshold view.

A Thresholdist might object by claiming that the evidence pertinent to setting credence levels will simply include that transmitted by logical entailment. Were this so, the mere fact that $\{B1...Bn\} \vdash C$ will ensure that the evidential support, and hence the credence level, of $\{B1...Bn\}$ will be transmitted to C. Though this, for all I have to say, may be a plausible view, two points should be noted. First, this seems to war with the motivation for Thresholdism, which is to take credence levels as fundamental and then to explain inferential relations in terms of the transmission of credence levels. (I discuss this aspect of the proposal below.) Were we simply to build inferential practice into the conception of evidence we would either leave adoption of that practice without rational motivation or we would provide it with a non-Threshold (one presumes semantic) justification. Neither option is appealing from the Thresholdist's point of view. Second, Thresholdism is supposed to acquire an advantage over Representationalism precisely because it adopts a novel understanding of inferential practice and one which rejects Logical Coherence (again, see below). On the current proposal it would forfeit these putative advantages.

2. Representationalism and Logical Coherence

It is no part of the contrast between the two conceptions of belief that they should react differently to the semantics for the logical constants and for inferential practice. So each party can accept that the semantic account of deductive consequence is correct, even if they differ over its explanatory function.

But in that case we can say that if $P1\ldots Pn \vdash C$ and $P1\ldots Pn$ are true then C is also true; but this means that if $\{P1\ldots Pn\}$ are taken to be a description of reality – are believed – then $\{P1\ldots Pn,C\}$ ought not be taken to be a description of a distinct way the world might be. So if S believes $\{P1\ldots Pn\}$ and knows that $P1\ldots Pn \vdash C$, S ought rationally to believe $\{P1\ldots Pn,C\}$. The reason for this is that S ought to reason (roughly) as follows: $\{P1\ldots Pn\}$ and $\{P1\ldots Pn,C\}$ represent the same way the world might be; $\{P1\ldots Pn\}$ represents reality; so $\{P1\ldots Pn, C\}$ represents reality. For S to draw this conclusion is for S to endorse that set of beliefs. Closure thus follows.

Also if $\{P1\ldots Pn\}$ are inconsistent then they cannot all be true so $\{P1\ldots Pn\}$ do not represent a way the world might be. Thus, since $\{P1\ldots Pn\}$ cannot play a representational role, those propositions ought not to be jointly believed. Consistency thus follows. And Representationalism requires Logical Coherence.

Simple though these arguments are, I think they are compelling. The reason why Thresholdists think that they can reconcile their view of belief with belief's representational role is that they see this task as being quite different to squaring the view with the semantic conception of deductive inference. They tend to suppose that, if they can show how practitioners' use of deductive inference is sanctioned on their account of belief, then that suffices to accommodate belief's representational role. But this is surely false; the task is not merely to accommodate actual inferential practice – we shall return to some of these issues later – the task also requires that we make sense of reflection on that practice. Reflecting in semantic terms on that practice – an enterprise which it ought to be no part of Thresholdism to reject – we quickly see that the representational role of belief requires Logical Coherence.

Christensen argues against an attempt to motivate Logical Coherence by appealing to the representational view of belief by arguing that even if we accept that our aim as investigators is to assert the error-free story of the world, we cannot use this to argue that it would be irrational to tolerate inconsistent sets of beliefs.[6] And he supports this view by appeal to actual practice, namely, our tolerance of Preface propositions – an issue that will soon move to centre-stage. Let us set aside the latter issue for the moment; Christensen's claim seems to be that, though a belief enters into an inconsistent set, we can still see that belief as entering into an error-free representation of the world. No doubt that is true; but, equally doubtlessly, it is devoid of any interest. So he claims more. He claims that a belief may be included in a *rationally tolerated* inconsistent set, yet still enter into the error-free representation of the world. The latter guarantees the belief's representational role; the former shows that Logical Coherence is not required by that role. Obviously for the argument to be completely persuasive we need to agree with Christensen that beliefs are, on occasion, included in rationally tolerated inconsistent sets. And that's why he provides us with Preface propositions which seem to generate inconsistency in rationally persuasive ways. And indeed we might reject his reading of these cases. But even without the helpful examples the account seems to succeed in driving a wedge between Representationalism and Logical Coherence. For unless we can show that there are no rationally tolerated inconsistent sets of belief, Logical Coherence seems to be one thing and representational role quite another.

We need to distinguish between different sorts of Representationalism. A weak version would claim that it is essential to belief that a belief *can* play a representational role; a stronger version would claim that it is essential to belief that a belief *ought* to play a representational role. Christensen secures at most weak Representationalism; but it is the stronger form that we are focused on. Our claim was that it is the proper role of a belief to enter into a description of the world; but it is quite clear that, although the beliefs Christensen draws our attention to can enter into such descriptions, that is no response to our semantic argument showing that they do not, in the envisaged circumstances, figure in such descriptions. And, since his claim is that such belief sets are rationally tolerated, he can't argue that in these circumstances the belief fails to fulfil its normative role. Should we be interested in strong rather than weak Representationalism? Yes, because the weak view is utterly anodyne. In effect it amounts to no more than the trivial claim that any belief is capable of being true. For, if a belief is apt to be true, then it is very hard to see why it should not be combined with other beliefs in a potential description of the way things are.

I suppose a Thresholdist might choose to reject the arguments by distancing the semantic, and, arguably, theoretical, machinery from pre-theoretic conceptions of representation. If she did so she might then deny the representational lessons drawn from the semantic account. But the cost is high; though semantic theory is *theory* it should be seen as an attempt to systematise notions relevant to representation, notions such as truth and falsity.[7] Most Thresholdists should thus concede that Representational conceptions of belief are wedded to Logical Coherence and thus are at odds with their conception of belief.

So it seems, provided that Logical Coherence is seen as an ingredient of Representationalism, we have genuinely competing conceptions of the normative role of belief. I turn now to the task of deciding between them. Here I use the capacity of each conception to deal with the (so-called)[8] Preface Paradox as something of a test of its adequacy.

3. The Preface Paradox

I've argued that Representationalism and Thresholdism are incompatible since the former requires Logical Coherence and Logical Coherence is incompatible with Thresholdism. So we need to choose between them and, in recent literature,[9] a number of writers have argued that the Preface Paradox (see Makinson 1965) shows that Logical Coherence is insupportable. If their contention is right then clearly the Preface Paradox shows that we should reject Representationalism. Moreover, the motive for rejecting Logical Coherence is one or another brand of Thresholdism, rejection of Representationalism thus goes along with acceptance of Thresholdism; so, though Representationalism doesn't explicitly enter the debate – or does so rarely – we can see the debate as instructive in the choice between these conceptions of belief.[10]

Here is a presentation of the paradox. Let S be the author of a book in which she makes the following claims: P1, P2, ..., Pn. S is sincere in her work and has been careful in writing her book; so S believes each of P1, ..., Pn. And let us suppose she is fully aware that she has these beliefs. But S also knows that it is unheard of for a book as ambitious as hers to be without error. So she has good reason to believe that at least one of P1, ..., Pn is false.[11] Call the proposition $\neg P1 \vee ... \vee \neg Pn$, *Preface*.

So we have:

S believes $\neg P1 \vee ... \vee \neg Pn$

S believes P1, ..., S believes Pn

By Logical Coherence, since S knows she has these beliefs:

S ought to believe $P1 \wedge ... \wedge Pn$[12]

By Logical Coherence again:

S ought to believe $(P1 \wedge ... \wedge Pn) \wedge (\neg P1 \vee ... \vee \neg Pn)$

But Logical Coherence again quickly shows that then S ought to believe an explicit contradiction, which is absurd.

This is the skeleton of the Preface Paradox, but it can be fleshed out in at least two importantly distinct ways – as Douven and Uffink 2003, 391 make clear. Each of the beliefs of the form *S believes Pi* will most likely have a level of credence which is less than certainty and one might see the level of credence of S's belief in *Preface* as reflecting no more than the aggregate of these uncertainties. So construed, the Preface and Lottery paradoxes are very similar and, perhaps, to be solved in the manner suggested by Douven and Uffink. I shall be concerned with a different version of the paradox namely that in which the *Preface* proposition has independent support drawn, say, from a knowledge of the history of scholarship or of one's own scholarship or, perhaps, theories in cognitive psychology. So the level of credence accorded to belief in *Preface* need not be a mere aggregate of the uncertainties in the beliefs in each Pi. It's clear that we might have Preface paradoxes which take this form and clear too from the intuitive plausibility that mathematicians – who may be justified in being certain of their propositions – no less than historians, may be struck by a well-supported humility when it comes to writing their prefaces.

How should we deal with the paradox? Well, faced with the absurd outcome of this piece of reasoning we have a number of options:

1. We might find fault with the inferential steps leading to the paradox.
2. We might relieve S of commitment to one of the propositions leading to the paradox.
3. We might explain away the appearance of paradox, while accepting the reasoning and premises which lead to a contradiction.

Some preliminary comments on each option:

- The most obvious way of implementing option (1) is to find fault with the steps of the argument which invoke Logical Coherence. And the most obvious motivation for this is to adopt a Threshold conception of belief.
- Since the assumption is that S believes each of the propositions of her book, option (2) needs to be implemented by finding a way for S to withhold belief in *Preface*.
- *Option (3) needs to explain why the development of a commitment to a contradiction is not sufficient for development of a troubling paradox.*
- Options (2) and (3), in contrast to option (1), involve acceptance of Logical Coherence.

I turn now to discussion of option (1). Deductive arguments, as we've noted, set a minimum on the credence level of the conclusion, given the credence levels of the premises. Since rational belief is governed by the threshold principle one may rationally believe the premises of such an argument yet rationally withhold belief in the conclusion because the credence level of the conclusion is below the threshold. If the premises of an argument are P1, ..., Pn and they are logically independent of one another, the conclusion is C and Cr(P) is the credence level of P then[13]:

$$Cr(C) \geq 1-(1-Cr(P1))- \ldots -(1-Cr(Pn))$$

Since $Cr(Pi)<1$, when Pi is not certain, the minimum credence level of C will tend to decrease as the number of non-certain premises increases. The Thresholdist now notices that in the Preface Paradox we are considering ambitious works, which, we may suppose, include large numbers of claims. Thus, though each claim may warrant rational belief, it is plausible to suppose that the conjunction of those claims – *Book*, the denial of *Preface* – may not warrant rational belief. So there is no rational commitment to a contradiction and the paradox is resolved.

But, since this position involves rationally condoning a set of beliefs which deductively yield a contradiction, it seems the Thresholdist has deprived herself of the ability to see the force of reductio arguments. 'Not so', she replies. We need to separate good from bad reductio arguments.[14] When the number of premises in a reductio argument is small, the argument shows rational incoherence in credence levels for anyone who takes the premises all to be above threshold value; when not, there is no rational incoherence in credence levels and thus, rationally, nothing amiss with the set of beliefs. So the effectiveness of a reductio argument is not a mere matter of form; rather it depends on the number of premises in the argument, their credence levels and the threshold set on rational belief.

Mark Kaplan (1996) attempts to argue against the view that the effectiveness of a reductio is linked to numbers in this way – numbers of premises and level of threshold – arguing that on occasion we can see the incoherence in a story yielding a contradiction, despite the fact that the story is made up of many independent claims. And indeed it seems implausible that any refutation of a complex theory with many premises will have to be, in effect, a refutation of part of the theory involving a small subset of its premises. Why should complex theories be resistant to refutation in a way that small theories are not?

It would seem that we have, in our use and conception of reductio arguments, a feature of belief which is supported only by the Representational conception. As I mentioned above, the Thresholdist doesn't see this because she thinks she has an account which meshes with actual use of reductio arguments. And maybe she does – that descriptive issue is hard to judge – but she doesn't appear to have an account which meshes with our reflective understanding of those arguments. For nothing about that understanding betrays a sensitivity to the number of premises in an argument.

Let me leave the debate about reductio arguments inconclusively at this point. I want, rather, to focus on two assumptions underlying the Thresholdist's account. The Preface Paradox stems from the plausible observation that ambitious works are apt to be mistaken in part and thereby to include falsities. The Thresholdist's solution to the paradox assumes that the relevant sense of ambition relates to the number of claims made. But there's no reason why we should go along with this assumption. Below I'll canvass reasons for rejecting it. Another assumption is that the level of credence in *Preface* is suitably related to the level of credence in *Book*, as established by deductive argument from the individual propositions forming the text. For the assumption is that when the level of credence in *Preface* exceeds the threshold, the minimum level of credence in *Book*, as established by deductive argument, is below the threshold, viz., if Cr(*Preface*)≥t then Cr(*Book*)<t (even though Cr(*Book*)≥1-(1-Cr(P1))-...-(1-Cr(Pn))), where t is the threshold value. So deductive argument only serves to confirm that Cr(*Book*) exceeds a value which may be below t. The Thresholdist simply *supposes* that it is below t. But this need not be so, since the *Preface* proposition – at least in the version of the paradox I am interested in – has *independent* support, there need be no suitable link between these credences. Let us turn to examine each assumption, starting with the first.

In at least some presentations of the Preface Paradox the author, reflecting on human or scholarly frailty, is struck by humility in light of the ambitions of her work. The upshot of her humble reflection is that she comes to believe that at least one of her claims is false. Now, in most presentations the ambition of the work relates to the number of claims it propounds, and the humble reflection to the likelihood of at least one of those claims being false. But this is surely incidental to the underlying problem, which simply has to do with reflection on one's cognitive frailty. Frailty may infect the way a claim is based non-inferentially on evidence but may also affect the complexity of inference and argument used in the attempt to establish a claim. Let's suppose that our author advances a relatively small number of claims, but uses elaborate argumentation in supporting each claim.[15] We may suppose too that each claim is surprising to most investigators in the relevant area. Now our author realises that given the complexity of her argumentation it is likely that at least one of her demonstrations is fallacious. She may also know that the history of the subject is that surprising claims advanced on the basis of inadequate demonstrations are generally false. So she advances the standard *Preface* proposition and thereby generates a Preface Paradox. But this is a paradox which seems unlikely to be resolved by the Thresholdist's methodology of rejecting Logical Coherence. For it seems highly likely that the level of credence warranted in *Book* will exceed the threshold and we will have a rationally sanctioned belief in a contradiction, or, at least, rationally sanctioned beliefs in contradictory propositions. Indeed the credence levels themselves will be incoherent.

Here's an illustration of this kind of counter-example. Suppose our author is a physicist whose limited number of claims are all derived from uncontroversial claims and thus warrant a credence level of close to 1. However the proofs are complex and the results surprising; so reasoning outside of physics the author is led to the *Preface* proposition. Since her claims all warrant a credence level of close to 1, deductive arguments based on those claims will confer a minimum credence level for their conclusions which is also close to 1. But here one of those conclusions – the conjunction of her claims, *Book* – is the denial of the

Preface proposition. Thresholdism cannot help her to find rational fault with endorsing these contradictory propositions.

Levels of credence are, let it be said, somewhat mysterious. However we can take them as (idealised) measures of the rational confidence one *should* have in a proposition, given one's evidence. That we should see them this way is encouraged by Thresholdist's accounts of, for instance, deductive inference. Consider the account we were given of the Thresholdist view of reductio arguments. The claim there was that the deductive argument establishes a minimum credence level for the conclusion given the credence levels of the premises; and that in the Preface case the credence level rationally established for the denial of the *Preface* proposition will be below the threshold value. So there is no rationally incoherent attribution of credence levels. Thus credence levels are constrained rationally – the effect here is universally taken to be that they comply with the laws of probability[16] – and independently of the agent's actual subjective confidences in her beliefs. The basis for the account will have to be a rationally constrained attribution of credence levels to propositions in light of the agent's evidence. Thus each $Cr(Pi)$ is an objective measure of the rational credence level warranted by the agent's evidence for Pi. $Cr(Preface)$ is, likewise, an objective measure of the rational level of credence warranted by the agent's evidence for *Preface*. But what is that evidence? Well, stories differ; but on the story one may tell, and may do so with good motivation, that evidence is related to the subjective likelihood of agents such as our author having made a mistake, many writers call this second or higher order evidence. And the point is that the credence level established by evidence relating to the subjective likelihood of a mistake may well come apart from the rational credences relating to each Pi. That is, we may well have a situation in which $Cr(Preface) \geq t$ yet $Cr(Book) \geq 1-(1-Cr(P1))-\ldots-(1-Cr(Pn)) \geq t$. And this would be paradoxical for a Thresholdist.

Here's an extreme case realising this kind of counter-example. Let's consider an arithmetician. She may well be warranted in having a credence level of 1 in $P1 \wedge \ldots \wedge Pn$; yet on other grounds – relating to the likelihood of her having made a mistake – warranted in having a rational credence in *Preface* which is also over the threshold. So her credence levels are rationally incoherent.

The upshot of the discussion is this. The Thresholdist succeeds in explaining away many likely cases of the Preface Paradox. But the cases above, which I've tried to argue are possible and which I've tried to illustrate, rely on the same intuitions which motivate those presentations of the paradox which, as it happens, lend themselves to Thresholdist treatment. So the Thresholdist has failed to address the source of the preface paradox.

Let us move on to look at the second two options, both of which involve accepting Logical Coherence and thus rejecting Thresholdism. First option (2), on which the author believes every proposition in her book and, because she accepts Logical Coherence, believes their conjunction, i.e., she believes *Book*.

But she doesn't believe *Preface*. Of course the higher order evidence that had been taken to support *Preface* is an uncontested feature of the paradox, so our author needs to find some way of rationally assimilating it. Seemingly the only plausible suggestion here is that argued for by Kaplan (1996): the evidence doesn't support *Preface* but does support the author's recognition that her belief in *Book* is unlikely to be true. Many have argued against the coherence of both having a belief and recognising that the belief is unlikely to be true. In itself this is an interesting enough issue. So it is tackled in its own section, which immediately follows.[17]

Beliefs that are Probably False

There appears to be an implausibility in conjoining the claims:

1. I believe that P.
2. The belief that P is probably false.

In fact, one might suspect that we are treading in territory overshadowed by Moore's paradox. But, whereas Moore's paradox conjured up a state of mind that it is impossible to make sense of, I don't think that the conjunction of the two claims above achieves the same. In Moore's case the claims are unacceptable because the speaker both commits herself to the truth of P and also revokes that commitment. And this incoherence makes it impossible to make sense of the speaker's overall commitments. In the present case no such incoherence appears to be in the offing. That this is so is partly confirmed by ordinary uses of language. Witness the following case: a (humble!) political analyst is asked during an interview what share of the vote he expects the ruling party to achieve in the next election. He replies that he expects it to be around 60%; but then immediately qualifies this, saying that he is probably wrong in this because he usually gets it wrong.[18] However he reaffirms that that is his expectation. The analyst's state of mind seems easy to make sense of. Telling a story about current patterns of voting and the likely events which will influence them, he arrives at his prediction of a 60% share for the ruling party. Telling a story about his own ability to predict these questions accurately, he comes to believe that he is not likely to be right, viz., that his belief is likely to be false. Nothing here throws up an incoherence. Of course the analyst's concerns about his own reliability might lead him to withhold judgement on the question; but, if it is important for him to tell a story about voting patterns, then those higher order concerns need not inevitably have this result. Having to tell a story exposes a believer to a risk of error; but that risk can be worth taking and there's certainly no purely epistemic or rational reason to avoid that risk completely; quite the reverse, achieving knowledge is an inevitably risky business.

And from the Representational perspective, the analyst's comments appear to be readily understandable. Acquiring evidence about his own epistemic reliability, helps him to tell a story about the likelihood of certain of his beliefs being true but doesn't help him to tell a story about patterns of voting which differs from his original story. So, again, if he is well-motivated to tell such a story, he need not (yet) have a reason for giving up the original.

The appearance of an intolerable tension arises, I think, as follows. If, in general, to believe that Q is to ascribe to Q a high probability of being true, then my belief in P requires ascribing a high probability to P's truth and my belief that my belief that P is probably false requires ascribing a high probability to the truth of the claim that P is probably false. But the latter naturally commits one to ascribing a high probability to the falsity of P itself, i.e., to ascribing a low probability to the truth of P. And these commitments are now in conflict. But the premise of the argument begs the question. Indeed, if credences reflect the probabilities one ought to ascribe to propositions, then the premise begs the question against Representationalism. For Representationalism entails Logical Coherence which can, on occasion, require commitment to beliefs which may fall below any chosen threshold in credence level.

The question is thus apt to be pushed further back: what kind of commitment can an agent jointly sustain in relation to the propositions that P and that P is probably false, which could justify ascribing to her the *beliefs* that P and that P is probably false. Thus far my answer has been that the agent might be committed by the demands of one explanatory programme (and supplementary premises) to P and by another (and supplementary premises) to 'P is probably false'. But obviously we would need to see her commitment to each explanatory programme as indicative of belief in the propositions it implicates. We might test the nature of these commitments by thinking about how the beliefs figure in action or in dispositions to participate in one or another betting situation. But once again, to accept that these are *essential* to the nature of belief is to beg the question against the Representationalist. Another sort of test, which doesn't prejudge the issue, might focus on sincere assertion and warranted ascription of the belief. And my point about relating the story of the political analyst is to make plausible that, on this kind of test, we may well have an agent who believes both that P and that P is probably false. She sincerely makes the assertions and we can make sense of her state of mind via ascriptions of those beliefs.

A generous reader might follow me thus far but protest that none of this *shows the rational admissibility* of the analyst's state of mind; exceptionally, we can be driven to ascribe incompatible beliefs to an agent, but this fails to show the rational acceptability of the agent holding those beliefs.[19] Fair enough; I rest my case on my assertion that the analyst's overall state of mind *seems* readily intelligible and, thus far, I can find no non-question-begging reason for rejecting this appearance as deceptive.

Let's briefly contrast the case with that of Moore's paradox. Suppose S asserts the sentence 'P but I don't believe P'. This appears paradoxical precisely because we cannot make sense of someone sincerely making the assertion, no matter how we elaborate the case. In contrast, I've described two (actual) cases where the relevant assertion is easily assimilated and seems to cause no fuss. Because

Moore's paradox strikes us as paradoxical we find ourselves having to explain why we cannot make sense of the (sincere) assertion and, at least in part, the reason is that we cannot answer the question whether S is committed, say, to a logical consequence of P. But in the case we envisage this simply isn't so: the agent is committed to any such consequence, but thereby derives no grounds for taking the consequence to be likely. At worst we simply generate another instance of the original position.

Another source of worry about beliefs known to be unlikely to be true is that one might well feel queasy about the extent of beliefs to which a believer is committed and about the inclusion of those beliefs in practical reasoning. Given a reasonably rich supply of well-supported beliefs a believer will find herself committed to all the (known) logical consequences of them, many of which may have a miniscule chance of being true.[20] And, to be sure, a believer is unlikely to avow having these beliefs and is unlikely to deploy them in practical reasoning. Indeed; but are these reasons to think that the believer isn't properly *committed* to these beliefs? I think not. Given the abstruse, unmotivated and often tedious reasoning needed to arrive at these beliefs it surely comes as no surprise that the believer doesn't actually form the bulk of them and is thus not in a position to avow having them. But this doesn't alter the fact that she is properly committed to them and should recognise this, if persuaded to follow the awkward reasoning. And, indeed, she should realise the importance of such commitments in reductio arguments, which lose none of their force as the reasoning takes in more and more premises.

It is also no surprise that such beliefs do not figure in practical reasoning and this for two reasons. First, as we've just noticed, the relevant beliefs are, by and large, commitments rather than acknowledged beliefs. And, second, given that they are known to be unlikely to be true the believer will know that actions based on them are unlikely to be successful. The issue now becomes very murky because opponents will question in what sense the relevant propositions are believed, if they properly do not figure in practical reasoning. But again, and as remarked above, the Representationalist can fall back on her view of the role of belief in forming a representation of how the world is: beliefs have a role in theoretical reasoning, which need not always be aligned with a role in practical reasoning. A better test than involvement in practical reasoning, for possession of such beliefs is sincere avowal and warranted ascription.

Christensen (2004, section 4.2) argues against versions of option (2) by questioning the coherence of the asymmetry in refusing to believe *Preface* in the case of one's *own* book whilst unproblematically doing so in similar circumstances when *another's* book is in question. The argument depends on viewing the two cases as analogous; but they are not. In one's own case one assimilates the evidence for *Preface* in light of one's commitment to *Book*; and the argument is that when one does so one can be led to appreciate that *Book* is unlikely to be true, nonetheless one is rationally committed to it. But in the case of someone else's book one has no commitment to the corresponding *Book* proposition. If, however, one reads and is convinced by one's colleague's book then the cases are analogous; in fact, they are essentially the same and one should refuse to believe *Preface*.

Let me admit that I'm unclear whether option (2) is ultimately defensible. There is an undoubted sense of strain in combining propositions (1) and (2) and more work than I've managed to do here needs to be done fully to dissipate that tension, to show that it betokens epistemic situations which are merely unusual and best avoided, rather than situations of incoherence. So let me provide a Representationalist defence of option (3).

The Nature of Paradoxes

Option (3) aims to dispel the air of paradox infecting the Preface Paradox. Accordingly we do not need to subscribe to beliefs which one recognises are improbable to be true. For, though option (3) adheres to Logical Coherence this only commits her to belief in (or commitment to) propositions which haven't been shown to have above threshold levels of credence. But this is not to accept beliefs which have been shown to have credence levels which are below the threshold value. Secondly, it is consistent with her position to deny credences as a way of making sense of the evidence for a proposition, or, perhaps better, she might presume inferential practice and allow that credences measure evidence for a proposition which includes that accruing through inference. So despite the fact that a narrow credence theorist might object to belief in a proposition, which is below threshold level in credence; she can insist that on a proper conception of evidence, on a broad credence view, the belief is well-supported.[21]

The Preface Paradox derives a contradiction from propositions which are apparently rationally believed by reasoning which appears to be rationally sanctioned. So if deriving a contradiction from propositions which are apparently rationally believed by reasoning which appears to be rationally sanctioned is to develop a paradox the Preface Paradox is a paradox. I know of no better definition of a paradox so, in support of option (3), I won't attempt to argue in favour of an alternative definition of the concept of paradoxicality, which fails to apply to the Preface Paradox; rather I want more simply to show how the Preface paradox is quite different in character from some other paradoxes.

Let's first contrast Russell's Paradox with the Sorites Paradox. Russell's Paradox is a single piece of reasoning which can be reproduced by any thinker; it always involves reasoning from the naive comprehension principle to a contradiction. Things change when we move to the Sorites Paradox. There it is clear that we can think of many versions of the paradox: some involve our use of colour predicates and envisage pails of paint, others stick with colour predicates but imagine various projections of light; and yet others involve the predicate 'child' and an individual at different stages of her life marked, say, by the number of her heart beats; still others involve the predicate 'bald' and a sequence of progressively more hairy men. What makes all these cases cases of the same paradox are *two* things: first, similar reasoning from similar premises is involved in each case and, second, there is reason to suppose that structurally similar solutions will apply in each case. So, if one has indeed solved the Sorites Paradox, then it should be obvious how the solution applies in each realisation of the paradox so as to dissolve the contradiction.

Now in this respect the Preface Paradox is far more like the Sorites than Russell's Paradox. For we can imagine a whole slew of realisations of it: Prefaces for history books, for physics books, for autobiographies; and, if my reasoning above is correct, *Preface* propositions based on the mere possibility of having made a mistaken observation and others involving the likelihood of errors in reasoning. So, if the paradox is interestingly akin to traditional paradoxes it is akin to Sorites-like paradoxes rather than paradoxes like Russell's. But is the paradox really akin to the Sorites? I claimed above that one of the reasons we thought the various realisations of the Sorites were instances of the same paradox was not merely a product of the common structure of the paradox in each case but also a sense that the same solution will apply in each instance. Though the structure of instances of the Preface Paradox are, indeed, similar; I don't see any reason to think that a single form of solution applies in each case.

Consider two realisations of the Preface Paradox: that involving a humble zoological author and that involving a similarly humble historical author. Each completes her book and asserts a relevant version of the *Preface* proposition, which, we do well to note, are different propositions alleging a falsity amongst different sets of propositions. Each goes on to realise that she is now trucking with a contradiction and thereby realises a need to revise her beliefs. But neither, as things stand, has any rational guidance on where the revision ought to be made. In order to make the appropriate revision the one author stands in need of zoological information and/or information about her reliability as a zoologist, the other historical information and/or information about her reliability as a historian. There is scant reason to think that a priori reasoning of the same pattern will dissolve the paradox in each case.

We are tempted to think otherwise; but the temptation is illusory. And here is how it emerges. Let's suppose that the zoologist does a little more work and she discovers that the claim made at the start of section 2.4 is false. So here's where the revision ought to be made and, in the second edition, the correction is implemented. Does this dissolve the paradox? The temptation is to say that it doesn't because the preface to the second edition will, no doubt, include a *Preface* proposition re-igniting the paradox. But this is mistaken; the zoologist hasn't escaped the general predicament but has a *different* task to find the apt revision in her beliefs. In effect, her task now is as different to the task she originally had, as was the historian's. Different information will be relevant and a revision quite unrelated to her previous one might take place in response to it.

So what we have is an inescapable predicament for our reflective author and, moreover, one which she can appreciate to be inescapable. But this, in itself, supplies no reason to suppose that the predicament requires anything like a uniform response; rather we have an endless series of problems generated in similar fashion but calling for quite different responses. So the Preface Paradox is, in this way, quite different from the Sorites and, so far as I can see, from all other traditional paradoxes. Though we may insist on calling it a paradox, we shouldn't let that fool us into supposing it has or requires a single solution.

As presented we know that option (3) is not consistent with Thresholdism because it accepts Logical Coherence. But we might wonder whether in its limited acceptance of an inconsistent set of beliefs it is consistent with Representationalism. It would be an unappealing version of Representationalism which required that all belief sets, qua *belief* sets, *be* consistent; since clearly a rational agent may well function with a set of beliefs which she doesn't know to be inconsistent. And indeed revelation of the inconsistency may take a good deal of insight, which the agent cannot be criticised for failing to achieve purely on grounds of rationality. But option (3) allows that an agent may function with a set of beliefs which she knows to be inconsistent; though, because she accepts Logical Coherence she will recognise that she ought not to do so and thus seeks an appropriate revision. The question is: does Representationalism require such an agent to cease believing in the propositions from the acknowledged inconsistent set? Does it require her to take *Book*-and-*Preface* off the shelf?

Agnosticism, in the circumstances, doesn't seem to be a consequence of Representationalism itself. Representationalism requires that it is essential to belief that it *ought* to play a representational role; a belief may fail to do so when for instance it enters into an inconsistent set, which is not known to be inconsistent. What Representationalism requires is that beliefs ought not to enter into such sets; and thus that a believer who knows that her belief set is inconsistent ought not to tolerate the situation. She can manifest her intolerance quite adequately by seeking a suitable revision in her beliefs; and can rationally argue against agnosticism by noting that, were that the right response, recognition of one's fallibility – that at least one of one's beliefs is false – would immediately and quite intolerably lead to rejection of all one's beliefs, to a suspension of belief *tout court*. The point is that Logical Coherence establishes an epistemic obligation on the agent, but it fails (in itself) to inform her about *how* she ought best to discharge that obligation. Thresholdism, in contrast, fails to discern an obligation because it fails to see any rational fault in the agent's belief set.

However, here is a niggling worry. How ought an agent to reason from her beliefs when she knows them to be inconsistent? Should she think herself entitled to infer to the truth of any arbitrary proposition? Many accounts of belief revision would require an agent to suspend belief in such cases, but, as I've just remarked, the pervasiveness of Preface situations militates against such a reaction. The agent has to revise her beliefs without suspending them, knowing too that they're inconsistent. Finding a satisfying response to how she ought to accomplish this is, I suggest, an important lesson of the Preface situation.

I cannot offer anything like a decent response here. But two things are worth noting. First, any theory of belief revision which invokes a principle of conservatism in belief revision – such as Quine's maxim of minimum mutilation[22] – will require retaining as many beliefs as is consistent with restoring consistency or expunging recalcitrance. Realising that a belief set is inconsistent requires revision in belief but – on pain of violating the maxim – cannot require blanket suspension of belief. I suppose one might argue that suspension of belief is simply a transitional step intervening between the discovery of recalcitrance and reinstatement of belief and that the maxim applies only to the initial and final stages. But it is by no means clear that this is feasible for two reasons. (i) As long as inferential moves go along with beliefs – about, for instance, the holding of conditionals – an agent will not both be able to suspend beliefs and carry out the requisite inferential manoeuvres in order to work out the repercussions of a change in belief. (ii) The agent will need to work out just which set of beliefs are those which need to be suspended, which, of course, she needs to do in advance of suspending belief in that set. Thus, in general, she will have to find a way logically to operate with a set of beliefs known to be problematic.[23] There are proposals which can help us here. For instance, on Tennant's proposal[24] discovery of a contradiction imposes revisions of belief determined by two things: (i) the relations of justification between beliefs mediated by inferential linkages, which delineate on what basis a belief was formed or is held; and (ii) the degree to which a belief is entrenched in one's scheme of beliefs. Given these two features, discovery of a contradiction will not trip off an immediate suspension of belief but will initiate a process of systematically withdrawing endorsement from a specific range of beliefs which averts commitment to the contradiction and does so while 'minimally mutilating' the existing belief scheme. So, provided a believer's system of beliefs is seen as a structured scheme rather than a mere set of beliefs, there are ways to deal with the epistemic situation short of blanket agnosticism.

Of course, as long as she maintains the beliefs in question, as long, that is, as she has not succeeded in finding a suitable revision in belief the agent will be committed to believing a contradiction. What sense are we to make of this? Well, given that the agent knows her beliefs are inconsistent she knows they jointly entail a contradiction and, thus, recognising the norm implicated in Logical Coherence, she knows she ought either to believe a contradiction or revise her beliefs. Since she is unable to believe a contradiction (and presumably realises this), she must recognise the obligation to revise her beliefs. So, as long as she avoids this, no doubt, substantial, task – which she may well do for lack of time, energy or inclination – she warrants a degree of epistemic censure. Of course, since she still functions with this set of beliefs in advance of making a suitable revision, there will be consequences of subsets of them that she discovers and thus ought to believe; and here she likely complies with the obligation by forming the relevant belief. The point is that the norm remains fully operative in all these cases. Of course, there is a humbling moral for a Representationalist: if she is properly aware of her epistemic frailty then any reasonably ambitious epistemic project will fail to deliver a belief set which, as a whole, represents reality. A goal of belief continually evades us and the norms governing belief are never fully satisfied. But perhaps this is an apt lesson to derive from knowledge of one's epistemic inadequacies.

A Hybrid Approach

A Thresholdist might react to my arguments against her solution to the Preface Paradox by conceding the point in the problematic cases I raised. In these cases credence levels have been assigned incoherently and thus a change in those attributions – with consequent revisions of belief – is called for. So in these cases she might choose to adopt a version of option (3) and might do so consistently with Thresholdism, precisely because Logical Coherence needn't drive the need for revision; rather incoherence in credence levels would do that work.

That position is certainly consistent but it concedes enough to render the Preface Paradox inert as a motive for adopting Thresholdism. For the Thresholdist's solution is itself incomplete and requires supplementation by a solution structurally analogous to one open to a Representationalist. Moreover it is hard to see how to motivate the hybrid view over the pure implementation of option (3) by the Representationalist. So as things stand the Preface Paradox, though not decisive, seems to provide some support for Representationalism in preference to Thresholdism.

Notes

1. So I'm thinking of credence as a measure of the confidence that a believer ought to have in the truth of a proposition, given her state of information in relation to that proposition.
2. The reason for taking this to be a normative requirement is that I shall want to allow that on a representational view beliefs can fail to participate in what deserves to be called a description of reality.
3. I imagine that there might be different forms of the view, each of which is distinguished by the ways in which it thinks beliefs need to 'hang together'. Plausibly these differences will be driven by differing metaphysical views about the nature of reality.
4. Thresholdism seems to align with a naturalistic view of belief – belief as an agent's reaction to the input of her surroundings – and Representationalism with the phenomenological tradition – belief as first personal account of one's world. Though this is highly suggestive, the story is likely to be far more complex.
5. There is, of course, considerable debate in the literature over whether normative principles derived from Consistency and Closure apply to belief. Macfarlane

(unpublished) provides an exhaustive discussion of these principles, which he dubs 'Bridging Principles'. Though he is sceptical about many forms of Bridging Principle, he is inclined to endorse a version according to which one should not disbelieve known logical consequences of one's beliefs. I don't think my discussion below is affected by the precise nature of accepted bridging Principles, since the Preface Paradox might be set up in a variety of ways, each of which targets a different Bridging Principle. I think my proposal can be adopted by an adherent of any plausible Bridging Principle. So I shall stick with the above as unpacking Logical Coherence.

6. See his 2004 sections 4.1 and 4.2.
7. To be sure, some semantic deflationists argue against the representational import of (one or another piece of) semantic theory, but: (i) their motivations for doing so have nothing to do with a Threshold conception of belief; (ii) while questioning the substance and/or explanatory power of semantic and representational notions, they do not reject those conceptions. So, though they might adopt a preferred construal of the representational role of belief, they need not reject such a view.
8. Reason for my caution here will emerge when I turn to discuss treatments of the issue.
9. See Christensen 2004; Sturgeon 2008; Weintraub 2001; Foley 1992 *inter alia*. The reasoning in some of these papers is applied to the Lottery rather than or as well as the Preface Paradox. When it is applied to the former there are obvious enough extensions to the latter.
10. Of course the Preface Paradox is just one arena in which Logical Coherence has been brought into question. Since there may be others, my argument cannot pretend to be exhaustive. Indeed the Lottery Paradox is often cited, in addition. I largely ignore it here because in many versions Logical Coherentists have a good response in arguing that we ought not to believe of each ticket that it won't win; and in other versions it raises much the same issues as the Preface Paradox.
11. Obviously this is an inconsistent set of beliefs. The logical machinery then kicks in simply to make the inconsistency explicit by deriving a contradiction.
12. I'll sometimes call the proposition believed here '*Book*'.
13. The easiest way to note this is to define the Risk of a proposition, R(P) as 1-Cr(P). Then $R(C) \leq R(P1)+\ldots+R(Pn)$, since C is only false when at least one of P1 to Pn is false. See Sturgeon, 2008.
14. See Sturgeon 2008.
15. We may suppose that this argumentation employs claims that are taken to be uncontroversial and certainly are not intended to fall within the scope of the author's *Preface* proposition.
16. To be sure Christensen has raised some doubts about this. I don't think these need detain us for the following reasons: (i) Christensen's reasons arise from thinking about how an agent should integrate her 'first order' credences with 'second order' beliefs about her own competence. But for the beliefs involved in *Book* this isn't relevant. (ii) Secondly, if we turn to the integration of the second order beliefs, we are essentially tackling the sort of problem thrown up by the Preface Paradox. I'm the process of arguing that belief, despite the Preface Paradox, requires Logical Coherence and to suppose that beliefs may fail to adhere to the laws of probability is to beg the question. In fact the example I go on to construct is near enough the same as the one Christensen uses to argue his point. (iii) I don't need the claim in full generality, just the claim that

credences are not purely subjective measures of confidence and the supposition that logical and mathematical truths warrant a credence of 1.
17. Let it be said that my experience is that the position does elicit some fierce incredulity. I'm tempted to say it expresses a belief that I have, but which is probably false.
18. Here's another such example, taken from the closing sentences of Dummett's *Truth and Other Enigmas*. Having presented his view that philosophy, since Frege, has at last found its true method Dummett admits that the history of such predictions is replete with disappointment and concludes thus: 'by far the safest bet would be that I was suffering from a similar illusion in making the same claim for Frege. To this I can offer only the banal reply which any prophet has to make to any sceptic: time will tell' (1978, 458). Clearly Dummett thinks that from a certain objective point of view his belief is likely to be false, but this doesn't lead him to relinquish it.
19. Note that my imagined generous reader would have to reject assimilation of the current scenario to those of Moore's Paradox. For in the latter scenarios the agent's state of mind is incomprehensible.
20. See Christensen 2004 for examples.
21. Recall, though, that in the section entitled 'Thresholdism and Logical Coherence' I argued against a combining Thresholdism with the broad conception of credences.
22. See Quine's classical statement (1953), also Quine and Ullian (1970, ch. 2) and Tennant (2012).
23. There is a third, more technical problem. Tennant (2006) argues that for finite schemes of belief it is false to suppose that systematic removal of a belief, p, followed by its replacement will restore the original situation in that all the original consequences of p (together with one's other beliefs) will flow back into the scheme of belief. What holds of a single belief will hold of whole systems of beliefs.
24. See his (2012).

Acknowledgements

The paper was presented in my department at the University of Cape Town and at a conference on naturalism and phenomenology held at the University of Johannesburg in 2014. I'd like to express my thanks to audiences at both of those events for their comments; to Jack Ritchie and David Papineau for their discussions; and, finally, to two anonymous reviewers for the journal for their feedback on a previous draft.

Disclosure statement

No potential conflict of interest was reported by the author.

References

Christensen, D. (2004) *Putting Logic in its Place: Formal Constraints on Rational Belief*, Oxford: Clarendon Press.

Douven, I., and J.Uffink (2003) 'The Preface Paradox Revisited', in *Erkenntnis* 59: 389–420.

Dummett, M. (1978) *Truth and Other Enigmas*, London: Duckworth.
Foley, R (1992) 'The Epistemology of Belief and the Epistemology of Degrees of Belief', *American Philosophical Quarterly*, 29(2): 111–124.
Kaplan, M. (1996) *Decision Theory as Philosophy*, Cambridge: Cambridge University Press.
MacFarlane, J. (unpublished) 'In What Sense (if any) is Logic Normative for Thought' presented at the Central Division APA 2004.
Makinson, D. (1965) 'The Paradox of the Preface', *Analysis*, 25: 205–207.
Quine, W. (1953) 'Two Dogmas of Empiricism', in *From a Logical Point of View*, 20–46, Cambridge, MA: Harvard University Press.
Quine, W., and J.S.Ullian (1970) *The Web of Belief*, 2nd edition, New York, NY: Random House.
Sturgeon, S. (2008) 'Reason and the Grain of Belief', *Noûs* 42(1): 139–165.
Tennant, N. (2006) 'A Degeneracy Theorem for the Full AGM-theory of Theory Revision', *Journal of Symbolic Logic* 71(2): 661–676.
Tennant, N. (2012) *Changes of Mind: An Essay on Rational Belief Revision*, Oxford: Oxford University Press.
Weintraub, R. (2001) 'The Lottery: A Paradox Regained and Resolved', *Synthese* 129: 439–449.

Index

Note: Page numbers followed with "n" refer to footnotes.

absolute deterritorialization 70
After Finitude (Meillassoux) 12, 17, 18–19
Aristotle 104

Badiou, Alain 1
Baker, Lynne 119–21
Baudin, Émile 16
Being and Time (Heidegger) 104
'biperspectivalist' approach 27
Bogost, I. 10
Book I of *Treatise* (Hume) 26, 28, 29, 32, 34, 36n7
Brassier, Ray 13, 17, 23n11
Bréhier, Emile 75
broadness, representationalism: conscious sensory experience 41–2; cosmic swampbrain 43, 44, 47, 58–9; inverted earth 42–4, 48; mental representations 43–4; particular objects 42, 44; transparency argument 49–50
Burge, Tyler 42, 118

Carroll, Lewis 73, 74
Cartesian Meditations (Husserl) 86, 116
Cerbone, David 3
Christensen, D. 132, 140, 146n16
Cogito 72
Contributions to Philosophy (Heidegger) 104
correlationism 9–10, 21n3; criticism of 15; scientific naturalism as form of 11
cosmic exile, rejection of 82–3
criticism of phenomenology 13, 14, 16
Critique of Judgment (Kant) 100
Critique of Pure Reason (Kant) 99, 105

Davidson, D. 17
De Caro, Mario 122
Deleuze, Gilles 1, 3; *Difference and Repetition* 68–70; Epicurean naturalism 65; and ethical naturalism 76–8; *Logic of Sense, The* 68, 73–5; metaphysical pluralism 65; methodological naturalism 67; nature of events 73–6; *Nietzsche and Philosophy* 66; ontological naturalism 67, 73–6; philosophy *vs.* science 71–3; pragmatism of 66; relation to naturalism 66–7; *Thousand Plateaus, A* 69–71
Deleuzian metaphysics 68
Descartes, René 7
Difference and Repetition (Deleuze) 66, 68–70, 76, 78n6
'disenchanted' conception of world 26–8, 36n4
Dretske, Fred 52
Dreyfus, H. 33

End of Phenomenology, The (Sparrow) 6
Epicurean naturalism 65
epistemology: naturalized 1, 26, 89–92, 96n5; phenomenology without 92–5
Essay on the Origin of Languages (Rousseau) 99
ethical naturalism 76–8
'experience,' Hume's sense of 28–31, 36n6

Fink, Eugen 82

Gallagher, Shaun 112, 113
Grand Design: New Answers to the Ultimate Questions of Life, The (Hawking and Mlodinow) 18
Guattari, Félix 66; machinic materialism 69–70

INDEX

Hardy, L. 15
Harman, Gilbert 52
Harman, Graham 10, 13, 16, 19, 22n5; anti-realism of phenomenology 12; scientific naturalism 11
Hegel, G.W.F. 4, 19, 22, 100, 101
Holmes, Brooke 78n4
Horgan, Terence 57, 61n12, 61n13
Hughes, Joe 78n3
human exceptionalism 11
Hume's naturalism 2; 'disenchanted' conception of world 26–8, 36n4; McDowell's conceptualism 32–3; 'Oxford view' 31, 36n9; sense of experience 28–31, 36n6; Todes' perception 31–4; *Treatise* 26, 28, 29, 32, 34, 36n7
Husserl, E. 5–8, 11, 15, 17, 37n21, 111–12, 114, 116; *Cartesian Meditations* 86; distinction between intentional and real objects 14; embraced transcendental idealism 17; multiform conscious processes 85, 87, 89, 93; phenomenological reduction 84, 87, 92; 'Philosophy as Rigorous Science' 83, 94, 95n2; transcendental phenomenology 83–9
hybrid and heretical phenomenology 4
hybrid and heretical version: methodological incompatibilism 111–13; minimal phenomenology *see* minimal phenomenology; ontological and scientific naturalism 119–22; overview of 109–10; 'phenomenological overbidding' 113–17; Précis 110–11

Kant and Phenomenology (Rockmore) 6
Kant, I. 9, 10, 18, 19, 22n4
Kant, Immanuel: Copernican Revolution 100; *Critique of Judgment* 100; *Critique of Pure Reason* 99, 105
Kaplan, David 60n1
Kaplan, Mark 135, 138
Kriegel, Uriah 56
Kripke, Saul 42

La structure du comportement (Merleau-Ponty) 5
Leiter, Brian 123
Lewis, David 27
liberal naturalism 122–3
logical coherence 4; Preface Paradox *see* Preface Paradox; representationalism and 131–3; thresholdism and 130–1

Logical Investigations (Husserl) 109
Logic of Sense, The (Deleuze) 68, 73–5
Logische Untersuchungen (Husserl) 14
Lottery Paradox 134, 146n10

Macarthur, David 122
McDowell, J. 27, 32, 35, 122
Meillassoux, Quentin 12–13, 16–18, 22n6
Merleau-Ponty, M. 5, 7, 22n5, 31–2, 104, 114, 126n2; 'phenomenology without epistemology' 92–5, 96n6
metaphysical realism 15
methodological naturalism 67, 68
minimal phenomenology 118–19; compatible with liberal naturalism 122–3; with methodological naturalism 123–5
Moore's paradox 138–40
Moran, Dermot 118
multiform conscious processes 85, 87, 89, 93

naturalism 5
naturalized epistemology 1, 26, 89–92, 96n5
naturalized phenomenology 5–6
Naturalizing Phenomenology (Varela) 5
Nature's Suit: Husserl's Phenomenological Philosophy of the Physical Sciences (Hardy) 15
Negri, Antonio 73
Nietzsche and Philosophy (Deleuze) 66
Nietzschean inversion 107
Nietzsche, Friedrich 103
nihilism 13
Nihil Unbound 13

objects and phenomena 85, 86
ontological naturalism 67, 73–6
'original epistemological problem' 90
Oxford Handbook of Contemporary Phenomenology, The (Zahavi) 20–1
'Oxford view' 31, 36n9

panpsychism 11
Papineau, David 2–3
Patton, Paul 3
Phenomenological Mind, The (Zahavi and Gallagher) 113
phenomenological reduction 84, 87, 92
Phenomenology of Perception (Merleau-Ponty) 7, 92, 114
'phenomenology without epistemology' 92–5
philosophy 11
'Philosophy as Rigorous Science' (Husserl) 83, 94, 95n2

INDEX

Philosophy of Nature (Hegel) 101
Plato 102
Preface Paradox 4; agnosticism 143; assumptions 135-6; belief revision theory 144; Bridging Principle 146n5; cognitive frailty 136; contradiction 144 credence levels 137; hybrid approach 145; Lottery Paradox 134, 146n10; Moore's paradox 138-40; preliminary comments 134; presentation of 133; Russell's Paradox 141, 142; Sorites Paradox 141, 142
psychologism 5
Putnam, H. 1, 2, 15-17, 19, 42, 122

Quine, W. V. O.: naturalized epistemology 1, 26, 89-92, 96n5; 'original epistemological problem' 90; rejection of cosmic exile 82-3; *Word and Object* 82

realism, forms of 13-17
Regulae ad directionem ingenii (Descartes) 7
relative deterritorialization 70
representationalism 2-3; accuracy 57-9; broadness *see* broadness, representationalism; and logical coherence 131-3; mind-independence 59-60; non-relationism 48-51; overview of 40-1; phenomenal intentionality 55-7; properties of 51-5; sensory awareness 50-1; singular experiential contents 45-7; *vs.* direct realist disjunctivism 53
'return to nature' 3-4, 97-107
Reynolds, Jack 4
Rockmore, Tom 6, 21n1
Rousseau, Jean-Jacques: *Essay on the Origin of Languages* 99; *Second Discourse* 98
Russell's Paradox 141, 142

Sallis, John 3-4
Schelling, F.W.J. 100, 101, 103
Schlick, Moritz 23n10
'science of human nature.' *see* Hume's naturalism

Sebold, Ricky 125n1
Second Discourse (Rousseau) 98, 107n1
Sellars, Wilfred 1
sense datum theory 49
Sixth Cartesian Meditation (Fink) 82
Sorites Paradox 141, 142
Sparrow, T. 19; *End of Phenomenology, The* 7-8; on speculative realism 10
speculative realism 2, 6; devastating criticism at phenomenology 19; end of 17-21; positive contribution 19-20; relation to phenomenology 6
speculative realists 9, 10
state of nature *(l'état de nature)* 98-9
stoic philosophy 73-4
Subjective, Intersubjective, Objective : (Davidson) 17

Thompson, Evan 117, 119
Thousand Plateaus, A (Guattari and Deleuze) 66, 69-71
thresholdism, and logical coherence 130-1, 145n4
Tienson, John 57, 61n12, 61n13
Timaeus (Plato) 102-3, 105, 106
Todes, Samuel 31-4
transcendental empiricism 68
transcendental phenomenology 18, 21n2, 83-9
Truth and Other Enigmas (Dummett) 147n18
Tye, Michael 52

Varela, Francisco 5

Walden (Thoreau) 101
Weiss, Bernhard 4
Williams, Michael 27
Wiltsche, H. 18
Winkler, Rafael 125n1
Word and Object (Quine) 82

Zahavi, Dan 2, 112, 113, 120
Zizek, Slavoj 1
Zourabichvili, François 65, 71